D1433169

Difference in View

Feminist Perspectives on The Past and Present Advisory Editorial Board

Lisa Adkins, *University of The West of England, UK*
Harriet Bradley, *University of Sunderland, UK*
Barbara Caine, *University of Sydney, Australia*
Sara Delamont, *University of Wales College of Cardiff, UK*
Mary Evans, *University of Kent at Canterbury, UK*
Gabriele Griffin, *Nene College, UK*
Jalna Hanmer, *University of Bradford, UK*
Maggie Humm, *University of East London, UK*
Sue Lees, *University of North London, UK*
Diana Leonard, *University of London, UK*
Terry Lovell, *University of Warwick, UK*
Maureen McNeil, *University of Birmingham, UK*
Ann Phoenix, *University of London, UK*
Caroline Ramazanoglu, *University of London, UK*
Sue Scott, *University of Manchester, UK*
Janet Siltanen, *University of Edinburgh, UK*
Dale Spender, *Australia*
Penny Summerfield, *University of Lancaster, UK*
Martha Vicinus, *University of Michigan, USA*
Claire Wallace, *University of Lancaster, UK*
Christine Zmroczek, *Roehampton Institute of Higher Education, UK*

English
XA 228, W6
GR1
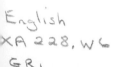

Difference in View:
Women and Modernism

Edited by

Gabriele Griffin

No GUL bookplates etc
(ASC)

Taylor & Francis
Publishers since 1798

UK   Taylor & Francis Ltd, 4 John St., London WC1N 2ET
USA   Taylor & Francis Inc., 1900 Frost Road, Suite 101, Bristol, PA 19007

©Selection and editorial material copyright Gabriele Griffin, 1994

All rights reserved. No part of this publication may be reproduced, stored in a retrieval system, or transmitted, in any form or by any means, electronic, mechanical, photocopying, recording, or otherwise, without permission in writing from the Publisher.

First published 1994

A Catalogue Record for this book is available from the British Library

ISBN 0 7484 0134 2
ISBN 0 7484 0135 0 (pbk)

Library of Congress Cataloging-in-Publication Data are available on request

Typeset in 11/13 pt CG Times Roman
by RGM Associates, Lord Street, Southport, England

Printed in Great Britain by Burgess Science Press, Basingstoke on paper which has a specified pH value on final paper manufacture of not less than 7.5 and is therefore 'acid free'.

94 - 1841

ADAM SMITH LIBRARY

Contents

for Hanna Zielke

a modern/ist woman

Acknowledgments

The contributors and editor would like to thank all those who supported the making of this volume. Specifically, Penelope Kenrick would like to thank Susan Hiller for granting permission to reproduce some of her work and for providing copies of that work. Katharine Cockin would like to acknowledge Dr. Clare Hanson for reading the manuscript of her chapter; Margaret Weare, custodian of the Ellen Terry Memorial Museum, and the National Trust for permission to quote from documents in the Edith Craig archive at the Ellen Terry Memorial Museum. Nikki Goode Shaughnessy wishes to thank Robert Shaughnessy, Treva Broughton and Nicole Ward for their support. Joss West-Burnham would like to thank Betty Princep, a colleague who many years ago introduced her to the Carolyn Heilbrun's work and to the writings of Vita Sackville-West and the participants of the 1991 'Gender and Modernism' conference at Nene College who helped her to clarify some of her ideas. Finally, Gabriele Griffin would like to thank Katia Stieglitz of the Artists' Rights Society, New York, for granting permission to reproduce Leonora Carrington's paintings *Femme et Oiseau* and *The Inn of the Dawn Horse*; Sylvia Hardy for conversations on modernism, support and help with the 'Gender and Modernism' conference in 1991, as well as enjoyable years of co-teaching the 'Edwardians and Moderns' course at Nene College; Nene College itself for supporting this project by granting remission from teaching and for facilitating the hosting of the 'Gender and Modernism' conference in 1991. Special thanks are also due to Comfort Jegede and Anthony Levings of Taylor and Francis for their editorial support.

Introduction

Gabriele Griffin

When you are writing before there is an audience anything
written is as important as any other thing and you cherish
anything and everything that you have written. After the
audience begins, naturally they create something, that is they
create you, and so not everything is so important, something is
more important than another thing, which is not true when you
were you that is when you were not you as your little dog knows
you.

(Gertrude Stein, 1990)

Modernism as Audience Effect

The audience effects Gertrude Stein talks about here, the notions that (1)
identity — whether personal or artistic — is not essential, but socially
constructed (by the audience), and that (2) it operates on the basis of
selectivity ('something is more important than another thing'),
constitute major issues for feminism (Hollway, 1992; Rothfield, 1990).
This is apparent in the context of *modernism*, definitions of which have
been subject to the scrutiny of feminist critics[1] seeking to reinscribe
women into a canon of artistic production which has marginalized all
but a select few whose work appears to exhibit certain, specific and
specifiable characteristics associated with experiment in language and a
heightened (self-)consciousness about the (inner) self and the
un/conscious. This selectivity, which has governed definitions of
modernism, is exemplified in Peter Faulkner's book, *A Modernist
Reader: Modernism in England 1910–1930* (1986) which, despite being
published in 1986,[2] at a time when modernism as a concept was already
under debate, begins with the following assertions.

> Looking back from the late twentieth century, we can see the arts of the period 1910–1930 as having a clear cultural identity to which the term 'Modernist' can reasonably be applied, although it was not a term used at the time. The characteristics of this movement, which affected all the arts and many countries,[3] have been the subject of much discussion, but perhaps the neatest formulation remains that of Stephen Spender in *The Struggle of the Modern* in 1963, where he writes of modern art as 'that in which the artist reflects awareness of an unprecedented modern situation in its form and idiom.' ... these new forms were triumphantly created ... by Picasso, by Stravinsky, by Proust ... by Pound, Eliot, Lawrence, Woolf, Joyce and Yeats. The masterpieces of that period rightly continue to attract our attention: we cannot find in other writers of the time anything to match the achievements of the Modernists.[4]
>
> (Faulkner, 1986, p. 13)

The assertion in the last sentence, of course, depends on who is looking and what that person is looking for. Faulkner does not register any self-consciousness about himself as audience. As a white, middle-class, professional male he assumes (expressed through the use of the first person plural 'we') a consensual community of readers who will concur in his representation of modernism. Both by his admission and in terms of Stein's comments, modernism is partly an audience effect rather than something essential, as epitomized (with one exception — Virginia Woolf) by 'the boys'. This is an indication of the looking-glass function[5] that artistic production may have for its audience. The audience wants to see reflected what it desires. Narcissism rules. Boys will see boys, especially if they look like themselves.

Misfits

This, of course, does nothing for those who do not fit the image. Predictably, for example, Faulkner (1986, p. 13) writes of D. H. Lawrence, who was not quite middle class (at least not at the beginning of his career) that 'Lawrence, in particular, can be seen as defining a characteristically independent position'. The presentation of modernism as possessing 'a clear cultural identity' is thus immediately undercut by the difference here ascribed to Lawrence. Indeed, proclamations of the specificity of modernism meet the resistance of difference already present in the work of modernist artists and writers in the form of fragmentation and tensions expressed as competing truths. This is as evident in W. B. Yeats's famous lines 'Things fall apart; the centre cannot hold' (*The Second Coming*) as it is in T. S. Eliot's notion, detailed in 'Tradition and the Individual Talent', of new works of art jostling for position among the old.

> The existing monuments form an ideal order among themselves, which is modified by the introduction of the new (the really new) work of art among them.
>
> (Eliot, 1934, p. 15)

Similarly, it is evident in the fragmentatious cubist work of Pablo Picasso, or the competing versions of the 'true' story in Sigmund Freud's case histories.

It is thus not only the fact that in the 1990s we live in a world governed by the tension of globalism versus regionalism, encouraging a sense of fragmentation and of the end of the grand narratives famously proclaimed by Lyotard (1984) — itself, the new grand narrative, the new orthodoxy — which has led to a revisioning of modernism; modernism's (or should it be: *modernisms*?) monuments themselves are full of faultlines which defy the 'clear cultural identity' some still seek to hold on to.

The Institutionalization of Modernism

These faultlines have not prevented the institutionalization of modernism as highlighted in Terry Eagleton's essay 'Capitalism, Modernism and Postmodernism' (1985), a process which manifests itself in the boundary-drawing necessary for the 'perpetuation of masculinist modernism' (Chow, 1992, p. 108) and which has the effect of creating precarious coherences that are themselves subject to the provisionalities of their audiences. Concretely, it has meant that modernism means different things and covers different periods in diverse subject areas: modernism is one thing for traditional art historians, but quite another for students of, say, English literature[6] — and, traditionally, 'never the twain shall meet'. Not only do different academic disciplines draw the boundaries of *their* modernisms differentially; even within a single discipline such as literature, divisions are manifest: many courses on modernism still focus virtually exclusively on the poetry, fiction and some theoretical, aesthetic writings by the celebrated few; they ignore, for example, the theatre work done during this period. Thus Gertrude Stein's poetry and lectures may be read but not her plays. Film and 'fine' art, likewise, are not regarded as the proper province of modernism on English literature courses.

The temporal specificity of modernism — are we talking about the period 1910-30, or about something much more extended? — is also under debate as part of the diversity of modernism's definition. However, these debates tend not to be admitted to within specific academic disciplines which often operate a system of 'splendid isolation'.

The discussions about postmodernism have, among other things (such as current debates about the boundaries of traditional academic disciplines), led to a questioning of narrow definitions of modernism, exploding the narrow early twentieth century timescale, for example, conventionally assigned it. Sandra Gilbert and Susan Gubar (Gilbert and Gubar, 1988) dig deep into the nineteenth century in order to trace the genealogy[7] and process of location of the woman writer in the early part of this century. As women, they are among those who have no investment in maintaining the 'clear cultural identity' ascribed to modernism by Faulkner for, as Patricia Waugh (1989) and others have demonstrated, women's investment in grand narratives and unified subject positions is different from that of men. In western patriarchal society, women's grand narrative is that of silence, of the white canvas. Women who 'may *never* have experienced a sense of full subjectivity in the first place' (Waugh, 1989, p. 2) cannot announce the death of their subjectivity. Rather, as Waugh (1989, p. 10) puts it:

> For Woolf, like many women writers positioned in a patriarchal society, a more appropriate question would be 'What represents me?'

What Represents Me?

This is, indeed, the question raised by many women artists from the modernist period. The attempt to answer this question leads Gertrude Stein to her experiments with language, and Djuna Barnes in *Nightwood* (1936) to construct characters who 'invent' their history complete with material 'proof' in the form of supposedly ancestral portraits bought in junk shops and the like. It leads Hermione in H. D.'s (1927) *Her* to reject the representations — science and mathematics — that shape the identity of her father and brother in favour of making her own marks on the white canvas as she walks across the snow, having made up her mind to leave America for Europe and to become a writer.

> Now the creator was Her's feet, narrow black crayon across the winter whiteness. *Art thou a ghost my sister white sister there, art thou a ghost who knows* . . . She trailed feet across a space of immaculate clarity, leaving her wavering hieroglyph as upon white parchment.
>
> (H. D., p. 223–4)

Her's literal enactment of her understanding that, in order to develop a sense of self, she has to make her own mark — resisting the sign systems she has been offered by the male members of her family — is expressive of feminists' perception before and since that 'if we do not define ourselves for ourselves, we will be defined by others — for their use and to our detriment' (Lorde, 1984, p. 45).[8]

Making Tracks

For many women in the early part of the twentieth century, attempting to define themselves meant literally — as it does for H. D.'s character Hermione — voting with their feet, making tracks, seeking self and change through movement. In the age of Isodora Duncan and Josephine Baker, not only female dancers were on the move. Women, particularly middle class women, were discovering ways of translating their sense of alienation within male-dominated culture into spatial dislocation. This constituted the actualization of the understanding that

> the phenomenological perception that 'I' am never at one with myself because always and ever already constituted by others according to whom, and yet outside of what, I take myself to be. For the woman writer, the further implication is that, if the 'I' is spoken or positioned in a discourse where subjectivity, the norm of human-ness, is male, then 'I' is doubly displaced, 'I can never in any material or metaphysical sense be at one with myself'.
>
> (Waugh, 1989, p. 11)

Gabriele Griffin

Identity, Nationalism, Internationalism

Actualizing this alienation through spatial displacement can, paradoxically, become a way of achieving some sense of identity. As Bryher (1963, p. 207), H. D.'s long-time companion, states in her autobiography: 'We were all exiles. We remain so to-day. It is our destiny'. Bryher links that sense of exile with the transformations she perceives to have affected her lifetime, specifically the move from a nineteenth century world (represented in her autobiography as a nursery of security, stable values, progress and purpose) to a twentieth century mentality (associated with 'rebellion' and the 'mockery of loyalty, duty and honour') which, according to Bryher (1963, p. 205), 'deprived the next generation of its proper roots'.[9] Bryher's vocabulary (and some of her ideas here) seem antiquated considered from a 1990s perspective, in part because her terminology has come to be associated with a concept which has been increasingly problematized[10] throughout the twentieth century — nationalism.[11] It also detracts slightly from the fact that it was precisely the *internationalism* of modernism, its happening 'in all the arts and many countries' as much as the geographical movement of people with whom it is associated, which empowered women in their artistic (self-)expression. As Bryher writes in *The Heart to Artemis:*

> It has been the custom throughout the ages to encourage an apprentice to leave home for a time as he is coming to maturity. It avoids much conflict with the older generation. The exiles in Paris were there for the same reason. They were throwing off the yoke, not of their country but of the small towns where they had grown up ... They could write, paint, love and be gay without recriminations from their elders ...
>
> (Bryher, 1963, p. 221)

As had been the case with certain Romantic writers — such as Mary Wollstonecraft and her daughter Mary Shelley — a century previously, women at the turn and in the early part of this century enacted their sense of displacement in patriarchal culture through spatial re-location, moving from their country of origin — in which they felt stifled[12] in their selves and their attempts at artistic self-expression — to another country which seemed to offer a sense of unfetteredness, thus enabling them to experiment in their lives as well as aesthetically.

Initially this movement was predominantly towards the east and the south, with American artists moving east to Europe, and many North

European artists being attracted to the southern and mediterranean parts of Europe, especially Italy, Spain and Greece. This was one major contributing factor to the internationalism of modernism. Another was the way in which geographical movement implied more than a spatial uprooting; it concretized a resistance to the history and traditions of these women's countries of origin, their social, cultural and familial backgrounds which, especially for women, had meant a positioning on the margins, now to be rejected. While many men struggled to hold on to those continuities — such as a sense of history as linear and evolutionary which had ensured their socio-cultural centrality — women in their work were interrogating these continuities and the precepts on which they had been founded. Some did so by portraying the (misguided) attempt to seek entry into the very positions, social and cultural, that had excluded them precisely because they were women: witness Radclyffe Hall's character Stephen Gordon's attempt to be accepted by the landed gentry of the home counties in *The Well of Loneliness*. Others, such as Djuna Barnes in *Nightwood*, re-constructed history, *his* story, not as one of continuity but of discontinuity, as one of selectivity and choice, with the individual responding to a psychological necessity, the need to belong, by inventing and furnishing a 'bespoke' history of which s/he wants to be a part, utilizing concrete objects to signify both the need and its expression. History here becomes an arbitrary phenomenon, founded in individual subjectivities. As such it paradoxically reflects the very arbitrariness of another history which simply excluded women and their experiences.

Other Being Different

History, and the self's relation to it, thus has a different meaning for women and men (Kelly, 1984). This is made evident in Chapter 5 where Montefiore demonstrates that whereas men constructed themselves as exemplary in their autobiographical texts, women frequently offered up an image of their marginality and their ordinariness as does Jean Rhys in her representations of female downward social mobility. Rhys' displaced characters are nonetheless typical, in their alienation, of an experience shared by vast quantities of women.

Rhys' female figures *are* atypical in terms of the canon of modernism as narrowly understood within English literature in that they are often of mixed race, and race as an issue does not feature in high modernism. It is worth noting that certain writers, originating from

America — such as T. S. Eliot who, of course, out-Englished the English (one way of compensating for displacement) — are routinely taught as part of English literature courses, while others are expected to find their place within American Studies. To these latter, significantly in my view, belong the writers subsumed under the category 'Harlem Renaissance' which instantly does away with an engagement with one set of Black writers in the context of modernism. The recent questioning of modernism's boundaries has promoted, among other things, the examination of Black writers within a framing discourse on modernism. This makes Mary Condé's essay on the image of Europe in the works of Nella Larsen and Jesse Redmon Fauset so important. The Black or mixed-race woman travelling to or in Europe experiences a multiple alienation: displaced within patriarchy; removed from her country or countries of origin; and singled out as exotic or freakish. Her multiple alienation raises with terrible clarity the question of the unitariness and authenticity of the self that preoccupies much of twentieth century thought. Whereas male writers strive after preserving an assumed wholeness of self, women begin to revel in their alienation. Some women writers start to celebrate a stance which refuses uniqueness in favour of a reclamation of a place within their female heritage which de-individualizes their position. Witness Joss West-Burnham's account of Vita Sackville-West's writerly engagement with her grandmother's and her mother's lives — the former, in particular, as a dancer, a Spaniard, a mistress to a British aristocrat whose children she bore being an example of the displaced female. Alternatively women choose to develop artistic techniques and images which undercut the individualism assumed in Romantic notions of creation in favour of highlighting the reproducibility of artwork.[13] Repetition and variation, two of the central components of Gertrude Stein's writerly technique (Stein, 1990) play a major role here and are as significant for *her* aesthetic as they are for the work of Susan Hiller, for example, discussed in Chapter 8 by Penelope Kenrick.

Encoding Difference

Hiller is very much alive and working today, as are several of the other artists such as Leonora Carrington whose work is examined in this book. Hiller serves as an example of an artist whose work indexes the problems of periodization in general and in relation to modernism in particular. As Penelope Kenrick indicates, Hiller's work, contemporary though it is, shows, quite literally, the traces of techniques like automatic writing which were *en vogue* during the early twentieth century, the period of 'high modernism'. These combine with mass-produced images such as photo-booth passport photos, to investigate and question the assumption critically interrogated by Rey Chow (1992, p. 108) that 'As the ruin of modernism, mass culture is the automatized site of the others, the site of automatized others, the site of automatons'. In so far as woman constitutes high modernism's other, Hiller's self-images reinforce the conflation between woman and mass culture made in the early twentieth century[14] and discussed by Chow. However, by literally over-writing these images, Hiller returns them to a logocentricity which queries their status as objects on the cultural margins.

Such oblique presentation of the female self in which that self is *not quite herself* is also typical for the work of Leonora Carrington whose writings and paintings from the period 1937–40 are discussed in this volume. Carrington's female selves come into being through merging with an animal other; human others (usually presented as parental authority figures) offer a threat to the young female self who takes refuge in the natural world assuming, erroneously, that this will facilitate the combating of a sense of estrangement from society.

The world Carrington presents is, in some respects, not dissimilar to that, for instance, of Virginia Woolf's (1927) *To the Lighthouse* where over-powering parental figures disable the younger generation with their spoken and unspoken demands, especially as regards the social conformity that validates their own, i.e. the parents', life choices. Whereas Woolf utilizes death as a way out of this dilemma, Carrington's figures become trapped in the moment of flight. Seemingly too young to leave the nest, their point of transformation turns into an unresolved state; becoming turns into being, the process or means becomes the end. Woman is thus constructed as subject-in-movement, as subject seeking to assume a sense of self.

The Search for a Female Self

Precisely this search for a sense of self is what motivates women's cultural production in the twentieth century. The need to find a female aesthetic (self) leads Woolf to write (Woolf, 1929, p. 74)

[a] great part must be played in [the] future so far as women are

concerned by physical conditions. The book has somehow to be adapted to the body, and at a venture one would say that women's books should be shorter, more concentrated, than those of men, and framed so that they do not need long hours of steady and uninterrupted work...

(This passage from *A Room of One's Own* seems slightly hilarious now, though its ideas are to some extent reinforced by the notion of an *écriture féminine* espoused by Hélène Cixous, for instance). Woolf makes a connection between women's material circumstances and physiological conditions and their cultural production which, while assuming an unchanging situation for women concerning their role as household managers and child rearers, highlights the conditionality of cultural production, its dialogic relation to the external world.

Given the different conditions of women's existence compared to that of men, it is not surprising that women's cultural production answers to a different aesthetic from that of men and that, when judged within a male frame of reference, it becomes invisible. This point is made in Elaine Aston's Chapter 11 on the theatre of Susan Glaspell whose work, not only because it is by a woman and comes in play form, has been marginalised within theatre history on the one hand and modernism on the other. Aston demonstrates Glaspell's encoding of women's specific experiences in her theatre work, indicating how these find both structural and stylistic expression in Glaspell's plays. A similar move is at play in Chapter 10 in Katharine Cockin's discussion of the performances of the Pioneer Players, a subscription theatre company of the early part of the twentieth century dominated by women. Their work questioned conventional gender roles through the plays they performed, a reversal of gender roles in these plays, and through the specificities of their productions. Both Cockin's and Aston's chapters, as do indeed a number of others such as Andrew Thacker's on Dora Marsden's involvement with the magazine *The Egoist*, Sue Wragg's on Lee Krasner, or Deborah Tyler-Bennett's on Djuna Barnes' short stories, raise the question of female (self-)representation, a female aesthetic and women finding their own voices in the context of the abiding binarism encoded in 'the battle of the sexes'.

Difference in View

Difference in View is appropriate in so far as such framing has been central to much of the cultural production of modernism; it establishes and perpetuates a dialectic interestingly critiqued by Bat-Ami Bar On (1993) whereby identity is constructed through difference, a difference perceived to be necessary for the maintenance of the self. This idea is unproblematic as long as it is not coupled with a hierarchy of values or operates a system of excluding and dominating difference. However, as suggested above, masculinist modernism has ascribed to women the looking-glass function while simultaneously excluding other differences as significant for the construction of the male self. Woman, to be precise, a certain sort of woman (white, middle class) is man's other and women, trying to extricate themselves from that exclusive hermeneutic duo, have both returned the gaze *and* turned to look elsewhere to find their own others, others who do not necessarily function as opposites, who are therefore not inevitably conceived of in hierarchical terms, but who, in their difference, approximate to women's position in society.

This emerges in Chapter 2, where Gregory Woods' piece on 'The Other Other or More of the Same? Women's Representations of Homosexual Men' describes Djuna Barnes' Dr. Matthew O'Connor of *Nightwood*, for instance, as '[constituting] a bridge between men and women'. Women's overall fairly sympathetic portrayal of male homosexuals, as discussed by Woods, may be read as their refusal to identify with the hierarchically oppositional, gendered categories embraced by the masculinist modernism of say a D. H. Lawrence or a T. S. Eliot.

What this chapter as well as the others in this volume explicitly and implicitly ask of the reader is to keep difference in view, to consider the implications of modernism as it is presented by Faulkner in terms of the exclusions and inclusions this entails. Keeping difference in view means remembering the multiple displacements that women have been or are subject to and the effects this has (had) on their work, their attempts at developing and embodying in their cultural production an aesthetic commensurate with their experienes. It means trying to understand the need for change expressed in their work, the refusal of traditions and boundaries, and the search for others that express their selves. As H. D. altruistically put it:

> My sign-posts are not yours, but if I blaze my own trail, it may
> help to give you confidence and urge you to get out of the

murky, dead, old, thousand-times explored old world, the dead
world of overworked emotions and thoughts.

(H. D., 1919, p. 24)

Notes

1   Among these are Shari Benstock, Susan Rubin Suleiman, Sandra M. Gilbert and
Susan Gubar, Gillian Hanscombe, and Rachel Du Blau Plessis.
2   In the first translation into English of Jean-François Lyotard (1984) *The
Postmodern Condition: A Report on Knowledge*, he questions the boundaries
taken for granted by, for example, Faulkner. A year later Terry Eagleton (1985,
p. 63) wrote that 'Lyotard's desire to see modernism and postmodernism as
continuous with one another is in part a refusal to confront the disturbing fact
that modernism proved prey to institutionalization'. Faulkner's book, in a sense,
celebrates this institutionalization.
3   For a brief discussion of the relative positions of first and third world countries
vis-à-vis modernism see Chow 'Postmodern Automatons'.
4   Suleiman (1990) can be read as a refutation of that claim to exclusivity.
5   Virginia Woolf discusses this looking-glass function at length in *A Room of One's
Own*, pp. 35–7.
6   Rey Chow (1992, p. 101) exposes this problematic in terms of first- versus third-
world debates, suggesting (and expanding upon the notion) that 'the more narrow
understanding of modernism . . . needs to be bracketed within an understanding of
modernity as a force of cultural expansionism whose foundations are not only
emancipatory but also Eurocentric and patriarchal'.
7   Contrast this with Michael H. Levenson's (1984) *A Genealogy of Modernism*,
Cambridge: Cambridge University Press, in which he focuses on the period
1908–22.
8   This is not just an assertion of epistemic privilege or 'better knowledge', as
appropriately critiqued by Bat-Ami Bar On (1993) but a recognition that power
differentials determine selectivity and that therefore women will have a different
investment, in voicing themselves and proclaiming their histories, than men.
9   Bryher's at times rather easy assertions about the differences between the
nineteenth and the twentieth centuries are interestingly reflected in Cora Kaplan's
introduction to *Aurora Leigh*, London: Women's Press, where Kaplan (1981,
p. 36) states: 'Our obsession is with the Victorian and Edwardian worlds
themselves. They are our middle-ages. There, in fancy dress, the still-present
hierarchies of class and gender are displayed without shame, unsuppressed by the
rhetoric of equality which glosses our own situation'.
10   As an aside (though relevant in the context of modernism) and on the issue of the
defence of values often associated with nationalism, it is worth noting that in 1916
the German playwright Bertolt Brecht was severely reprimanded at his school for
decrying Horace's line 'Dulce et decorum est pro patria mori' as propaganda
(Mittenzwei, W. 1987, *Das Leben des Bertolt Brecht*, Vol. 1, Berlin: Aufbau-
Verlag, pp. 42–44).
11   Ernest Gellner's (1983) *Nations and Nationalism*, Oxford: Basil Blackwell, offers
an introduction to some of the issues around the problematization of nationalism.
12   Those who stayed at home or allowed themselves to be taken over by social
convention or to live in the shadow of men were/are often portrayed as enacting
their sense of incarceration by denying the self (sexually) — e.g. in Radclyffe
Hall's *The Unlit Lamp*, Joan Ogden's staying in one room (the conventional

interpretation of the nineteenth century poet Emily Dickinson's life), getting laid up (see Alice James' *Diary*), or committing suicide.

13 The implications of this reproducibility have been famously explored by Walter Benjamin, 1977, in *Das Kunstwerk im Zeitalter seiner Reproduzierbarkeit*, Frankfurt/Main: Suhrkamp.

14 An interesting fictional example of this is presented in Dorothy Cowlin's novel, 1942, *Winter Solstice*, London: Merlin Press, 1991, in which the female characters are presented as *au fait* with technological innovations of the early twentieth century such as the cinema and the aeroplane but most of the male characters are rooted in a pre-industrial state.

References

BAR ON, B.-A. (1993) 'Marginality and epistemic privilege' in ALCOFF, L. and POTTER, E. (Eds) *Feminist Epistemologies*, London, Routledge, pp. 83–100.

BARNES, D. (1936, reprinted 1987) *Nightwood*, London, Faber and Faber.

BRADBURY, M. and McFARLANE, J. (Eds) (1976) *Modernism 1890–1930*, Harmondsworth, Penguin.

BROE, M. and INGRAM, A. (Eds) (1989) *Women's Writing in Exile*, Chapel Hill, University of North Carolina P.

BRYHER (1963) *The Heart to Artemis: A Writer's Memoir*, London, Collins.

CHOW, R. (1992) 'Postmodern automatons', in BUTLER, J. and SCOTT, J. W. (Eds) *Feminists Theorize the Political*, London, Routledge, pp. 101–17.

D.(OOLITTLE) H.(ILDA), (1927, reprinted 1984) *Her*, London, Virago.

D.(OOLITTLE) H.(ILDA), (1919, reprinted 1988) *Notes on Thought and Vision and The Wise Sappho*, London, Peter Owen.

EAGLETON, T. (1985) 'Capitalism, modernism and postmodernism', *New Left Review*, 152, pp. 60–73.

ELIOT, T. S. (1934) 'Tradition and the individual talent', *Selected Essays*, London, Faber & Faber, pp. 13–22.

FAULKNER, P. (Ed.) (1986) *A Modernist Reader: Modernism in England 1910–1930*, London, Batsford.

GILBERT, S. M. and GUBAR, S. (1988) *No Man's Land: The Place of the Woman Writer in the Twentieth Century*, New Haven, Yale University Press.

HALL, R. (1928, reprinted 1982) *The Well of Loneliness*, London, Virago.

HALL, R. (1924, reprinted 1934) *The Unlit Lamp*, London, Jonathan Cape.

HOLLWAY, W. (1992) 'Gender difference and the production of subjectivity', in CROWLEY, H. and HIMMELWEIT, S. (Eds) *Knowing Women: Feminism and Knowledge*, Milton Keynes, Open University Press, pp. 240–74.

JAMES, A. (1934, reprinted 1965) *The Diary of Alice James*, London, Rupert Hart-Davis.

KELLY, J. (1984) 'The social relation of the sexes: methodological implications of women's history', *Women, History, and Theory*, Chicago, University of Chicago Press, pp. 1–18.

LORDE, A. (1984) 'Scratching the surface: some notes on barriers to women and loving', *Sister Outsider: Essays and Speeches*, Trumansburg, Crossing P., pp. 45–52.

LYOTARD, J.-F. (1984) *The Postmodern Condition: A Report on Knowledge*, Manchester University Press.

ROTHFIELD, P. (1990) 'Feminism, subjectivity, and sexual experience', in GUNEW, S. (Ed.) *Feminist Knowledge: Critique and Construction*, London, Routledge, pp. 121–44.

SCOTT, B.K. (Ed.) (1990) *The Gender of Modernism*, Bloomington, Indiana University Press.

STEIN, G. (reprinted 1990) 'What are master-pieces and why there are so few of them', *Look at Me Now and Here I Am: Writings and Lectures 1909–45*, London, Penguin, pp. 148–56.

SULEIMAN, S.R. (1990) *Subversive Intent: Gender, Politics and the Avant-Garde*, Cambridge, MA, Harvard University Press.

WAUGH, P. (1989) *Feminine Fictions: Revisiting the Postmodern*, London, Routledge.

WOOLF, V. (1929, reprinted 1983) *A Room of One's Own*, London, Granada.

WOOLF, V. (1927, reprinted 1983) *To the Lighthouse*, London, Granada.

Chapter 1

Europe in the Novels of
Jessie Redmon Fauset and Nella Larsen

Mary Condé

Deeply embedded in American thought is the idea that happiness is a place. The songs hope for somewhere over the rainbow, somewhere a place for us; but what American literature tells us is that no matter how far Natty Bumppo may move out west, or however hard Huck Finn may try to light out for the territory, there is nowhere. When Newland Archer tells Ellen Olenska (Wharton, 1920, p. 242) that he wants to go with her somewhere where they can be just two people in love, she asks him, 'Ah, my dear — where is that country? Have you ever been there?'

Newland clearly supposes the good place to be in Europe, and France, especially, is desired by Wharton's American characters as a land of civilized values affording freedom from the vulgar materialism of America. In Wharton (1923), as in Cather (1922), France does provide the lonely, alienated protagonist with a redemptive dream of beauty, but only at the very moment that this beauty is being destroyed. Even more pessimistic about Europe as a solution for their characters are two African–American writers, Jessie Redmon Fauset (1882–1961), author of *There is Confusion* (1924), *Plum Bun* (1929), *The Chinaberry Tree* (1931) and *Comedy: American Style* (1933), and Nella Larsen (1893–1963), author of *Quicksand* (1928) and *Passing* (1929). Fauset's and Larsen's preoccupations are not with dreams of beauty, but with the possibilities of work, and workable social identities, for their heroines.

Neither writer is interested in Africa. Nella Larsen, born of a Danish mother and a West Indian father, presumably felt her own connection with Africa to be remote. Jessie Redmon Fauset certainly felt hers to be so, coming, as do most of her characters, from a long-established American family. In her foreword to *The Chinaberry Tree* (p. x), she makes it clear that the prosperous middle-class American of whom her fiction treats, sees himself as part of a very early wave of immigration:

> ...he started out as a slave but he rarely thinks of that. To himself he is a citizen of the United States whose ancestors came over not along with the emigrants in the Mayflower, it is true, but merely a little earlier in the good year, 1619.

In *There is Confusion* (p. 182) Peter Bye's friend, Tom Mason, tells him that he is considering settling in France with his sister, and Peter replies,

> I don't want to leave America. It's mine, my people helped make it. These very orchards we're passing now used to be the famous Bye orchards. My grandfather and great-grandfather helped to cultivate them.

Significantly, Tom loses his 'sudden respectful interest' when he realizes that the Byes cultivated the orchards as slaves. Throughout her fiction, however, Fauset insists on the shared history of black and white Americans and on their shared investment in America. This shared investment is not only economic but intellectual and it is strictly a Mayflower, European one. The critic Elizabeth Ammons has referred to Fauset's own 'access to the great texts of western civilization' as 'virtually unlimited' (Ammons, 1991, p. 141). In *Plum Bun* (p. 133), the racist white Roger's declaration that he would send all black Americans back to Africa if he could, is not only hateful but ridiculous, since there is in Faucet's work no sense of Africa as a place of origin with any continuing meaning. Readers looking for a celebration of African heritage will be disappointed, as will readers looking for a celebration, or even some account, of the black American working class. Joyce Flynn remarks on

> [Marita] Bonner's early interest in telling the stories of the black working class, stories largely neglected in the writings of her Afro-American contemporaries such as Jessie Fauset and Nella Larsen.
>
> (Flynn and Stricklin, 1987)

The word *neglected* here implies a shameful omission. Fauset in particular has been accused of narrow, exclusively middle-class sympathies. Bernard W. Bell says disapprovingly of Fauset's first novel *There is Confusion* that 'neither the characters nor the author-narrator has much sympathy for commonplace minds or people.' (Bell, 1987, p. 107) Conversely Deborah E. McDowell (in Larsen, 1928) has been disappointed by the novel's 'unconvincing' ending, the heroine's renunciation of a successful stage career for a commonplace marriage. Fauset does not fulfil any conventional expectations that she should be concerned with Africa, or with the black working-class, or that she should be a feminist. Barbara Christian has drawn attention to Fauset's acute consciousness of audience:

> She, together with Nella Larsen, wanted to correct the impression most white people had that all black people lived in Harlem dives or in picturesque, abject poverty.
>
> (Christian, 1985, p. 173)

Ironically, however, this almost deprived Fauset of an audience altogether, since the first publisher to whom she submitted her first novel rejected it because 'white readers just don't expect Negroes to be like this.' (Sylvander, 1981, p. 73).

Part of what white readers just did not expect was the educational background of Fauset's characters, and of their creator. Michel Fabre speaks of 'her rather snobbish delight' in using French titles for her poems (Fabre, 1991, p. 118). In an introduction to a selection of her poems published in the 1927 *Caroling Dusk* anthology, Fauset enlists Chaucer's help to boast about knowing 'the difference between the French of Stratford-atte-Bowe and that of Paris' (Cullen, p. 118). Reviewing Langston Hughes in 1926, she feels compelled to validate one of his poems by a reference to Latin, German and English poetry (Scott, 1990, p. 165). All this is part of her assertion of her identity as a cultured American, her refusal to play the part of the 'other'.

Elizabeth Ammons quotes Fauset's words of 1923, addressed to would-be writers and teachers of writing in the black community:

> Do our colored pupils read the great writers and stylists? Are they ever shown the prose of Shaw, Galsworthy, Mrs. Wharton, Du Bois or Conrad, or that old master of exquisite phrase and imaginative incident — Walter Pater?
>
> (Ammons, 1991, p. 140)

Ammons is struck by the absence of any white male American from this list. Also striking is the fact that four out of the six are Europeans. In Fauset's own work, it is European poetry (particularly the English Romantics and especially Wordsworth and the 'Immortality Ode') rather than European prose which is quoted by author and characters. A rare exception is her reference to a French novel of 1902. When Fauset moves her scene to Chambéry during the First World War in *There Is Confusion*, she identifies it as the scene of a novel by Henri Bordeaux, *La Peur de Vivre* (Bordeaux, 1902), the story of a young girl who, afraid to face the perils of life, forfeited therefore its pleasures (Fauset, 1924).

She then goes on to make a connection between one of Bordeaux's characters and one of her own:

> Certainly Alice Du Laurens, the young woman of Bordeaux's novel, would have been no more astonished to find herself in New York than Maggie Ellersley, whom she so closely resembled in character, was to find herself in Chambéry.
>
> (Fauset, 1924, p. 254)

What is curious about this reference is that Maggie is not in the least like Alice, as her very presence in a foreign country proves, but almost her opposite. Alice is far too weak to contemplate going to Algeria with Marcel, her true love, whom she abandons because she is dominated by her mother — as Maggie dominates hers. Maggie, essentially a worker, always acts on impulse — Alice feebly lets her opportunities slide away from her. Alice signally fails to become the widow of the man she loves — Maggie, because of her determination, triumphantly succeeds. Perhaps Fauset had genuinely forgotten the gist of the Bordeaux novel or perhaps she meant to say that Alice and Maggie resembled each other in appearance: they do both look fragile and pale. Oddly enough, Alice is extremely like Teresa in Fauset's last novel (Fauset, 1933).

Whatever the reasons for Fauset's strange lapse, it occurs in a very characteristic passage, in which she is writing about *knowing*: about how far Americans know Chambéry at all, and the various ways in which they might know it (as the location of the château of the old dukes of Savoy, as Rousseau's birthplace, as a First World War 'rest center for colored soldiers', as a place where you cannot get a lost telegram repeated, but you can get excellent, cheap manicures and delicious little cakes). Fauset is consistently concerned with the meanings Europe has for her characters. One meaning it never has is *home*.

Maggie looks every night at the huge cross on top of the Mont du Nivrolet, but what she is planning is her chain of American Beauty

Shops (pp. 261–2). Maggie and Philip finally decide to marry as they meet in the chapel of the old Dukes of Savoy, but their brief married life is to be in New York (p. 268). *Plum Bun*, Fauset's second and best-known novel, ends in Paris with the happy reunion of Angela Murray and Anthony Cross, but it is clear that they will not settle there. Angela is halfway through her year studying art in Paris, and 'within those six months she had lost forever the blind optimism of youth' (p. 376). She does not appear to meet anyone except other Americans, and Paris, which 'at first charmed and wooed her' (p. 374), ceases to charm as the autumn sets in.

> Paris, so beautiful in the summer, so gay with its thronging thousands, its hosts bent on pleasure, took on another garb in the sullen greyness of late autumn. The tourists disappeared and the hard steady grind of labour, the intent application to the business of living, so noticeable in the French, took the place of a transient, careless freedom.
>
> (Fauset, 1929, p. 376)

Angela recognizes this as 'good discipline', but it destroys the magic of France for her. If Fauset's delight in France were entirely 'snobbish', her heroine would prefer Paris without the tourists. Fauset, however, indicates that an American's business in Paris is to be a tourist, or at least a merely temporary visitor — and then to go home. Houston A. Baker classes Angela's 'European exile' at the end of *Plum Bun* with Helga's despair at the end of *Quicksand* and Clare Kendry's death at the end of *Passing* (Baker, 1991, p. 35).

Fauset's last novel, *Comedy: American Style*, presents the grimmest of all her pictures of Americans in France. France has here become the living hell to which Olivia, the 'confirmed Negro-hater' and her fatally weak daughter Teresa are consigned as punishment. Everything the country had appeared to offer is bitterly transformed. The 'traditional fondness of the French for the Negro' (p. 223) becomes the appraisal of the Senegalese as 'all right as cannon fodder' (p. 182). Teresa's French husband's useful energy in driving a shrewd bargain becomes his horrific meanness about money, which he defines in all seriousness, indeed, in a towering fury, as 'the most precious thing on earth!' (p. 325). His sublime competence as a tour guide is revealed as a hateful insularity: he likes only his home-town, Toulouse, and Toulon because its fortresses gratify his aggressive patriotism (pp. 180–2).

Olivia, stranded for life in Paris, now finds all the little details of

French life which might have delighted her as a tourist alien and repulsive: 'the horrid little stuffed larks' in the delicatessen, the 'sickeningly sweet *sirop*' (pp. 322–3). She meets absolutely no one but another American expatriate, Mrs Reynolds, who urges her to get back to America as soon as she can because 'it made her sick to see a woman, past middle age, with a home and husband in God's country, pass them up for the fabled freedom of Paris' (p. 324). We know that Olivia has always failed to provide a home for her children and has been bitterly loathed by her husband since she drove her black-skinned son Oliver to suicide. So we can enjoy without compunction the irony of her surviving son's reply when he is asked where Olivia has gone: 'Why, to Europe of course. She's completely hipped on foreign life' (p. 315). Olivia's desire for Europe has always been a contaminated one, ever since she passed for white as an Italian girl in America at the age of nine (pp. 5–6). It is part of the horror of her daughter Teresa's exile that her racist French husband believes her to be white.

Teresa's desire for Europe is, in Fauset's terms, perfectly wholesome, for two reasons: she wanted to come only for a few months, to perfect her French, and not to settle for life, and she wanted to gain a qualification so that she could earn her own living. If, like Maggie Ellersley, or Angela Murray after the end of *Plum Bun*, she had returned home knowing more of the beauties of Europe, but more capable of working in America, she would have had the best of the Old and the New Worlds. As it is, she is reduced to taking in sewing from the American students she previously invited as guests; and she is tied to a man who, although 'indifferent, miserly and hard-headed with the cold pitiless logic of the French' (p. 324), is without even the ambition to become a full professor at the University of Toulouse where he teaches.

It is no accident that Fauset's heroines' distancing of themselves from emotional ties has European connotations. Joanna Marshall in *There Is Confusion* replies impatiently to Peter when he asks her for reassurance, ' . . . But, Peter, I have so much to think about — my tour, my booking, you know, my lessons in French and Italian, my dancing . . . ' (pp. 132–3). The 'bit from an old Italian song' she sings him after their first kiss is about parting — 'You'll make me cry', says Peter (p. 105) — and in the first long love-letter she sends him, which comes too late, she can express her erotic feelings only through quoting Goethe. When Angela Murray in *Plum Bun* decides to pass for white and rejects her sister Virginia (whose name suggests not only innocence but an American state), she changes her own name to a mixture of French and Spanish, Angèle Mory.

Again and again Europe is presented as a dishonest escape route. In *There Is Confusion* the old white Meriwether Bye offers to take the small black Meriwether Bye away from his parents to Paris and Vienna (p. 294). Laurentine in *The Chinaberry Tree* (1931) could have chosen to desert her unhappy mother by going to Paris (p. 13).

One reason for Europe's construction as a place feeding escapism is Fauset's attitude to work. The title of *There Is Confusion* has its direct source in the epigraph, taken from Tennyson's poem *The Lotus Eaters*:

There is confusion worse than death,
Trouble on trouble; pain on pain, —

lines which continue but are not quoted in Fauset,

Long labour unto aged breath

which is 'worse than death' in the eyes of lotus-eaters who take a dishonest escape route into utter lethargy. The most eloquent argument against African–Americans leaving for Europe is, for Fauset, the work they have invested in America. Yet this work need not bring fame or material gain. Joanna Marshall, whose sinking into a comfortable marriage at the expense of a stage career Deborah E. McDowell has deprecated (Fauset, 1929), has in Fauset's eyes already achieved greatness by her literal representation of America on stage. Joanna does this wearing a mask, theatrically passing for white, but when at the end of one performance 'America' is asked to unmask, and reveals herself as black, Joanna trenchantly claims her place in American history:

I hardly need to tell you that there is no one in the audience more American than I am. My great-grandfather fought in the Revolution, my uncle fought in the Civil War, and my brother is 'over there' now.

(Fauset, 1929, p. 232)

Most African–American women writers of the 1920s and 1930s were unlike Fauset in their almost complete lack of interest in Europe. Marita Bonner stresses the importance of European immigration for American life. In 'Nothing New', her first story with an explicitly Chicago setting, she writes:

You have been down on Frye Street. You know ... How it lisps in French, how it babbles in Italian, how it gurgles in German, . . .

(Bonner, 1987, p. 69)

But Bonner locates none of her fiction in Europe itself and other writers have found Europe merely a convenient offstage device. In Mercedes Gilbert (1938, p. 221), it is the white plantation owner's year's absence in Europe which makes possible the wrongful imprisonment of the black hero Jim. In Zora Neale Hurston (1934, p. 235), France exists only as a place from which demobbed black men return demanding their meals 'Toot sweet'. In Zara Wright's *Black and White Tangled Threads* (1920a) and its sequel *Kenneth* (1920b), England provides the solution for the problems of the white-skinned black Americans, Zoleeta and Kenneth, who become members of 'the royal family of Blankleighs' (*Kenneth*, p. 338), a surname which indicates the perfunctory nature of this conclusion. Equally, these writers are unlike Fauset in their lack of interest in American history. They are concerned with the aftermath of slavery, but not with America as a developing nation. Gilbert and Hurston argue for the special identity of black people; they do not claim that 'there is no one in the audience more American than I am'.

Nella Larsen saw the dangers of a special identity for black people. In Paris in 1925, for example, the spectacular success of the *Revue nègre* at the Theâtre des Champs-Elysées coincided with the establishment of the new French Institut d'Ethnologie (Clifford, 1988, p. 122). This suggests that the social freedom of African–Americans in Paris was likely to be compromised by their labelling as exotic and 'other'. Even in Harlem, the 'Legendary Capital' of black Americans, as James de Jongh calls it in his analysis of Harlem and the literary imagination (de Jongh, 1990, p. 5), white voyeurs intruded. In *Passing* Larsen describes a dance in Harlem in 1927 which leads her protagonist Irene Redfield to muse on the feelings which the dark-skinned provoke in their white admirers. She says,

I think that what they feel is — well, a kind of emotional excitement. You know, the sort of thing you feel in the presence of something strange, and even, perhaps, a bit repugnant to you; something so different that it's really at the opposite end of the pole from all your accustomed notions of beauty.

(Larsen, 1929, p. 205)

But it is in Denmark that the heroine of *Quicksand*, Helga Crane, experiences the full force of this 'emotional excitement'. Having left Harlem where the music at a nightclub makes her feel like a 'jungle creature' (Larsen, 1928, p. 59), she enjoys in Copenhagen the dubious pleasure of the status of 'some new and strange species of a pet dog being proudly exhibited' (p. 70). The portrait-painter Axel Olsen paints a picture of her as 'some disgusting sensual creature with her features' (p. 89).

Helga is both prized and relegated to a subhuman level in Copenhagen precisely because of her rarity. Her uncle, indignant that she has turned down Olsen's proposal of marriage, cannot believe that she has reasons connected with race, and urges on her the uniqueness of her position, since it is not

> as if there were hundreds of mulattoes here. That, I can understand, might make it a little different. But there's only you.
>
> (Larsen, 1928, p. 91)

Ironically, Helga had always prized both her own idiosyncratic elegance and 'rare and intensely personal taste' (p. 1) and the variety of African–American skin-tones:

> sooty black, shiny black, taupe, mahogany, bronze, copper, gold, orange, yellow, peach, ivory, pinky white, pastry white.
>
> (Larsen, 1928, p. 59)

In Copenhagen she gradually loses all sense of worth either as an individual or as a member of a black race. A special identity for black people has become no identity at all.

Quicksand is more profoundly pessimistic than any of Fauset's novels. Like Fauset, Larsen presents honest work as a necessary good, but makes this almost impossible for her heroine to achieve. Helga works as a teacher for almost two years in a 'machine' (p. 4) of a school in the South and lives for two years in idle luxury in Copenhagen. In between, she exists in anxious poverty in Chicago where 'a few men, both white and black, offered her money, but the price of the money was too dear. Helga Crane did not feel inclined to pay it' (p. 34). She also lives in New York, where she works as a secretary with a Negro insurance company, but has ultimately different plans.

> Some day she intended to marry one of those alluring brown or yellow men who danced attendance on her. Already financially

successful, any one of them could give her the things which she had now come to desire, a home like Anne's, cars of expensive makes such as lined the avenue, clothes and furs from Bendel's and Revillon Frères', servants and leisure.

(Larsen, 1928, p. 45)

Leisure, a 'peacock's life' (p. 81), seems to be hers when she lives in Denmark with her aunt and uncle, but Helga is forced to learn that it is leisure with a harsh, commercial purpose. The moral climate is no different from Chicago's — or New York's. Her aunt advises her to capture Olsen, the portrait painter, as a husband, 'or else stop wasting your time, Helga' (p. 80). Olsen, when he finally does offer Helga marriage, puts it even more bluntly: '... you have, I fear, the soul of a prostitute. You sell yourself to the highest buyer' (p. 87).

Whether in America or Denmark, then, Helga is a commodity. The difference is that in America she is acutely conscious of it. In Denmark she is treated like a child who does not even choose her own clothes. Her suitor Olsen is reduced to a childlike state when Helga refuses him: he looks like 'a puzzled baby' just as Roger in *Plum Bun* looks like 'a cross baby' (p. 322) when Angela refuses his offer of marriage, but this does not bring Helga any corresponding power. The only solution is to leave Denmark, which is no solution at all, since the return to America brings her only misery and an utter waste of her life in a degraded marriage. She is still considered an alien, but now not even a beautiful exotic one. She has sold herself — and to the lowest buyer.

Another element in *Quicksand*'s profound pessimism is that Helga is trapped not only racially but biologically. Her degraded marriage is the result of a violent but temporary sexual appetite, and her utter despair the result of the agony of childbirth (p. 130). She cannot leave her hateful husband because of her ties to her children and she is trapped in a hellish cycle of childbearing and drudgery.

Helga opens the novel, although discontented, much more firmly in control than she ever will be again. She is earning her own living; she is young, beautiful, and healthy and delights in choosing the lovely, elegant clothes which express her individuality (p. 18) — a far cry from the clothes in Denmark which express her only as the manipulated 'other'. Her descent from this unsullied potential in one part of the South to her unmitigated ruin in another is registered by her choice of two European texts. In Naxos she decides on Marmaduke Pickthall's best-selling picaresque English novel *Said the Fisherman* (1903) much admired by E. M. Forster (1936, p. 250) and D. H. Lawrence (1936, pp. 351–4), which celebrates the lure and adventurous possibilities of oriental life. In Alabama she asks for Anatole France's (1923) 'The Procurator of Judea' (p. 131), an ironic study of the gap between results and intentions. But Europe is not, as in Fauset's fiction, offered as an experience to use or misuse, since Helga is already on her downward path. The tourist details of the scenery are presented blandly and the Danish people are shown to be as cold at heart as Fauset's French, but there is no crisis here. There is no right way in which Helga could have tackled Denmark and there is no good America to which she can return. It is hard to imagine that Larsen's projected third novel, set in France and Spain, would have been an optimistic one. Both Fauset and Larsen stress the culture, the physical beauty and the infinite variety of African–American women and much of the impetus of their fiction comes from their attempt to draw them into the centre from the margins of American society. But Helga Crane, born in a Chicago slum (p. 21) of half-Danish parentage, is closer to Marita Bonner's immigrants in her near and uneasy relationship to Europe. Unlike the white-skinned black women in Larsen's own novel *Passing* and in Fauset's novels, whose racial mixture is a product of America's history, Helga's mixed race is the result of a recent collision with Europe. It is Europe, in the person of her Danish mother, which has constructed her as the mulatto 'other', whereas to Fauset's characters it is Europe which paradoxically defines their American identity.

Nella Larsen and Jessie Redmon Fauset both insist that Europe is no stopping-place for black Americans. But Fauset's hopeful emphasis on the redemptive qualities of hard work, properly fuelled by the European encounter, highlights the hopelessness of Larsen's conclusions about the fate of African–American women. Fauset, like Edith Wharton and Willa Cather, realized that there is no good place, but believed that the encounter with Europe could make America a better place. Larsen felt that the African–American woman's complex legacy of oppression had compromised her too deeply for any happiness.

References

AMMONS, E. (1991) *Conflicting Stories: American Women Writers at the Turn into the Twentieth Century*, New York and Oxford, Oxford University Press.
BAKER, H. A., Jr. (1991) *Workings of the Spine: The Poetics of Afro-American Women's Writing*, Chicago and London, University of Chicago Press.

BELL, B. W. (1987) *The Afro-American Novel and Its Tradition*, Amherst, University of Massachusetts Press.

BONNER, M. (1987) *Frye Street and Environs: The Collected Works of Marita Bonner*, FLYNN, J. and STRICKLIN, J. O. (Eds) Boston, Beacon Press.

BORDEAUX, H. (1902, reprinted 1912) *La Peur de Vivre*, Paris, Librairie Plon.

CATHER, W. (1922) *One of Ours*, London, Virago Press (reprinted 1987 with introduction by Hermione Lee).

CHRISTIAN, B. (1985) *Black Feminist Criticism: Perspectives on Black Women Writers*, New York and Oxford: Pergamon Press.

CLIFFORD, J. (1988) *The Predicament of Culture: Twentieth-Century Ethnography, Literature, and Art*, Cambridge, MA and London, Harvard University Press.

CULLEN, C. (Ed.) (1927) *Caroling Dusk*, New York, Harper.

DE JONGH, J. (1990) *Vicious Modernism: Black Harlem and the Literary Imagination*, Cambridge University Press.

FABRE, M. (1991) *From Harlem to Paris: Black American Writers in France, 1840–1980*, Urbana and Chicago, University of Illinois Press.

FAUSET, J. R. (1924), *There Is Confusion*, New York, Boni and Liveright.

FAUSET J. R. (1926), *Crisis*, review of Langston Hughes' *The Weary Blues* (1926), reprinted in SCOTT, B. K. (Ed.) (1990) *The Gender of Modernism: A Critical Anthology*, Bloomington and Indianapolis: Indiana University Press.

FAUSET, J. R. (1929) *Plum Bun: A Novel Without A Moral*. London, Pandora Press (reprinted 1985 with introduction by McDOWELL, D. E.).

FAUSET, J. R. (1931) *The Chinaberry Tree: A Novel of American Life*, New York, Frederick A. Stokes.

FAUSET, J. R. (1933) *Comedy: American Style*, New York, Frederick A. Stokes.

FLYNN, J. and STRICKLIN, J. O. (Eds) (1987) *Frye Street and Environs: The Collected Works of Marita Bonner*, Boston, Beacon Press.

FRANCE, A. (1923) 'Le Procurateur de Judée', *L'Etui de Nacre*, Paris, Calmann-Levy, pp. 1–27.

FORSTER, E. M. (1936) 'Salute to the Orient!' *Abinger Harvest*, London, Edward Arnold, pp. 247–62.

GILBERT, M. (1938) *Aunt Sara's Wooden God*, with foreword by LANGSTON HUGHES, College Park, Maryland, McGrath Publishing.

HURSTON, Z. N. (1934) *Jonah's Gourd Vine*, London, Virago Press (reprinted 1987 with afterword by Holly Eley).

LARSEN, N. (1928) *Quicksand*, New Brunswick, NJ, Rutgers University Press (reprinted 1986 with introduction by McDOWELL, D. E.).

LARSEN, N. (1929) *Passing*, New Brunswick, NJ, Rutgers University Press (reprinted 1986 with introduction by McDOWELL, D. E.).

LAWRENCE, D. H. (1936) 'Said the Fisherman', by Marmaduke Pickthall' in *Phoenix: The Posthumous Papers of D. H. Lawrence*, (Ed.) with introduction by McDONALD, E. D. London, Heinemann, pp. 351–4.

PICKTHALL, M. (1903) *Said the Fisherman*, London, Methuen (reprinted 1986 with introduction by CLARK, P.).

SCOTT, K., 1990 (See Fauset, J. R., 1926).

SYLVANDER, C. W. (1981) *Jessie Redmon Fauset, Black American Writer*, Troy, NY, Whitson.

WHARTON, E. (1920) *The Age of Innocence*, Harmondsworth, Penguin.

WHARTON, E. (1923) *A Son at the Front*, London, Macmillan.

WRIGHT, Z. (1920a, reprinted 1975) *Black and White Tangled Threads*; (1920b) *Kenneth*, New York: AMS Press.

Chapter 2

The Other Other or More of the Same? Women's Representations of Homosexual Men

Gregory Woods

I make no apology for speaking about character, or, indeed, about characters, plural. In as far as it is useful to think of 'gay fiction' as being about rather than necessarily by homosexual people, one is forced to consider, in the first instance, representations of homosexual characters. Books themselves do not, strictly speaking, have sexualities; but the people in them do. What we call gay fiction has been written primarily in order to satisfy a need for narratives about how homosexual people live and die. Such narratives are intended for homosexual readers, to show them themselves, as it were, reflected in a literature of their own; or for heterosexual readers, to broaden their minds; or for both — the main point being, in any case, to render the homosexual individual visible.

The Modernist period slightly post-dates the mental health movement's invention of the concepts 'homosexual' and 'heterosexual', but coincides with the subsequent cultural formation of personal identities based on sexuality (*the* homosexual, *the* heterosexual), as well as with the emergence of homosexual people as a self-conscious minority with a collective identity to shape and rights to be demanded and won. So it is during the same period that the character with a stable homosexual identity first appears in fiction, whether as a minor figure (like the Greek sailor in James Joyce's *Ulysses*) or as a novel's main focus (like E. M. Forster's eponymous *Maurice*). Many of the classic early fictional representations of homosexual men were written by women and it is on these that I mean to concentrate.[1]

As with male writers, so with female. The 'private' lives of those who practise sodomy on and in each other's persons are not fit material for public speech. The British Empire preferred to think of itself, like Brezhnev's Soviet Union or Deng's China, as an astringent desert of manly virtue surrounded by an otherwise effeminate oasis. It was easier for writers to set novels about homosexuality either far from Britain or in some equally distant period in the past. Like many male writers of the inter-war period, and of times since, Naomi Mitchison found the cultures of classical Greece and Rome an apt arena — safely neutral territory — in which to display aspects of male love. Her Greek stories *Krypteia* and *O Lucky Thessaly!* (Mitchison, 1928, pp. 16-25, 27-56) and the Roman story *A Matter of No Importance* (Mitchison, 1929, pp. 81-95) read like preparatory studies for the later and more ambitious gay fictions of women like Mary Renault and Marguerite Yourcenar. Although all three of Mitchison's stories end unhappily, with the parting of the lovers, it is clear that the author does not believe that the temporary griefs she portrays are at all a necessary part of homosexual love, as homophobic myth, then as now, would dictate. At no point does she kill off her characters to punish their sin, as many other writers in this century have chosen, or felt they were forced, to do. To that extent and further, these early stories are positive in an exemplary manner.[2]

Similarly distant from the British social context of its day, Sylvia Townsend Warner's short novel *Mr Fortune's Maggot* (1927) is set on a South Sea Island, far from the restraints of Anglo-Saxon morality. In tone and atmosphere, the story partakes of some of the camp exoticism and eroticism of Ronald Firbank's *Prancing Nigger* (1924). But Warner's book is, at heart, far more seriously charged: it has much to say about religious imperialism and, in general, the disruption of the equilibrium of primitive societies by the civilizing zeal of the developed world. It is also acutely conscious of how love itself is, so often, a colonizing process, ultimately as destructive to lover as to beloved. At the same time, it provides about the nearest we get to a rhapsodic version of man–boy love from the pen of anyone other than a man who loves boys.

However, although Warner was willing privately to refer to the book's central character, a missionary, as being 'fatally sodomitic' (Harman, 1989, pp. 69-70), in the novel itself, Mr. Fortune describes his love for the boy Lueli not as 'what is accounted a criminal love' but as a 'spiritual desire' (pp. 192-3). It is to the book's credit, though, that its subjects are harmony and hope, not the depradations of repression. The genteel missionary eventually leaves the island and his beloved boy behind, but he leaves enchanted and enriched. Having lost his faith through contact with the humane paganism of the islanders, he feels liberated into a truer spirituality, unencumbered by the church. He leaves his God, or what is left of him, on the island as a souvenir for the boy. He also carves the boy an idol to adore. On the boat back to civilization, he receives the news of the Great War, the ultimate sign of what horrors virility can contrive to support its own vanity (p. 247).

Of novels set in Britain at the time of their writing, one might have expected those most fully involved in the Modernist experiment with representations of consciousness to provide fruitful explorations of deviant states of mind. But this is not necessarily so. Virginia Woolf, for instance, seems to take her preoccupation with psychological reality as an excuse for representing love between men as a private affair, so emphatically divorced from the social realm as not to require the definition 'homosexual'. In *The Waves* (1931), she represents Neville's love of Percival as a life-long obsession — perhaps a less traumatized form of the kind of obsession which ties Septimus Warren Smith to his dead wartime comrade, Evans, in *Mrs Dalloway* (1925) — from which Neville never emerges for long enough even to label himself homosexual. It is true that, on leaving school, he is aware that he will 'pass, incredible as it seems, into other lives', and that his love of Percival is 'a prelude only' (p. 43). But, even though Neville does later have a lover, he still thinks constantly of Percival as his lost ideal; the lover, in any case, is faithless (pp. 126–7). Louis, who himself goes through a boy-loving phase at school, predicts Neville's future life as a stable but intense sequence of comfortable scenes 'with many books and one friend' (p. 48). What he fails to predict is the degree of the intensity: the friend will always be the same boy, even long after his accidental death.

There is certainly no awareness at any point in the book, none in any of the book's characters, that male homosexual acts were illegal. There is no sense of oppression, but, rather, of a suppression of overt feeling voluntarily inflicted by Neville on himself, and the consequent image of him, within the minds of the other characters, as one whose destiny is irredeemably sad. When the news arrives that Percival has died in India, Neville says to himself: 'From this moment I am solitary. No one will know me now' (p. 108).

What Woolf depicts here — though she shows no clear sign of being aware of the fact — is male homosexuality at its most palatable to the British status quo (by which I mean, to the values of the upper-middle and upper classes). The Neville/Percival relationship is an entirely conventional public (private) school romance: unrequited, sublimated, with the desired boy conveniently killed off and remembered thereafter, by the boy who desired him, in sentimentally nostalgic soft-focus.

Neville's sexual identity really only takes shape in fantasy. He daydreams of Mediterranean boys sprawling naked in the dust beneath fig trees. He imagines Percival thrashing little boys with a birch (p. 25). He thinks of Percival 'naked, tumbled, hot' on his bed in the moonlight (p. 35). Later in life, he has a recurring fantasy about naked cabin boys squirting each other with hoses (pp. 128, 140). But unlike other bourgeois, homosexual characters of the period (Forster's Maurice, for instance), who meet their sexual needs among the working class, Neville is too much of a snob to soil his bookish, pseudo-classical dreams with the vulgarity of real life. In a characteristic moment he says, 'I cannot read in the presence of horse-dealers and plumbers. . . . They will make it impossible for me always to read Catullus in a third-class railway carriage' (p. 51). Forster, like Lawrence, would have had him trying to strike up a conversation, at least. After all, a horse-dealer or a plumber might, more vividly even than Catullus himself, bring fantasy to life.

That other great Modernist, Gertrude Stein, was far less interested than Woolf in fictional character, so it is not surprising that one does not find in her work the kinds of representation with which this essay is concerned. In any case, Stein's attitude to homosexual men — or rather, in the customary manner of homophobes, to what homosexual men do with each other — was negative. Ernest Hemingway says she told him: 'The main thing is that the act male homosexuals commit is ugly and repugnant and afterwards they are disgusted with themselves. They drink and take drugs to palliate this, but they are disgusted with the act and they are always changing partners and cannot be really happy . . . In women it is the opposite. They do nothing that they are disgusted by and nothing that is repulsive and afterwards they are happy and can lead happy lives together' (Hemingway, 1964, pp. 25–6).[3] Stein's only written representation of homosexual men is in a short piece called *Men*, in which a trio of men enact an emotional drama involving kisses, tears and physical violence (Stein, 1951, pp. 310–15). In her characteristic fashion, Stein teases out the meanings of phrases by repetition and revision, until meaning itself seems an indulgence. But she does, here, grant significance to what singles these men out from others:

> He was meaning again and again in being such a one and he was remembering that he had meaning again and again that he was such a one. He was remembering again and again that he was such a one and he was remembering again and again that he was having meaning. He was such a one.
>
> (Stein, 1951, pp. 314–15)

One thing that the piece makes clear, intentionally or not, is that the three creatures Stein portrays are quite alien to Stein's own equilibrium. Her verbal patterns have the effect of distancing her voice from the men's emotions, with which, as a lesbian, she does not even begin to identify.

By and large, the homosexual characters in men's novels have been tragic loners, outcast in their own land. One has to turn to the non-Modernist women writers for a substantial development of the idea of solidarity between oppressed groups.[4] Even lesbians have appeared only relatively rarely in the male literature. But a number of women's novels, during and between the wars, made a point of discussing the commonality of interests between such groups as female and male homosexuals, the Irish in Britain, black people, Jews, pacifists and the working class. The bravest of these is *Despised and Rejected* by A.T. Fitzroy (1918), whose publisher was convicted for publishing, not an obscenity, but a book likely to prejudice the recruiting of persons to serve in His Majesty's Forces and their training and discipline. Indeed, questions of homosexuality and pacifism have to wait to be so seriously yoked together again until Mary Renault's *The Charioteer* (1956). Fitzroy's sophisticated association of the rituals of heterosexual courtship with social pressures on men to go to war proves a perfect context for her liberal arguments on sexuality. Hers is a more broadly conceived, *social* vision of virility, love and warfare than is found in more personal writings such as Wilfred Owen's poems.

Whereas, in men's fiction, it is often seen as being important to represent homosexual men, at least for part of the narrative, from the viewpoint of the heterosexual homophobe, women writers are generally more concerned to offer the viewpoint of a sympathetic woman character, perhaps representative of the author herself. The clearest example of this type is June Westbrook, in *Strange Brother* by Blair Niles (1932). Healthily curious — or perhaps, at times, inquisitive to the point of intrusiveness — she observes, and then seeks out, homosexual men in Harlem bars. She questions and studies them. When she has won their trust, she is supportive. Her friendship with one, Mark Thornton, becomes the main relationship in the book:

> They were friends without any complication of sex. It was a different relationship from any that June had ever known before, closer than any which had ever existed between her and a woman friend, and more serene, June felt, than would ever be possible in any equally close friendship with a normal man.
>
> (Niles, 1932, p. 193)

31

It is she who makes the link between black and homosexual people as similarly outcast. And it is through her female normality, rather than Mark's male deviance, that the book's pleas for tolerance are voiced.

Far more notorious — and therefore, perhaps, more effective — is Radclyffe Hall's novel *The Well of Loneliness* (1928), which has no mediating hetero voice to comfort the reader who seeks touchstones of normality.[5] Hall's main portrait of a homosexual man, Jonathan Brockett, is no less of a stereotype than the manly lesbian Stephen Gordon herself; if perhaps no more so, either. Although brilliant, he is 'curiously foolish and puerile' at times, and his hands are 'as white and soft as a woman's' (p. 227). When he is in his foolish mood, his hands make 'odd little gestures' and his laugh becomes too high, his movements too small, for his unquestionably male physique. He is liable to compromise his body even further by playing such tricks as putting on the parlourmaid's apron and cap (p. 230). Not unexpectedly, he is an aesthete: art is said to be the one thing in life he respects (p. 233). Be that as it may, his favourite activity is gossip — a fact which Hall even finds symbolically reflected in his appearance: he is described as having 'sharp eyes that were glued to other people's keyholes' (p. 235). When he gossips, his voice takes on an 'effeminate timbre' which Stephen hates (p. 245). Unstoppable, he gushes 'on and on like a brook in spring flood' (p. 247).

This is not to say that Hall is insensitive to the situation of such a man in such an era. Her account of Brockett's changing moods carefully registers his reactions to oppression. There are times when he gets sick of 'subterfuge and pretences' (p. 241); and if he is cynical it is because he spends much of his time 'secretly hating the world which he knew hated him in secret' (p. 242). When he speaks of heterosexual people ('the so-called normal'), his voice, not unreasonably, becomes 'aggressive and bitter' (p. 350).

As a lesbian, Stephen Gordon observes Brockett from a certain distance, but also with sympathetic identification. When they first meet she feels at ease with him, 'perhaps because her instinct divined that this man would never require of her more than she could give — that the most he would ask for at any time would be friendship' (p. 228). But when the Great War breaks out, she discovers that, for all his marginalization and difference as a homosexual man, he is still privileged *as a man*: he is allowed by his country to enlist in its service. (Hall does not mention that he would have been rejected had he been open about his sexuality when enlisting.) Whatever he may think of this dubious honour, the reaction of a patriotic but redundant woman is clear: 'Stephen had never thought to feel envious of a man like Jonathan Brockett' (p. 271). There is, of course, a good deal of disdain in this sentiment: for Stephen usually only envies 'real' men. But in time of war, despite his effeminacy, Brockett is officially considered man enough to die for King and Country — which Stephen is not.

After the War, when Stephen has, after all, distinguished herself in a women's ambulance unit and won the Croix de Guerre and Brockett too has returned, changed in all aspects except 'those white and soft-skinned hands of a woman' (p. 333), Stephen seems increasingly to resent, but forced to accept, a sense of fellowship with other queer people. Near the end of the book there is a complex, depressive scene in a gay bar — a kind of *Purgatorio* for melancholy inverts — where a grey-faced youth whispers to Stephen, 'Ma soeur' (my sister). Her immediate, macho impulse is to hit him in the face with her fist but, although she thinks of him as 'it', a mere creature, barely human at all, she restrains herself, apparently realizing that she has no choice but to identify with him. Digging her nails into her own palms, she reluctantly replies, 'Mon frère' (p. 394). It takes the cultivated Jew Adolphe Blanc to calm her down and persuade her that the men in the bar are fully human. She never loses this antagonistic relation to effeminate men. Indeed, the book virtually closes with a dream in which a cluster of reproachful pansies accuses her of having stolen their masculine birthright of strength (p. 446).

The ostentatiously feminine man is, of course, always a problem to women if his performance ever threatens to slip over from self-expression into parody. And yet, on the other hand, women writers have often shown admiration for men who, even if they do despise the feminity they adopt, hate masculinity even more. So the shameless sodomite is always a useful character for highlighting both antagonisms and potential alliances between women and men. Djuna Barnes provides one such, Dr Matthew O'Connor, in *Nightwood* (1936). He is an unlicensed gynaecologist who goes to bed in full drag: nightgown, wig and make-up. His bedroom is chock-a-block with old scent bottles and rusty gynaecological instruments. At the head of his bed is a bucket 'brimming with abominations'. The whole room has taken on the air of its occupant's ambisexuality: it is described as 'a cross between a *chambre à coucher* and a boxer's training camp'. It no more resembles a real woman's boudoir than it does a real man's (p. 116).

However, what seems to interest Barnes most about the doctor is his way of speaking. He is, of course, pathologically indiscreet. He is sometimes heard to shout after a man's departing shadow in the street,

'Aren't you the beauty!' (p. 49). Asked what he remembers of Vienna, he describes Austrian boys on their way to school, 'rosy-cheeked, bright-eyed, with damp rosy mouths, smelling of the herd childhood' (p. 33). He claims to be able to tell men apart in pitch darkness and even what quarter they frequent, by the 'size and excellence' of, one supposes, their genitals. Some 'come as handsome as *mortadellas* slung on a table' (p. 136). Above all, he talks to women about men, on whose sex lives he is an authority. His knowledge is arcane and expansive but is just as likely to be sharpened down to the point of a paradox: 'It's the boys that look as innocent as the bottom of a plate that get you into trouble' (p. 231).

In this case, then, the homosexual man constitutes a bridge across the gap between men and women, conveying information about the former to the latter, at once enthusing about men as sexual partners and proving their peculiarities alien and exotic. But he is, above all, an untrustworthy informant, far too much of a man: deceitful in bed, when dragged-up to be penetrated by men, and deceitful at work, when penetrating women under false pretences. Shari Benstock speaks of how the 'gossipy and garrulous' doctor 'parodies woman's language, steals her stories and her images in order to teach her about herself' (Benstock, 1987, p. 266). The problem is that, however sincere and convincing his drag, it still conceals the phallus; however brightly lipsticked his mouth, it still contains a patriarchal tongue. Even as an unlicensed doctor in a frock, he has learned to speak with the authority in which doctors are wont to dress up their speculations. Although demonstrably 'other' than heterosexual, heterosexist man, from the perceptive point of view of female otherness, he is nonetheless *the same*. He is homosexual, but a man.

Women writers have not, of course, been immune to homophobia, as its carriers any less than its victims. For instance, there is a somewhat gratuitous passage in Winifred Holtby's *South Riding* (1936) which explains the unpleasantness of Alderman Snaith by identifying him as a survivor of predatory homosexual child abuse. Snaith watches, mesmerised, as his cat gives birth on his hearth rug and is impressed by the 'neatness and economy' of the natural process. ('This, then, was nature — this amusing, tidy and rather charming process.') As the cat finishes licking her kittens clean, Snaith feels released from a burden of suppressed memory:

> Within that brief period of time a thousand half-formed images had been destroyed, a hundred nightmares broken. A serenity of

liberation began to dissolve the horror surrounding all thoughts of mating and procreation haunting him since that one hideous initiation, when, a little pink and white boy, brought up by a maiden aunt, too soft and pretty and innocent for safety in Kingsport streets, he had fallen into the hands of evil men and fled from them too late, a psychological cripple for life.

(Holtby, 1936, pp. 134–5)

While a passage like this clearly reflects a general female concern about the consequences of child abuse, it performs two negative tasks as well. Firstly, given its brevity but the decisive confidence of its last five words, it somewhat ambiguously both absolves Snaith of responsibility, and yet blames him, for his subsequent personality and deeds, flashing into the reader's consciousness with a virtually subliminal insistence, which takes no real account of the complexities of such a case. Secondly, as the novel's only reference to male–male sexual relations, its formulations of the conquest of nature by unnature, child by adult and innocence by evil takes on a stereotypical resonance, echoing the most negative representations of homosexuality within the society to which the book claims reference; the result being, in an otherwise consistently reformist and liberal text, to suggest that anti-homophile vigilance can itself have significant reforming powers, eventually, to rid local communities and councils of the likes of Alderman Snaith.

In this final text, then, if woman herself is 'other', the homosexual man is more other still. His distance from woman is used, if only in passing, to punctuate the argument that heterosexual women and men have a close commonality of interests and should, therefore, share equally in the privileges of democracy. Only then can women, as mothers, adequately protect boys, as sons and potential fathers, from being raped by sonless men.

If I overstate the case, here, by isolating this passage from its humane contexts, I do so, not to accuse Holtby of an uncommon malice, but to offer a mundane example of how women writers too, even the most aware, may fail their gay readers by using homosexuality as a representative evil. This is a careless moment, from which I do not seek to excuse Holtby, but in contrast with which I would prefer to affirm the superiority of the rest of her book. It is, however, a suitable place to end. For what was the 'homosexual' century, between inversion and gayness, if not a hundred years of homophobic representation? The few exceptions, some of which I have named here, are part of the proof.

Notes

1 The terms *homosexual* and *homosexuality* first occurred in German, in two pamphlets by Karl Maria Kertbeny (real name Benkert) published in 1869. The new terminology was given greater currency by Richard von Krafft-Ebing in his *Psychopathia sexualis* of 1887, a translator of which, Charles Gilbert Chaddock, first used the word *homo-sexuality* in English in 1892.
2 Another, later, short story worth reading is Karen Blixen's *The Sailor-Boy's Tale*, in which male love is represented as being at least as dangerous as it may be enigmatic and even magical (Dinesen, 1942, pp. 89–103).
3 In fairness to Stein, one ought to acknowledge the possibility that, in making these ludicrous remarks, she may have been deceiving Hemingway. The stated view about homosexual men is so close to what he would have wanted to hear, that he may have overlooked any trace of irony in its tone.
4 By the shorthand term 'non-Modernist' I mean, in brief, writers who were content to write realist fiction on predominantly social themes, without much concerning themselves with the kinds of innovation which one associates with the fiction of the inner individual as practised by Virginia Woolf, or the reflexive stylistic experimentation of writers like Gertrude Stein.
5 It is true that Stephen Gordon is sufficiently maladjusted to her lesbianism to be constantly pleading the cause of normality, but the fact remains that she has to admire the garden of the norm from the other side of the fence.

References

Dates of references cited within the text refer to dates of original publication. As many of these 'obscure' publications have latterly been republished, the dates given in this list refer to the latest edition of the text.

BARNES, D. (1979) *Nightwood*, London, Faber.
BENSTOCK, S. (1987) *Women of the Left Bank: Paris, 1900–1940*, London, Virago.
DINESEN, I. (1942) *Winter's Tales*, New York, Random House.
FITZROY, A. T. (1988) *Despised and Rejected*, London, GMP.
HALL, R. (1982) *The Well of Loneliness*, London, Virago.
HARMAN, C. (1989) *Sylvia Townsend Warner: A Biography*, London, Chatto and Windus.
HEMINGWAY, E. (1964) *A Moveable Feast*, London, Cape.
HOLTBY, W. (1936) *South Riding*, London, Collins.
MITCHISON, N. (1928) *Black Sparta: Greek Stories*, London, Cape.
MITCHISON, N. (1929) *Barbarian Stories*, London, Cape.
NILES, B. (1991) *Strange Brother*, London, GMP.
STEIN, G. (1951) *Two: Gertrude Stein and Her Brother and Other Early Portraits* [*1908–12*] New Haven, Yale University Press.
WARNER, S. T. (1978) *Mr. Fortune's Maggot*, London, Virago.
WOOLF, V. (1963) *The Waves*, London, Hogarth.

Chapter 3

'Twinned Pairs of Eternal Opposites': The Opposing Selves of Vita Sackville-West

Joss West-Burnham

This essay is concerned to discuss Vita Sackville-West (1892–1962) as a writer within the modernist period, through a reading of her novel *All Passion Spent* (1983) and of the biography *Pepita* (1986). Both texts — centred as they are on the lives of particular individual women (the aged Lady Slane in the novel and the flamboyant figure of Vita Sackville-West's grandmother, Pepita, in the latter) — appear as examples of the ways in which 'female modernism challenged the white, male, heterosexual ethic underlying the modernist aesthetic of "impersonality"' (Benstock, 1988, p. 21). For rather than distance herself from the materials in her work, Vita Sackville-West offers us in each of these very different books an opposing view of her own self. As Gillian Hanscombe and Virginia Smyers suggest in *Writing for Their Lives*: 'modernist woman is not unconventional, she is anti-conventional, wishing her creative energy to take every form of expression possible to her' (Hanscombe and Smyers, 1987, p. 11).

This experimentation with 'every form of expression possible' of genre, form, narrative voices and language is a constant feature in the writings of Vita Sackville-West. Although there appears to be a dearth of critical interest in her work, the continued motivating force and desire in her life was to write, 'to be a good writer' and to be regarded as such by others. This ambition is recorded in her diary: 'I will get myself into English Literature. Somehow or other' (Glendinning, 1983, p. 167). Her prolific productions (Glendinning, 1983) as reviewer, novelist, dramatist, journalist, biographer, travel writer and poet bear testimony to such ambitions.

However, with hindsight it can be argued in a number of ways that

Vita Sackville-West did not make it into English Literature. The interest in her has been fuelled by her own life rather than by her writing: her unconventional marriage to Harold Nicolson, their bi-sexuality made public and Vita, the woman, famous as a result of their son's publication in 1973 of *Portrait of a Marriage*. This text was subsequently hailed as a modern classic and marketed by the BBC as a television series as 'an extra-ordinary love story' or, as *The Times Literary Supplement* remarked, 'one of the most absorbing stories, built around two very remarkable people to stray from Gothic fiction into real life'. One can only assume that one Gothic element here is to do with the perception of their dual sexuality as 'other' which, in itself, could provide the impetus for further work on the reception and subsequent construction of Vita Sackville-West and her work.

Interest in the life of Vita Sackville-West has continued with the publication in 1989 by Methuen of *Violet to Vita: The Letters of Violet Trefusis to Vita Sackville-West*. This was also greeted with acclaim by critics and reviewers.[1] The private life of Vita Sackville-West, rather than her works, has become a very public story. I suspect that she herself was partly expectant of this outcome for as early in her writing career as 1923 she wrote the following in her introduction to *The Diary of Lady Ann Clifford*:

> We should ourselves be sorry to think that posterity should judge us by a patchwork of our letters, preserved by chance, independent of their context, written perhaps in a fit of despondency or irritation, divorced above all, from the myriad little strands which colour and compose our peculiar existence, and which in their multiplicity, their variety and their triviality, are vivid to ourselves alone, uncommunicable even to those nearest to us, sharing our daily life...
>
> (Glendinning, 1983, p. 167)

This from someone who, all her life, had no desire to come out openly about her unconventional marriage and her love for women. Victoria Glendinning records how the correspondence between Harold and Vita provides an insight into their dual lives, for in their letters of self-disclosure to each other, in their diaries 'in their different writing selves, they could write what they could not say' (Glendinning, 1983, p. 59). This practice of correspondence provided a support for their marriage and it can also be suggested that Vita's writing elsewhere also provided both support as well as disclosure.[2]

In some senses this essay perhaps adds to the patchwork process Vita Sackville-West referred to, by restricting its focus to only two of her works for it also presumes to build upon the autobiographical mining already discussed in its attempt to analyse the 'twinned pairs of eternal opposites' that were Vita Sackville-West. The pronounced interest in Vita's life can be more fruitfully exploited in relation to her work as one investigates the paradoxical relationship between continuity and discontinuity throughout. For not only as a woman but also as a woman *writer* was Vita Sackville-West positioned within her culture as 'other' during this period of literary history. However, this positioning (as 'other' was contributed to by Vita herself, as well as by her friends. She and they recognized her as having duality — dual selves, opposing characteristics, apparent eternal opposites. And these oppositions and contradictions are present in her writings — sometimes twinned but more often isolated or separated in the use of different forms, different narrative techniques, different genres.

Instead of the writing moment being that which 'promises to seal the self and to heal a divided subject, it instead opens a seam in the ''autobiographical'' text exposing what Felicity Nussbaum terms ''a fissure of female discontinuity'' that escapes the boundaries of any given theory of self-hood and writing practice' (Benstock, 1988, p. 9). This fissure or splitting, or separation disguised by the pretence of portraying unitary selves through the device of autobiography, is a constant feature of Vita Sackville-West's productions, fictional and factual.

Essential, at this point, I think, is to discuss my use of 'autobiography/autobiographical'. Here I follow Carolyn Heilbrun's (1989) *Writing a Woman's Life*, more specifically her methodological approach of traversing between texts and life — life as texts' arguments. Heilbrun works to establish the importance and significance of the cultural contexts in which women are writing and how these can constrain as well as empower. For instance, Heilbrun suggests that it is often very difficult for women to write directly about themselves, particularly with respect to feelings of anger and/or difference. Therefore women have adopted different strategies and devices to accommodate this which we are only just beginning to acknowledge (p. 15). She suggests that there are four ways to write a woman's life: autobiography, fiction, biography and finally a text in which a woman unconsciously writes her life in advance of living it (p. 14). In keeping with my subject material I want to make a pairing of these categories with the texts I have chosen: *All Passion Spent* and *Pepita*. The first is a novel and hence fiction but also a demonstration of what I think Heilbrun means by 'unconscious' writing of the self. *Pepita* on the other hand is offered as biography but like all texts is constructed and hence can be read also as autobiography and fiction.

In *All Passion Spent* it is possible I think to read the main character, Lady Slane, as a version of Vita Sackville-West, particularly as a projection of herself in later life. This then fulfils Heilbrun's category of 'unconscious' writing of the life before actually living it. In this novel Lady Slane, at 88, is at the end of her full life, reflecting on her past. We are told that Lady Slane 'all her life long, gracious and gentle — had been wholly submissive — an appendage' but then the expectations of what an old woman should or ought to be are challenged for, as Glendinning notes in her introduction to the Virago edition: 'this novel reverses the usual order of things. It is the children (nearly all of whom are in their 60s I should add!) who are staid and narrow-minded and their gentle mother who turns out to be revolutionary' (Sackville-West, 1983, p. ix).

The revolutionary act that Lady Slane takes is the decision on the death of her husband not to live with her children or to acquiesce to the plans they have for her but to live alone and await her death in contemplation — in solitude — in passivity. And, in this sense, the novel appears to be a prolepsis for Vita Sackville-West's own old age. For she was only 38 when she wrote *All Passion Spent* but in her imagination appears to fulfil Heilbrun's category of writing her life in advance as she herself chose to spend the end of her days in solitude in her tower at Sissinghurst. This re-making of the self at the end of the day/life is echoed in the poem 'Solitude', conceived at the same period as *All Passion Spent*:

> Night came again to heal my daily scars;
> Shreds of myself returned again to me;
> Shreds of myself, that others took and wove
> Into themselves, till I had ceased to be.
> Poor patchwork of myself was all unripped
> And stitched again into some harmony
> Like the pure purpose of an orchestra.
> I rode my horse across a moonlit cove
> And found therein my chained Andromeda.
>
> (Glendinning, 1983, p. 296)

If by comparison we consider the biography *Pepita*, Heilbrun's categories of autobiography and biography appear apposite. One could also include it in the category of fiction, for Roland Barthes (1977) has called biography 'a novel that dare not speak its name' — a construction — a fiction created by the biographer.[3] And here *Pepita* is an extremely fruitful text. For ostensibly it is the biography of Vita Sackville-West's Spanish grandmother, Pepita, but in actuality the text shifts from Pepita's life to the life of Vita Sackville-West's mother, Victoria. *Pepita* can also be read with respect to the 'fissures of female discontinuity' as they apply to the writer of the life, Vita Sackville-West (Benstock, 1988, p. 30). *Pepita* is therefore often paradoxical because, whilst it demonstrates certain elements of continuity in women's lives shared by the grandmother, mother, daughter, it also works to assert differences and 'female discontinuity'.

Vita Sackville-West's presence throughout this biography, as our guide through other texts and evidence, our interpreter of other cultures and languages, our witness to moments in history, is so strong that by the end the story we have read becomes that of the construction of the narrative of the self of Vita. *Pepita* can be seen as an apologia and/or a means of making sense of Vita's own life rather than purely a discussion or description of her grandmother and her mother. *Pepita* thus becomes a process by which a particular construction of Vita is achieved, a Vita who is Spanish, a granddaughter, a daughter, a writer.

What also ◦ecomes apparent in reading *All Passion Spent* and *Pepita* alongside each other is the presentation of similar material which is used in different ways because of the different forms used. This begs questions such as, why are the different forms used? What was Vita Sackville-West concerned to achieve in these texts by way of writing the self — using different languages for telling what ultimately is the same story — the story of herself as she works through the significance of the many contradictions in her inheritance and her character?

As I have briefly mentioned earlier, Alison Hennegan in her introduction to the Virago edition of *Pepita* uses the notion of opposites to discuss Vita Sackville-West. She suggests that 'in her mixed ancestry she (Vita) found, in part created, twinned pairs of eternal opposites' and that these provided sources and reassurance for some of her more bewildering conflicts (Sackville-West, 1986). Hennegan then lists some possibilities for these twinned pairs: 'Spanish versus English; gypsy versus aristocrat; Latin passion versus English reticence; the volatility of Spain's peasant working class versus the punctiliously ranked and ordered line of Sackville's ancestors; childlike spontaneity — happy amorality versus sexual relationships which are carefully codified and ratified by legal sanction' (Sackville-West, 1986). In *Pepita* and *All*

Passion Spent we have the embodiment of these 'twinned pairs of eternal opposites'. Each in a different way allows Vita Sackville-West to explore her self as 'other' — her opposing and contradictory selves.

Let us look first in detail at *All Passion Spent* and its story of the life of Lady Slane who represents quintessential Englishness, an aristocrat, the wife of a successful politician who has, on the surface, had a privileged life of plenty and who, at the start of the novel, has been recently widowed. Through third person narration we are offered 'an indirect, softness of approach' (Sackville-West, 1983, p. x). But Lady Slane is also represented as 'a lonely woman at variance with the creeds to which she had apparently conformed' (p. 135).

And throughout the novel we are presented with a critique of the world as it is — established with the masculine as the norm, woman as other. The polarities of femininity and masculinity are diagnosed in relation to individual lives, in particular those of Lady Slane and her husband Henry. The exploration of what happens to a woman in a society where the social norm is that of marriage is at the centre of this text.[4] But there are also other elements interwoven into this patchwork, in particular the processes of ageing for a woman and the consequences of living a life of thwarted or foresaken youthful ambitions and desires.

We have on the one hand an old woman's lament as her body becomes 'her companion' and a constant reminder to her 'of the tyranny' it had always threatened (p. 194) whilst on the other, a fairly substantial critique of a society that restricts women through its obsession with image, looks and beauty. As Lady Slane muses, 'What a queer thing appearance was, and how unfair. It dictated the terms of people's estimate throughout one's whole life. If one looked insignificant, one was set down as insignificant . . . ' (p. 26)

The novel's ulterior narration constructs a character as split into a past and a present self: 'For Lady Slane was in a fortunate position of seeing into the heart of the girl who had been herself . . . ' (p. 148). It is interesting to note the emphasis on 'who **had** been herself'. In the extraordinary passage (p. 148) which follows we are told:

> her young thoughts were of an extravagance to do credit even to
> a wild young man. They were thoughts of nothing less than
> escape and disguise; a changed name, a travestied sex, and
> freedom in some foreign city — schemes on a par with the
> schemes of a boy about to run away to sea.

But this is not all — for the young Lady Slane had also wished to be a painter, to create. These young thoughts, ambitions, selves however were thwarted by the only one employment open to women — marriage.

Victoria Glendinning notes that Vita Sackville-West built into *All Passion Spent* 'her lifelong anger about the way society distorts and inhibits the individual, particularly if that individual is a woman' (Sackville-West, 1983, p. x) and, I would add, particularly if the woman is middle class and married.

Lady Slane's thoughts on love and marriage centre on the internal and external transformations of her 'self' that were required of her. Prior to marriage 'she had her own name: Deborah Lee, not Deborah Holland, not Deborah Slane' (p. 146). On marriage:

> She knew only that she remained completely alien to all this fuss about the wonderful opportunity which was hers. She supposed that she was not in love with Henry, but, even had she been in love with him, she could see, therein no reason for foregoing the whole of her separate existence. Henry was in love with her, but no one proposed that he should forego his. On the contrary, it appeared that in acquiring her — he was merely adding something extra to it (p. 160).

The result is that 'her love for him had been a straight black line through her life. It had hurt her, it had damaged her, it had diminished her . . . (that) her self had drained away to flow into the veins of another person' (p. 174). Lady Slane then asks 'Who was she, the 'I' that had loved?' and she decides (p. 175):

> That self was hard to get at; obscured by the too familiar trappings of voice, name, appearance, occupation, circumstance, even the fleeting perception of self became blunted or confused. And there were many selves. She could never be the same self with him as when she was alone; and even that solitary self which she pursued shifted, changed, melted away as she approached it, she could never drive it into a dark corner, and there like a robber in the night, hold it by the throat against the wall, the hard core of self chased into a blind alley of refuge.

The self remains illusive, constantly changeable and even an act of violence cannot contain it.

Towards the end of the novel we are offered a different way of looking at the self through Lady Slanes's face to face encounter with the personification of her earlier other self, her great grand-daughter, Deborah, (same name, same desire for freedom) who wants to be a musician rather than marry. But 'This child, this Deborah, this self, this other self, this projection of herself, was firm and certain' (p. 283). Immediately after these revelations that things are different, more hopeful for future generations of young women, Lady Slane dies quietly and the novel closes.

The links between generations of women were also to become a main feature of *Pepita* — grandmother, mother, daughter, are explored and portrayed in relation to each other. This seems highly significant with respect to Vita Sackville-West's own sense of identity or construction and re-construction of self: '...a woman's sense of identity, as well as her view of her place in society, is likely to be largely shaped in response to her relationship with the woman who has served as her earliest model be it mother, grandmother or another woman.' (Park and Heaton, 1988, p. xi). Vita Sackville-West never knew or met her grandmother; she was but a reconstruction, a fantasy, perhaps an alter ego? She also had a very difficult relationship with her mother. Simone de Beauvoir in *The Second Sex* notes how 'the mother–daughter relationship has a particular quality for, the daughter is for the mother at once her double and another person' (de Beauvoir, 1974, p. 496) and I want to suggest that this is exactly the situation in *Pepita*, a text that could only be written in Vita's own middle years, after the death of her mother. In this text Vita, writer, grand-daughter, daughter, 'other' brings judgement to bear on her subjects in their relation to her — as the role models they did or did not provide for her. Glendinning (1983) suggests that we can read *Pepita* as the moment in Vita's life when she finally exorcizes the Spanish, passionate side of her self and settles into her English inheritance but I am not sure that this can be said to be the case for it assumes that *Pepita* as a text strives towards unity when in fact it appears to thrive on being the opposite to this. It has no investment in creating a cohesive self over time. If anything, it works to exploit differences and change over sameness and identity both through the story of Pepita and of Victoria.

At the beginning of *Pepita*, we are told quite categorically by the author, 'I should like to explain here that nothing in the following pages is either invested or even embellished. Down to the smallest, the very smallest particular, it is all absolutely and strictly true' (p. 14). This claim that the book is the truth and nothing but the truth is given further weight as the author reveals the evidence used to write it: legal documents and 'eye' witness reports collected in 1896 by Vita's grandfather's solicitors in Spain in order to fight the court case to prove that her grandmother had, in fact, been married to her grandfather and thus prove her mother's legitimacy.

The story of Pepita's life is, briefly, that she was the daughter of Catilina, the illegitimate daughter of a Duke descended from the Spanish branch of the Borgias family. At '19 Pepita was dark, quiet and beautiful with a face divine' (p. 17). Catilina is portrayed as forceful and domineering but the daughter/mother relationship is one of adoration. We are told that 'Pepita's devotion to her mother was of a nature to be considered excessive by their friends, who on occasions did not hesitate to describe Catilina as Pepita's evil angel' (p. 19). Vita, the author, comments on this mother/daughter relationship throughout, undercutting her original assertions of truth and authenticity. Catilina's ambition for her daughter is to be a dancer. Pepita succeeds in this, marries a Spanish dancer, Juan Antonio Gabriel de la Oliva, and then leaves him and has an affair — which is to last all her life — with Lionel Sackville-West, a diplomat. She has children by him, travels the world but cannot inhabit the public world with him as she is regarded as not respectable.

The text then shifts to focus upon the life of Vita's mother — again with interventionary comments from the author. Victoria's mother, Pepita, dies when Vita is only eight and her father Lionel abandons his children and flees to Buenos Aires to take up a post as British Minister. Victoria is sent to a convent until at eighteen she is 'reclaimed' by her English family and becomes eventually her father's social hostess. Victoria is described as 'lovely, ingenuous and irresistibly charming' (p. 161). She copes with her rags to riches turn admirably. Vita comments: 'Yes, her life was a romance indeed' (p. 183). We are told how this beautiful creature could have had the pick of hundreds of men for a husband but instead falls in love with her first cousin — another Lionel Sackville-West. She then has a privileged life at Knole as well as travelling around the world — in fact the life of Lady Slane in *All Passion Spent*. Victoria comes across to us as a snob, someone unconcerned about the world of politics or social issues or at least this is how Vita portrays her to us. We are told, 'she never thought much, she merely lived' (p. 201), for herself.

It is through such judgements that *Pepita* can be read as an attempt by Vita Sackville-West to explore herself in relation to these two women. *Pepita* is therefore a text which stresses self-disclosure — self as an authority in her own being, her other self, even though this self is often decentred, often actually absent. Vita's anxieties about what kind of self to create of/for her grand/mother can be found in the text itself. Thus she writes, 'Pepita, can I re-create you? Come to me. Make yourself alive again. Vitality such as yours cannot perish' (p. 32) and later asks:

> why should I be afraid of invoking you or my own mother, who are both dead though you were both once so much alive — more vividly and troublesomely alive than most people? You both made trouble for everybody connected with you. You were both that sort of person. Yet you were both adored (p. 33).

Two pages later we are told how she wants to recreate them as 'jolly raggle-taggle Bohemians' — free, sexual spirits who followed their passions, lived unorthodox lives and yet were still loved and adored. The over-arching concern for Vita is to tell the stories of women's lives which are unorthodox, different and yet have not left them lonely and unloved. It may be a way of suggesting that even though she too is different she is still lovable. An alternative reading would be that which fits into the *apologia* mode whereby Vita can reconstruct her self by demonstrating that her behaviour, particularly with respect to her sexuality, is not her fault but that her passionate self has been inherited. It was in the genes of these two women. Therefore, whilst it is tempting to see a complete separation or distinction between Vita Sackville-West's attempts to create or recreate the lives of others, from the possibilities of *Pepita* as self-disclosure this is impossible. The two are inextricably connected.

Pepita ends with Vita's critique of her mother and by inference her grandmother too: 'She was too Latin, somehow; too unreal; too fantastic altogether; too un-English' (p. 225). This serves, in part, to establish Vita's position as other to this — English, realistic and ordinary in some kind of traditional sense, a woman perhaps very much like Lady Slane. However, it can be concluded that within both *Pepita* and *All Passion Spent* the lives of the women presented to us, the self that is at the heart of these books, is in fact Vita who proclaims at the very end of *Pepita* that the motto for any life is 'to thine own self be true', even if that self is different, or secret.

Notes

1 This interest continues: witness the sell-out of Suzanne Raitt's *Vita and Virginia* (Oxford University Press, 1993) concerned with the friendship between Vita

Sackville-West and Virginia Woolf; the hype surrounding the film version of Woolf's novel, *Orlando* (which is supposed to be a tribute to Vita Sackville-West).
2 Alison Hennegan, Introduction to the Virago edition of *Pepita*.
3 The temptation here of course is to forge a relationship between this phrase and a love that dare not speak its name and to extend the work on Vita's anxieties in relation to her bi-sexuality.
4 In both her introduction to the Virago edition of *All Passion Spent* and in her biography of Vita Sackville-West, Victoria Glendinning notes the similarity between this fictional representation of a woman's life and the issues discussed by Virginia Woolf in *A Room of One's Own* and *Three Guineas*. Both latter texts are contemporary to those of Vita Sackville-West. Woolf and West were also friends at this time.

References

BARTHES, R. (1977) *Image, Music, Text* (Translated by Stephen Heath), New York, Hill and Wang.

BENSTOCK, S. (1988) (Ed.) *The Private Self: Theory and Practice of Women's Autobiographical Writings*, Chapel Hill & London, The University of Carolina Press.

DE BEAUVOIR, S. (1974 edn) *The Second Sex* (Translated by H. M. Parshley), London, Vintage.

GLENDINNING, V. (1983) *Vita: The Life of Vita Sackville-West*, Harmondsworth, Penguin Books.

HANSCOMBE, G. and SMYERS, V. (1987) *Writing for Their Lives: The Modernist Woman 1910–1940*, London, The Women's Press.

HEILBRUN, C. (1989) *Writing a Woman's Life*, London, The Women's Press.

LEASKA, M. A. and PHILLIPS, J. (Eds) (1989) *Violet to Vita: The Letters of Violet Trufusis to Vita Sackville-West*, London, Mandarin.

NICHOLSON, N. (1973) *Portrait of a Marriage*, London, Weidenfeld & Nicholson.

PARK, C. and HEATON, C. (1988) *Close Company*, London, Virago.

SACKVILLE-WEST, V. (1983) *All Passion Spent*, London, Virago.

SACKVILLE-WEST, V. (1986) *Pepita*, London, Virago.

WOOLFE, V. (1929) *A Room of One's Own*, (Granada edition, 1977), London, Hogarth Press.

WOOLFE, V. (1938) Three Guineas, (Penguin edition, 1977), London, Hogarth Press.

Chapter 4

'The Museum of Their Encounter': The Collision of Past and Present in the Fiction of Djuna Barnes

Deborah Tyler-Bennett

Djuna Barnes was born in 1892 in New York State and died in Greenwich Village in 1982. Although spending seventy years of her life in America, she is chiefly remembered for her sojourn in Paris during the 1920s. She is termed a modernist writer and is compared with other modernists such as Eliot and Joyce. Yet her work bears little relation to theirs, being closer to that of women writers of the period such as Natalie Clifford Barney and Mina Loy. How useful the term modernist is in relation to Barnes's expansive career remains a matter for speculation.

Barnes published widely both for well known magazines, such as *Vanity Fair*, and 'little' magazines, such as *Transition*. This diversity of publication can be linked to her aesthetic, as it matched the eclectic pastiche of her texts. Barnes's move to Europe (*c.* 1920) was a direct result of what she regarded as the commercialisation of Greenwich Village. Her move back to America (*c.* 1939) was due both to wartime pressures and the atmosphere of tourism in Paris. It was 'the crowd' (so prevalent in works by modernists) which in the end disgusted her.

Inhabitants of the fictional realms created by Djuna Barnes in the 1920s and 30s often seem to be confronted with problems of identity. This is frequently linked to the influence of the past upon the present. In many of her works, the hold of the past upon individuals living in the present is foregrounded. The struggle of personal consciousness against objects from history is often symbolised, in both Barnes's fiction and in her drama, by the rooms and apartments which the individual occupies. I wish to discuss the relationship between the individual, gender identity and the space which they occupy in this chapter, using the short stories *Cassation*, 1962, and *Vagaries Malicieux*, 1974, by way of illustration.

As much of Barnes's fiction deploys the symbolism of rooms which are at once inherited and created by the individual, it would be simple to impose a Freudian interpretation upon them.[1] Yet it is my contention that Barnes's fiction remains resistant to such a reading, just as it eludes most other critical constructs. For Djuna Barnes, artistic creation seems to have presented a possibility of evading being categorised. Her complex texts resist both the discourse of psycho-analysis and the imposition of a theoretical structure upon them. This leaves the feminist in a position which is at once difficult and rewarding because Barnes's texts inhabit a space which is both marginal and free. This can be seen as a deliberate ploy on the part of an author for whom categorisation came to represent a denial of the self.[2]

Many of Barnes's characters are not confronted by physical death but by the burden of continuing to live. The knowledge that it is life, not death, which haunts most of humanity seems to be central to her texts. It could be argued that it is this knowledge which forms a back-drop to the emotional dramas which are played out in the private sphere of the rooms within these texts. The rooms here referred to, which are linked to the creation and the destruction of the self, are redolent with the past which 'freezes' the present of the individual. In *Nightwood* (1936), the novel for which Barnes is best known, the room inhabited by Nora Flood and Robin Vote is described (p. 85) in terms of the objects which fill it.

There were circus chairs, wooden horses from the ring of an old merry-go-round ... Chandeliers from the flea-fair, stage-drops from Munich, cherubim from Vienna, ecclesiastical hangings from Rome, a spinet from England and a miscellaneous collection of music-boxes from many countries; such was the museum of their encounter.

This 'museum' has been linked by Jane Marcus (1991) to the Bakhtinian concept of carnival and it has also been discussed as indicating Nora's desire to create an un-American space which she and Robin can inhabit as well as highlighting the imposition of heterosexual objects upon a lesbian relationship.[3] It could also be interpreted as Nora's attempt to create a space which is other: an eclectic mixture of the religious and the secular, which is intensely personal.

This room constitutes what Maggie Humm (1991) has termed a 'border crossing,' as it creates a pastiche of other rooms, past and present, by blending religious iconography with home comforts and carnival with domestic objects. It is, in some ways, a 'museum' of the relationship between the two women, as it is a collection which parodies domestic conventions. Useful domestic objects, for example, such as chairs are displaced by circus chairs. The mundane is thus replaced by the carnivalesque. The room is also a pastiche of high and low art, as a classical instrument (the spinet) occupies the same space as do the music boxes. Theatrical trappings lie alongside religious objects and thus it is suggested that religion constitutes a type of personal theatre. Modernity and the past are here inextricably linked. The desire to blend past and present barely conceals the intimation that one is cut adrift in a mechanistic city, living a life without coherence.[4]

For many characters, the resultant feeling of rootlessness seems to manifest itself in a collecting of objects from the past which is at once compulsive and arbitrary. These objects have little to do with personal histories but rather allow individuals to create a façade. These created pasts, embodied by objects, are façades which, as time passes, certain characters come to believe. In *Nightwood*, 1936, for example, Felix Volkbein, a Jewish character, turns his back on his roots and creates an aristocratic pedigree for himself. To illustrate this pedigree he carries with him a series of family trees, seals and genealogies. Felix carries these throughout the novel as emblems of the past which he has created for himself. He continues to bear them long after most characters have ceased to believe that they are his. This 'faked' family history results in a disjuncture between Felix's self and his environment. He, like many other characters in works by Barnes, renders himself 'unplaceable.' The question of what comes to be believed, façade or actual past, is one which haunts Barnes's fiction.

Both *Vagaries Malicieux* and *Cassation* explore the themes of the past, gender-roles and the created self. Rooms in both stories are artificial spaces, opposed to the organic growth of the natural world. *Cassation,* which is narrated by a woman in Paris who tells a tale of her past life in Berlin (where Barnes stayed in the early 1920s) is a story which studies the loneliness of the individual. The narrator, an expatriate Russian, tells the story to an unknown listener whose reactions are not revealed to the reader. Thus the tale is one told by someone aware of her role as an exile. She recounts details of her life with Gaya, a woman whom she once loved. The physical presence of Gaya offers a centre of futile activity (p. 13):

> Something purposeful and dramatic came in with her, as if she were the centre of a whirlpool, and her clothes were a temporary debris.

This activity is placed in direct opposition to the 'frozen life' which exists within the dream-like environment of Gaya's house. Gaya is 'savage' with jewels, and to enhance this appearance of wealth, the house is filled with opulent *objects d'art*. Yet, despite these small details, the exact location of the house remains unknown. As with Seymour Menton's (1983) discussion of the use of houses in magic realist painting,[5] the house remains 'the big house' without either name or street number to locate it (Barnes, 1962, p. 13). The house exists stranded within the iconography of the text, as much as buildings are marooned in the paintings of Remedios Varo. As with many literary works of magic realism, the vague nature of the building's exterior is directly contrasted with the heightened, overtly sharpened focus on its interior.

In order to define herself, Gaya collects, under her roof, a bizarre selection of objects. Her shelves are lined with expensive books, signifiers both of knowledge and wealth. These are, says Barnes, 'bound with red morocco, on the back of each, in gold, was stamped a coat of arms, intricate and oppressive' (p. 13). In Gaya's bedroom, this 'intricate and oppressive' atmosphere is magnified. The room itself seems to symbolize a vast battle between the sexes, where inanimate objects develop the same force possessed by Gaya's clothing (p. 13):

> A great war painting hung over the bed; the painting and the bed ran together in encounter, the huge rumps of the stallions reigned into the pillows. Generals with foreign helmets and dripping swords, raging through rolling smoke and the bleeding ranks of the dying, seemed to be charging the bed, so large, so rumpled, so devastated. The sheets were trailing, the counterpane hung torn, and feathers shivered along the floor, trembling in the slight wind from the open window.

The masculine, militaristic nature of the war canvas possesses a vital and destructive quality which 'does battle' with the feminine elements in the room, the sheets and counterpane. So violent is this encounter that it sends feathers blowing across the floor. The epic sweep of the painting is contrasted with the slight movement of the feathers; yet both the epic and the domestic are equally important to the dynamic of the room.

The scene appears to possess infinitely more reality for the narrator than Valentin, Gaya's ironically named, disabled child. Valentin is described as lying in the bed, making a barely human 'buzzing' sound. The child is truly dispossessed as, lying amid the violence of a gendered battle, she is rendered mute. This battle however, appears to remain rooted in the bed, as Gaya and Ludwig, her husband, 'a little man, quite dreamy and uncertain', seem to live amicably (p. 13).

Time, in Gaya's environment, seems to have been arrested. Once within the walls of the house, the narrator seems to be trapped in a state of limbo. Once begun, the love between Gaya and the 'girl' seems likewise to have frozen. As Jenny Petherbridge attempts in *Nightwood*, Gaya seems to wish to entrap the beloved in a house full of opulent objects, objects which both define and obscure the self. Eventually, the reader comes to realize that the narrator has broken free from the web of the past and has rejected the gender battle, which the bed represents, for a certain kind of personal autonomy. In confronting both the encounter between bed and picture and the mute child, she is able to explore her own otherness in relation to these and gains the strength to escape. Gaya, however, remains trapped, a prisoner in her house full of objects. The painting, from which the narrator is able to liberate herself, remains Gaya's nemesis. Unlike the narrator, Gaya cannot embrace her otherness but remains with Ludwig and Valentin, compromising her gender and thus her life. The reader, therefore, has to decide whether the battle of the sexes which the room appears to resemble is no more than an ironic commentary on the actual relationship between Gaya (the 'masculine' woman) and Ludwig (the 'feminine' man). Is the idea of this battle (where masculinity wins via militaristic force) therefore a fantasy? Is Gaya the dominant partner? The fact remains that Gaya does not leave with her lover but stays with Ludwig. Thus the painting might suggest that, despite Gaya's obvious strength, Ludwig maintains the upper-hand as patriarchy is on his side. He does not need to display this strength because he is sanctioned by behavioural codes which are symbolized, in their most overt form, by epic paintings such as the one which dominates the bedroom. In leaving for Paris, the narrator makes a personal choice, which is indicative of her new-found sense of self. In this context, Gaya's sense of self is denied by objects such as the painting.

The experience of the woman in *Cassation* is, in part, mirrored by the unidentified protagonist of the tale *Vagaries Malicieux*. This time the place is Paris and the central character is a young writer who has gone there to find the city of James Joyce. The narrator is complacent, possessing a set of expectations concerning the city. The narrator also has a set of gender expectations based on a heterosexual model, where 'masculinity' and 'femininity' are stereotypically defined. These expectations are shaken to their foundations as the narrator meets actual Parisians and is plunged into a world which is unknowable. Two women of the city, one young and one old, live in a house which, again, is cluttered with rich objects from the past. Among these are portraits and statues which depict women from the family's history:

> On the satin-covered walls hung hundreds of gilt-frames, in which winsome women, of an earlier age, put up their back-hair for someone, and still others disclosed such busts as are dreamt of only by starved lithographers.
>
> (Barnes, 1974, p. 21)

These images define a femininity which does not fit the living women. Daily they confront the two women who live in the house, lessening the reality of their lives. The women move silently around the house, as if they are guests in it. Unlike the war painting in *Cassation*, these portraits are static but, like that painting, they condition the lives of the house's occupants. In this context, the past is brought into sharp focus, while the present seems to be blurred. The images of women within the rooms have been created by male artists, the history of the sitters' lives is, presumably, forgotten.

In Barnes's text these gendered images crush both men and women. Upon walking to Napoleon's tomb, the narrator describes it as being like 'a cannon, fired over a lake of corpses' (p. 21). The memory of war (both the recent 1914–18 war and wars long past) is an oppressive reminder of male militarism. These visions of old conflicts define masculinity just as the portraits define femininity. In the city itself, this issue is amplified and the echoes of the dead dominating the women's rooms, are also present in urban parks and gardens. The nameless narrator is displaced, alone in the city and promenading in public gardens (p. 24):

> where half-destroyed satyrs and virgins lie among the long grass, as unmolested as the dead, for children and nursemaids play about them with a reverence which needs no civic reminder.

The narrator has hitherto been complacent concerning gender but is shaken by the encounters within and without the house. In the park, this sense of instability is re-inforced. The dead within the text cling voraciously to the living, making the individual feel like a charlatan who is imposing, as might a bad guest, upon the past. As with Gaya, both the narrator of this Parisian tale and the women live cloistered by opulent images. In the park, the statues remain essentially unmolested whereas the living are constantly hounded by a past which, despite their assertions otherwise, defines their identity. This image of the statues being unmolested can be linked both to the treatment of childhood sexual abuse in Barnes's fiction and also to the idea that the living are continuously molested by memories of the dead.[6] It is the dead who remain free of the abuse which might have been their lot in life, and the statues marking their memorials which remain tranquilly unaffected by change. The instability of the present in the face of a past, which raises questions about identity and juxtaposes a present façade with a past existence whose meaning is inferred rather than affirmed, is a central concern of Barnes's work. In her texts, rooms act as constant reminders of a gendered past, a past which threatens to engulf the present. Even when a character seems to have escaped this past, such as the narrator of *Cassation*, the rooms live on in the imagination forcing the individual to confront not only the lure of history but the uncertain present of the self.

Notes

1 Barnes often appears to parody Freudian concepts in her texts; thus to read them within such a framework is often to ignore this parodic stance. Although early criticisms, such as those by Alexander Woolcott, linked Barnes with Freudian ideas, the works resist such a critical framework by parodying the notion of the room as a space linked to intimations of the womb.

2 Barnes refused many interviews, did not enjoy discussing her work and did not write an autobiography. Her texts, by defying categories (*The Ladies Almanack*, 1928, could be termed an almanac, a novel, an illustrated chap-book, a lesbian satire, a Picaresque romance, a lesbian hagiography), elude strictly literary definitions.

3 Marcus comments on the fact that the seeming 'misrule' provides an alternative voice to the escalating voice of totalitarianism. She regards this as no coincidence as the characters in *Nightwood* (1936) are the very individuals who would be destroyed under fascism.

4 This might be considered as being typical of women's writing of the period, as the short fiction of Katherine Mansfield (where individuals are often isolated in cafés and pensions) demonstrates.

5 Menton maintains that these houses often exist in isolation, as in paintings by De Chirico and that they are depicted in sharp focus but without identifying features.

6 Louise de Salvo (1991) has suggested that Barnes deployed images of childhood abuse in order to explore and come to terms with the childhood abuse which she undoubtedly suffered at the hands of Wald Barnes, her father. Examples of this can be found in Barnes's major play, *The Antiphon* (1958), in which scenes containing the father's rape of the daughter were cut by T. S. Eliot. An excellent analysis of Eliot's destruction of Barnes's play has been provided by Lynda Curry (1991).

References

BARNES, D. (1928) *Ladies Almanack*, Dijon, Darrantiere.
BARNES, D. (1936) *Nightwood*, London, Faber and Faber.
BARNES, D. (1958) *The Antiphon*, London, Faber and Faber.
BARNES, D. (1962) 'Cassation', *Selected Works*, London, Faber and Faber, pp. 12–20.
BARNES, D. (1974) 'Vagaries Malicieux', *Vagaries Malicieux*, New York, Frank Hallman, pp. 5–28.
CURRY, L. (1991) 'Tom Take Mercy: Djuna Barnes's Drafts of *The Antiphon*', in BROE, M. L. (Ed.), *Silence and Power: A Re-evaluation of Djuna Barnes*. Illinois, South Illinois University Press, pp. 286–99.
DE SALVO, L. (1991) 'To Make Her Mutton at Sixteen: Rape, Incest and Child Abuse in *The Antiphon*', in BROE, M. L. (Ed.) *Silence and Power: A Re-evaluation of Djuna Barnes*. Illinois, South Illinois University Press, pp. 300–15.
HUMM, M. (1991) *Border Traffic: Strategies of Contemporary Women Writers*, Manchester, Manchester University Press.
MARCUS, J. (1991) 'Laughing at Leviticus: "*Nightwood*" as a Woman's Circus Epic,' in BROE, M. L. (Ed.) *Silence and Power: A Re-evaluation of Djuna Barnes*, Illinois, Southern Illinois University Press, pp. 221–52.
MENTON, S. (1983) *Magic Realism Rediscovered*, New York, Alliance.
TATE, T. and ADAMS, B. (1991) *That Kind of Woman*, London, Virago.

Further Reading

These texts are not cited in this chapter but may be of use for further reading.

BROE, M. L. (1989) 'My Art Belongs to Daddy: Incest as Exile, the Textual Economies of Hayford Hall', in BROE, M. L. and INGRAM, S. (Eds) *Women's Writing in Exile*, Carolina, Carolina University Press, pp. 41–86.
HIPKISS, R. (1968) 'Djuna Barnes: A Bibliography', in *Twentieth Century Literature*, pp. 161–3.
MESSERLI, D. (1977) *Djuna Barnes: A Bibliography*, New York, New York University Press.
MESSERLI, D. (1985) 'The Early Newspaper Stories of Djuna Barnes', *Smoke*, London, Virago, p. ix.

Chapter 5

Case-histories versus the 'Undeliberate Dream': Men and Women Writing the Self in the 1930s

Jan Montefiore

A child may ask when our strange epoch passes,
    During a history lesson, 'Please sir, what's
An intellectual of the middle classes?
    Is he a maker of ceramic pots,
    Or does he choose his king by drawing lots?'
                    (W. H. Auden and L. MacNeice, 1937, p. 201)

On the other side . . . is nothing but the Oh no, Oh no, no, no, no, of the undeliberate dream that is to be endured and yet resisted, the horror of refusal with no power of refusal, Oh no. Oh no. No, no, no.
                    (Stevie Smith, 1938, p. 70)

Case-histories from the Auden Generation

'No other decade can have produced so much autobiography as the ten years between 1930 and 1940'. This remark by Virginia Woolf in her essay on the young male writers of the 1930s (Woolf, 1966, 2, p. 177) condemned their work as written in bad faith and 'spoilt by the voice of the loudspeaker' (p. 175). Her only praise for 'Mr Auden, Mr Spender, Mr Isherwood, Mr MacNeice' (p. 174) was that they did write well about themselves: the egoism which disfigures their work is also, she argues, its only redeeming feature. 'They have been incapable of giving us great plays, great novels, great poems . . . But they have had a power which, if literature continues, may prove to be of great value. They have been great egotists' (p. 177). Posterity might, she thought, owe much to their 'creative and honest egoism'.

Although Virginia Woolf's recognition of the dominance of the autobiographical mode among writers of the 1930s is astute — and even prophetic, given the volume of post-war memoirs of the 1930s[1] — her insight has not been much noticed by literary historians of the decade, perhaps because the young men whose names she specifies published no book-length memoirs before 1940, apart from Christopher Isherwood's *Lions and Shadows* (1938). But the poets Stephen Spender, Louis MacNeice, Cecil Day-Lewis and (more indirectly) W. H. Auden all wrote strongly autobiographical poems and plays;[2] George Orwell chose the form of personal testimony for his non-fiction; Edward Upward's published fiction in the 1930s was all autobiographical; Isherwood and Graham Greene used travel writing as a way of revisiting their youth. When these men produced studies of literature, history and society, they constantly resorted to the autobiographical mode, usually by invoking the writer's own illustrative case-history. Louis MacNeice's study *Modern Poetry* (1938) includes three chapters about his own development, called *My Case-Book* (pp. 32–74); the third part of Cyril Connolly's *Enemies of Promise* (1938) also consists of the writer's case-history of his Eton schooldays. George Orwell inserted an account of his own socializing into his analysis of English society in *The Road to Wigan Pier* (1936). Graham Greene (1939) prefaces his account of the persecution of Catholics in Mexico with a memoir of his miserable schooldays in Berkhamstead. And in *Letter to Lord Byron* (Auden and Macneice), Auden follows up his virtuoso potted histories of English society and European literature with an account of himself as a typical 'intellectual of the middle classes'. It is these fragmentary case-histories of typical intellectuals of the middle classes that concern me in the first part of this paper.

All of these memoirs are of the writers' schooldays and all insist on the representative quality of these experiences. (Even Graham Greene, who writes in Catholic rather than sociological terms, insists on the representative quality of his hellish schooldays as instances of the miserable human condition.) Though they mostly deal with the period 1910–25, these educational case-histories are very much of the thirties, the writers' focus moving between the trauma of the Great War and the moment of writing in 1936 or 1937, represented as a time of political crisis which retrospectively illuminates the writers' youthful illusions. So even when these memoirs describe an expensive education or a world of privileged security, they are bounded by an awareness of historical catastrophe and crisis: much of their intellectual energy lies in the writers' ironic awareness of themselves as historical subjects. In the discursive writings of what Samuel Hynes has called the 'Auden generation' of the 1930s, the personal memoir of life at school functions rhetorically as the signifier of the collective experience of that generation of ex-public schoolboys who, to quote Hynes again, 'were born between 1900 and 1914, were at school during the First World War and came to adulthood in the 1920s and to their early maturity in the thirties' (Hynes, 1976, p. 9).

To regard one's own life as an exemplary case-history is modest because it assumes the determining importance of the writer's social environment; it is also potentially arrogant in claiming a universal status for particular forms of subjection. Public school followed by Oxbridge was not the standard educational experience for middle-class girls, however bright (Woolf, 1928, 1938) — nor even for most middle-class boys, though one might not think so from reading these memoirs. As narratives they are quite similar, usually consisting of a brief glimpse of a nursery Eden, contemplating arum lilies (Connolly, 1938, p. 146), enjoying nursery rhymes and hymns (MacNeice, 1938, pp. 36–8) or innocently admiring 'fishermen and blacksmiths and bricklayers' (Orwell, 1983, p. 232), followed by fairly detailed accounts of public school and (sometimes) Oxbridge education before, during and after the Great War. These are usually shot through with irony at the youthful self's pretensions, snobbery or cowardice. Although this self-irony earned Woolf's praise for the writers' honesty in 'telling the unpleasant truths about themselves' (Woolf, 1966, **2**, p. 177), their memoirs today appear exceedingly reticent. Isherwood's *Lions and Shadows*, with its discreet hinting at repressed homosexuality and anonymous lumping together of the writer's younger brother, dead father and formidable mother into a vaguely apprehended 'my family' (or 'my female relative', 1947, p. 179) now looks disingenuous compared with the candid rhetoric of Isherwood's latest memoirs (1971, 1974). Other writers are almost equally silent about families and bodily desires, mentioning the latter only in the context of frustration ('I was eighteen and a half . . . I had never masturbated': Connolly, 1949, p. 250), or of revulsion, as when Greene recalls the stink of the lavatories at Berkhamstead and 'Collifax, who practised torments with dividers' (Greene, 1982, p. 14) and when Orwell describes his fascinated horror at the dirty bodies of navvies in their sweat-stained clothes (Orwell, 1983, pp. 234–5). Only Auden recalls the pleasurable passions of adolescence, and that briefly: 'Like other boys, I lost my taste for sweets/ Discovered sunsets, passion, God and Keats' (Auden and MacNeice, 1937, p. 208).

'Like other boys' Auden insists on himself as representative, not as exceptional, an emphasis shared by all these autobiographers. Schooling is the key experience in all these memoirs, because of its crucial role in the social construction of an upper middle-class individual. At the public schools boys learned the values of class, nation and empire as well as the skills and knowledge that enabled them to become officials, administrators or teachers (a point repeatedly made by the contributors to Graham Greene's well-known 1934 anthology of memoirs *The Old School*). And as the commentators on the left-wing writers of the thirties have frequently observed (Symons 1990, Bergonzi 1978), their rebellion against these values only defined their identities more sharply as ex-public schoolboys — particularly since all these writers were intellectually gifted and often very successful students. In *Autumn Journal*, Louis MacNeice spells out these contradictions in a passage which reflects on the complacency and arrogance which he, like others, learnt along with Latin and Greek: 'Not but what I am glad to have my comforts;/ Better authentic mammon than a bogus god/ If it were not for Lit. Hum. I might be climbing/ A ladder with a hod' (MacNeice, 1939, part XII, p. 49).[3] All these writers emphasize their youthful subjection to false values. Orwell's autobiographical passages in *The Road to Wigan Pier* are part of a generalizing argument about the psychology of middle-class snobbery: the writer offers his own history as an example of this pathology, describing his young self as typically, not exceptionally class-conscious: 'When I was fourteen or fifteen I was an odious little snob, but no worse than other boys of my own age and class' (Orwell, 1983, p. 240). When he argues that middle-class people are repelled by workers because they learn in childhood that '*the lower classes smell*' (p. 234), he offers his own childish obsession with dirty, alien working-class bodies as evidence of that psychology (and his outgrowing of it as evidence that this 'mind-set' can be transcended). Cyril Connolly uses an overt rhetoric of scientific objectivity to make the same case: 'A critic is an instrument which registers certain observations; before the reader can judge of their value he must know sufficient of the accuracy of the instrument to allow for the margin of error. We grow up among theories and illusions common to our class, our race, our time' (Connolly, 1938, p. 141). Similarly, Isherwood insists in the foreword to *Lions and Shadows* (1938) that the subject is simply 'a young man, living in a certain European country at a certain period . . . subjected to a certain kind of environment, certain stimuli . . .

In such matters, everyone must be his own guinea-pig' (Isherwood, 1947, p. 7).

This scientific rhetoric, like Orwell's argument, begs the question of the writer's present subjectivity (not to mention the reader's) — an insoluble problem, neatly evaded by these objective analogies of vivisection or calibration. Isherwood handles the difficulty with elegant, ingenious reticence, classifying his young self as a sad example of public-school pathology, not because he is snobbish but because he is possessed by what Auden condemned in his elegy for Freud as 'our dishonest mood of denial' (Auden, 1940, p. 42). Isherwood treats his young self less with objectivity than with affectionate contempt, constantly exposing the young man's pretensions to being heroic and exceptional by exposing his timid conventionality, as when he plans to defy the Establishment at a college feast: 'Needless to say, what really happened was that we had an excellent dinner and that I got drunk' (1947, p. 115). These anti-climactic self-ironies, often signalled by the phrase 'needless to say' (Isherwood, 1947, pp. 35, 69, 79, 95, 115, 138, 305) trap their object in a structure of superior ironic knowledge, emphasizing his subjection to the environment against which he rebels. This appears particularly in the well-known passage where Isherwood writes about his failed first novel *Lions and Shadows*, using the same scientific/sociological language as the foreword to the 'mature' book in 1938: the adolescent book was, he says, the symptomatic behaviour of 'a member of a certain class, living in a certain country, and subjected to a certain system of education' (Isherwood, 1947, p. 74). Its unconscious, censored subject was the War: 'we young writers of the middle 'twenties were all suffering, more or less subconsciously, from a feeling of shame that we hadn't been old enough to take part in the European war... Like most of my generation, I was obsessed by a complex of terrors and longings connected with the idea "War" ' (Isherwood, 1947, pp. 74-5).

This definition of 'my generation' of course assumes that only boys count — an assumption shared by Isherwood's male contemporaries in the 1930s, and indeed by subsequent historians of the decade (Symons 1965, 1990; Hynes, 1976; Bergonzi, 1978; Lucas, 1979; Kermode, 1988; Cunningham, 1988). He is alert and imaginative — and writes well — in representing himself as subject to history, but cannot, it seems, imagine significant subjectivity except in the most emphatically masculine — and class-bound — terms. The obsession with a 'test' felt by the men who were too young to fight in the War — which Isherwood persuasively claims was common to 'all of us young writers of the "twenties" ' (Isherwood, 1947, p. 74) — is a specifically masculine anxiety defined as universal:[4] a blind spot shared by Isherwood's peers. This universalized masculinity is not confined to the autobiographers' own stories; it is repeated by the discursive texts in which all the memoirs except Isherwood's are embedded. The patriarchal bias of Orwell's *The Road to Wigan Pier* is by now notorious;[5] and it is fairly typical. No women are to be found in the lighthearted summaries of social history, Mr Average, the post-Romantic hangover and Auden's own development in 'Letter to Lord Byron', apart from the poet's mother, and a few camp abstractions like England, 'the Mater, on occasions, of the Free' (Auden and MacNeice, 1937, p. 233) and Modern Art ('Because it's true Art feels a trifle sick/ You mustn't think the old girl's lost her kick', p. 107). In the stanza I have quoted as epigraph, the imagined child of a future Utopia has never heard of class hierarchies and thinks monarchs are democratically chosen, but calls his teacher 'Sir' and knows that all societies consist of men: 'Is he a maker... Does he choose his king?' (Auden and MacNeice, 1937, p. 201). Louis MacNeice's *Modern Poetry* insists on the masculinity of poetry ('we are working back towards the normal virile efficiency of Dryden or Chaucer' p. 152); he barely mentions contemporary women apart from Edith Sitwell (p. 61), Stevie Smith and Dorothy Parker, who are lumped together inaccurately as 'hard-boiled Americans' (MacNeice, 1938, p. 148). *Autumn Journal* (1939) does of course mention women, but only as objects of desire. The account of modernist writing in Connolly's *Enemies of Promise* (1949) acknowledges a few women (Daisy Ashford, Stein, Woolf, and H.D., pp. 27–9); plus Bowen, Cather, Compton-Burnett, Lehmann and Mansfield in the 'production chart' on pp. 61–3; Stein is noted as an influence on Hemingway (Connolly, 1949, p. 59), *Orlando* is criticized and *The Waves* praised (Connolly, 1949, pp. 48–9). But all the close readings are of male writers, and the account of the writer's problems assumes that women are, at best, 'intelligent and unselfish' wives who understand 'that there is no more sombre enemy of good art than the pram in the hall' (Connolly, 1949, p. 116).

Women In and Out of History

So far, I have said nothing about women writers. Of course, women were writing autobiographically in the 1930s, and with no less consciousness of their historical and political context than their male colleagues; but they wrote differently, often from an assumption of feminine marginality and usually choosing fiction rather than memoir.

Virtually none of this work has, however, as yet been acknowledged in the available histories of the 1930s. Female writers have been less noticed than working-class male writers[6] by the literary historians of that decade, who have taken at face value the very questionable claims to representative status made by the 'Auden Generation', ignoring the work of Elizabeth Bowen, Vera Brittain, Katharine Burdekin,[7] Nancy Cunard, Winifred Holtby, Storm Jameson, Rosamond Lehmann, Naomi Mitchison, Kathleen Raine, Jean Rhys, Stevie Smith, Christina Stead, Sylvia Townsend Warner, Rebecca West, Antonia White and Virginia Woolf — to cite only the most distinguished names of women writers active in the 1930s (Montefiore, 1987, pp. 30–4).

Almost all of these writers belong, like the Auden Group, to the educated professional middle classes. But very few of their life-histories, early or late, correspond to the typical experiences of the male 'Auden Generation', partly because of gendered differences in education and partly because almost all are older. Of the sixteen writers I have listed, only a handful were born after 1900: Elizabeth Bowen, Rosamond Lehmann, Kathleen Raine, Stevie Smith and Christina Stead. The others, apart from Woolf, were all born in the 1890s, came of age during the First World War and established themselves as writers during the 1920s (apart from Rebecca West who achieved distinction as a very young woman). None of these women was uneducated; the majority had at least some experience of good academic schooling, and Sylvia Townsend Warner and Nancy Cunard, both educated privately, came from cultivated homes, but only a handful — Brittain, Holtby, Jameson, Lehmann and Raine — were university graduates, and of these only Lehmann and Holtby seem to have been admitted to college without a struggle.[8]

The autobiographical writings of these women do not fit the thirties mould, not only because of the authors' sex and age, but because of their literary form. Almost all of the women whose names I have cited were novelists, many of whom took their material from their own lives, though, apart from Vera Brittain's *Testament of Youth* (1933) and Jameson's *No Time Like the Present* (1932), they published fictions rather than memoirs (Woolf's (1976) memoir *Moments of Being* was posthumously published). The obvious differences from the fragmentary male autobiographies are firstly that, apart from Antonia White, women writers do not focus on their schooldays and secondly that they are less inclined than the men to represent their experiences as typical except, significantly, when they deal with the War. Storm Jameson writes that 'What happened to me happened in greater or smaller degree to the rest of us who in 1914 were the young generation' (Jameson, 1932, p. 101); Vera Brittain (1933) makes a similar claim. Yet both women write as witnesses and survivors, rather than exemplary specimens of their class, sex and caste and neither treats her young self with the irony which characterizes their male colleagues.

But it is the autobiographical novels by women, rather than their memoirs, that I am dealing with here. Formally, these divide into two modes: on the one hand, traditionally written social novels using the writer's own experiences of marriage, love and family to articulate a panoramic chronicle of the present or the recent past; on the other, experimental novels exploring the subjectivities of single women, usually by means of fantasy or reverie. These autobiographical novels all differ considerably in plot, both because the writers' collective social range varies from near-upper class (Naomi Mitchison, Virginia Woolf) through the fairly well-to-do (Stevie Smith, Vera Brittain, Winifred Holtby) to the hard-up or seedy lower margins (Storm Jameson, Jean Rhys), and partly because the realist writers concentrate on marriage and sexual love (usually during the First World War or in its immediate aftermath), experiences which are more subject to chance variation than public school educations in this period. Neither kind of book obviously conforms to the case-history model — that is, they do not articulate the experiences of a typical or representative self.

The realist novels, now largely forgotten, include Naomi Mitchison's *We Have Been Warned* (1935), whose action runs from 1931 to 1933, Storm Jameson's *Mirror In Darkness* trilogy (1933–36), which begins in 1919 and ends with the General Strike in 1926 (plus a post-war sequel: Jameson 1945), and Vera Brittain's *Honourable Estate* (1936), a chronicle novel covering the history of two families from 1890 to the early 1920s. Ruth Alleyndene, the heroine of the second half of the novel, is given the same experiences of losing a lover and a brother in the War as the young Brittain. Similarly, Naomi Mitchison's heroine Dione Galton, socialist daughter of a Scottish landowning family, mother of five children, wife of an Oxford don standing as a Labour Party candidate in an industrial constituency, Communist sympathiser, visitor to the USSR, pioneer in sexual liberation, and Cassandra-like visionary, is transparently a self-portrait, though the book looks outward rather than inward. The fact that Dione's social identity is constituted by a wide variety of social relationships means that her story can also be a panoramic account of liberal England in the early 1930s; even the fantasy dream-sequences experienced by Dione and her sister are condensed, symbolic representations of the perennial social forces of good versus evil, progress versus reaction, rather than explorations of an unknown self. This outward autobiographical focus is also found in Jameson's *Mirror in Darkness* trilogy, in that the story of the main female character, Hervey Russell, is Storm Jameson's own, and yet the novels are not primarily an exploration of her own life. Hervey's early marriage to an irresponsible weakling who refuses to support her or his child; the badly-paid advertising work she undertakes to support her son who is looked after by relatives in Whitby; her discovery of her husband's adultery and her decision to divorce him; her eventual literary success, and her difficult but rewarding affair and second marriage: all these exactly match Storm Jameson's own personal history as she tells it in her autobiography (Jameson, 1984). But Hervey Russell's life is only one among a large and socially varied cast of characters who between them represent the major trends in post-war British politics — that is, the ruling class Establishment, their victims, opponents and allies. Her story is the main unifying narrative in this chronicle, but its principal theme is the slow defeat of the Left.

It is not surprising that heroines modelled so closely on their pioneering originals should all be exceptional women. Mitchison's Dione is consciously adventurous, pushing back the boundaries of acceptable sexual behaviour and smuggling a Communist assassin out of the country; Brittain's Ruth achieves the fulfilment in work of which her mother's generation could only dream, while the apparent diffidence of Storm Jameson's Hervey masks a survivor's arrogant self-sufficiency. Whereas male writers like Isherwood or Orwell emphasize, with the irony of hindsight, their own historical subjection to corrupt and commonplace values, these novels insist on their heroines' stubborn refusal to be like other girls. Yet they do not set out to explore the consciousness of these exceptional women. Even in *We Have Been Warned* (Mitchison, 1935), where the heroine's experiences and her running commentary on them constitute most of the narrative, the focus is on what she sees, not on how she sees it. There is, however, one major and telling exception to this rule: all the realist female autobiographical narratives insist strongly on the crucial determining effect of the War on the minds of the civilian non-combatants who lived through it. The intelligent, sensitive heroines of Vera Brittain and Storm Jameson respond to the proximity of mass death with a sexualized intensity which the novels represent as a particular symptom of a widespread corruption of the spirit, though this is recognized not by the young women themselves but by the mature narrators.

Marginal Subjectivities

A different autobiographical tradition, emphasizing a problematic female subjectivity, was established in the 1920s and 1930s by novelists such as Virginia Woolf, Dorothy Richardson, and later Stevie Smith and Jean Rhys. Three classics from this period: Virginia Woolf's *The Years* (1937), Jean Rhys' *Voyage in the Dark* (1934) and Stevie Smith's *Over The Frontier* (1938), all foreground the subjectivities of underprivileged, marginal single women — the chorus girl turned kept mistress in *Voyage in the Dark*, the powerless and sometimes poverty-stricken Pargiter girls in *The Years*, and Pompey, secretary to Sir Phoebus, whose verdict on her official duties is 'How boring, how unfree... How *kind* of him to have me?' (Smith, 1982, p. 85). The marginalized subjectivities of the bored secretary, the downwardly mobile 'kept' woman or the spinster on a small fixed income exist in a more or less overtly political context: British imperialism is an important, ambivalent theme for all three writers, while Stevie Smith's novel engages with the growing power of fascism (also noted by Woolf, 1990, pp. 288–9). But when these women engage with history, with the discourses of imperialism or political activism, they do so by memory, reverie or fantasy, not by action.

This is particularly obvious in *The Years*, Woolf's overtly feminist chronicle of the Pargiter family over 57 years. The female Pargiters are impoverished and marginalized by economic dependence, by lack of access to education and to the institutions of British power, and by their fathers' mean provision for them. When Digby Pargiter dies, the untrained, uneducated Sara and Maggie Pargiter have to move from the West End of London to a slum, in contrast to their male cousins who have become dons, lawyers or colonial administrators. The only prospect for the girls is marriage, which is not necessarily an escape: the fortunate Maggie marries a nice radical Frenchman, but Delia, out of hero-worship for Parnell, marries an Irishman who turns out to be a dim-witted sporting Unionist.

Although *The Years* may sound in summary like a feminist chronicle of domestic oppression, it is actually a kind of historical novel. It contradicts the dominant narratives of recent English history by deliberately marginalizing them, covering the years 1880–1937 as experienced by an upper-middle-class English family without mentioning the Boer war, the death of Queen Victoria, the rise of the trades unions or the Labour Party (i.e. the increasing political significance of the working class) nor the collapse of the Liberals. The suffragette movement is touched on — Rose Pargiter is a militant and gets jailed; Eleanor and another cousin belong to the moderate suffragist lobby — but only in the interstices of reveries and conversations: we are not shown Rose in action. Similarly, the First World War is given just one scene (an evening in London during the Zeppelin raids of 1917).

Clearly, the subject of politics in the traditional, recognizable guise of power struggles between representative individuals (as in Storm Jameson's novels, for instance) is conspicuous by its absence from *The Years*. And yet the book is preoccupied, if not with power struggles, certainly with the institutions of power — the universities, the law-courts, the colonial civil service Army: all male preserves ultimately belonging to the British Empire — and all barred to women. The institutions of imperialism are shown indirectly, not through the minds of the rulers or administrators, but through their silent female audience whose capacity for imagination bears an inverse relationship to their power and knowledge. Eleanor's mind is full of vivid images when she reads her brother Martin's tight-lipped letter about his experiences 'in the jungle' on her way to watch yet another brother's performance as a barrister, so that 'flames for a moment danced over the vast funereal mass of the Law Courts' (Woolf, 1990, p. 93). Throughout *The Years*, the minds of the unmarried female Pargiters — Eleanor and Sara, as well as Maggie, Kitty, Delia and Rose as young girls — dominate the narrative, all endowed with far more vivid imaginations than their privileged, conventionally successful brothers. This is particularly true of Sara, imaginatively the most gifted of her family and economically the most unlucky, being unmarriageable as well as hard up. The opposition between male imperial privilege and marginal female vision is brought out most sharply through her and her cousin Edward's differing responses to Sophocles' *Antigone*. The gender contrast is constructed around educational privilege and the classics as a male preserve, rather than the British Empire as defended by Colonel Pargiter or administered by his son Martin, but these are of course connected as institutions of power. Edward is shown as an Oxford undergraduate preparing for the Fellowship examination which will determine his future, reading Sophocles with intense concentration, comprehensive knowledge, and precision: 'he made another note; *that* was the meaning. His own dexterity in catching the phrase plum in the middle gave him a little thrill of excitement' (Woolf, 1990, p. 42). Edward's knowledge of the text is characterized by authority, possession of meaning and a Little-Jack-Hornerish pleasure in his own decoding skills. Twenty-seven years later, his cousin Sara reads his verse translation of the play during the pauses of watching a garden-party she does not attend and is possessed by a vision of the heroine:

> Antigone...stood there letting fall white dust over the blackened foot. Then behold! there were more clouds; dark clouds; the horsemen leapt down; she was seized; her wrists were bound with withies; and they bore her, thus bound...where?
>   There was a roar of laughter from the garden. She looked up. Where did they take her? she asked... 'To the estimable court of the respected ruler?' she murmured, picking up a word or two at random, for she was still looking out into the garden. The man's name was Creon. He buried her. It was a moonlit night. The blades of the cactuses were sharp silver. The man in the loincloth gave three sharp taps with his mallet on the brick. She was buried alive... Straight out in a brick tomb, she said.
>   (Woolf, 1990, pp. 117–18)

This counterpointing of text and context is even sharper than the scene of Eleanor's intense absorption in her brother's letter. And in some ways, Sara imagines the play as wrongly as Eleanor does the jungle (which she thinks of as 'stunted little trees' p. 92). She reads *Antigone* vaguely, as a narrative not a drama — 'scenes rose quickly, inaccurately, as she skipped' (p. 117) — and ignorantly, since she can approach the text only through Edward's dull-sounding translation, from which that unappealing line 'the estimable court of the respected ruler' is presumably quoted. The highly trained, skilful Edward knows the words of the play as Sara never can, but her vision of its tragic violence has a power that he never approaches. She is a poet *manquée*, yet throughout the book her poetry consists of half-articulated reveries like this one, or else ephemera thrown off in conversation.

Nevertheless, Sara's reading of *Antigone* in translation is not, so to speak, the author's own. Virginia Woolf, who read Sophocles in the original, wrote in 'On Not Knowing Greek' that 'it is useless...to read Greek in translations', and warned readers against glamorizing the classics in a 'haze of associations...reading into Greek poetry not what they have but what we lack' (Woolf, 1966, 1, p. 11) — criticisms which would certainly invalidate Sara's romanticism. Furthermore, Sara's vision of primitive violence is itself determined by the discourse of imperialism. The scene she imagines, with its vultures, sandclouds, cactuses and fierce horsemen, sounds more like North Africa than Greece (possibly because she is mixing up Sophocles' Thebes with Egyptian Thebes), and Creon 'in a loincloth' burying a woman alive is not only a more nearly naked embodiment of male power than Sir William Watney who boasts of being worshipped in his 'old riding-breeches' by a credulous herd of 'good people' (Woolf, 1990, p. 175); he is constructed by an imperialist iconography of alien races as savage, primitive, violent. Sara imagines Antigone solely as a victim; she never notices the famously defiant dialogue between Antigone and Creon, a passage praised by Woolf in the near-contemporary *Three Guineas*, 1938. The creative potential of the powerless, marginal female Pargiters appears in their fantasies of the institutions of power (the colonial jungle) and knowledge (Greek poetry and philosophy) from which they are barred; and yet the terms of their imaginations are defined — and limited — by those institutions of power.

Unlike Sara's reveries, the daydreams of Anna Morgan, who narrates Jean Rhys' novel *Voyage in the Dark* (1934) are overtly determined by the facts of imperialism, since they are not based on fantasy but on her memories of childhood in one of Britain's Caribbean colonies. Anna, a *déclassée* single girl without even a small fixed income, is even more socially marginal than the Pargiter spinsters. The English see Anna only as a tart; her true, unknowable identity is represented by her nostalgic memories of her Caribbean home (she is a dispossessed ex-member of the planter class). Anna's incommunicable desire for warmth, richness and colour becomes a mental retreat from the cold brutality, hypocrisy and ugliness which she encounters in England. Her memories, always prompted by adversity, have the escapist quality of fantasy and, as she falls lower socially, reveries and daydreams come to dominate the narrative. She constantly recalls the paradisal sensual appeal of her island: the night-blooming lilies, the waterfalls, the sunshine — 'The light is gold and when you shut your eyes you see fire-colour' (Rhys, 1967, p. 43). But people's lives in the glamorous Caribbean island are as much determined by racism and imperialism as the grim commercialized English towns where the people hate 'dirty foreigners' (*ibid.*, p. 110). Anna's feelings about black people are an unstable mixture of attraction, envy, superiority and guilt. As a child, she says, 'I always wanted to be black . . . Being black is warm and gay, being white is cold and sad' (*ibid.*, p. 31). These oppositions are represented, almost allegorically, by the two female figures in her adolescence: Hester, her viciously respectable, racist English stepmother, and Anna's best friend, the black servant Francine — 'that dreadful girl Francine' as Hester calls her — full of sensual vitality and physical strength. Anna watches the black people with admiration, but always separately; she firmly identifies herself as white against her stepmother's insinuations: ' "You're trying to make out that my mother was coloured," I said. "You always did try to make that out. And she wasn't" ' (*ibid.*, p. 65). She feels guilt about her family's past; she insists 'I'm the fifth generation born out there, on my mother's side', and as she speaks, she remembers seeing old slave-lists: 'Maillot Boyd, aged 18, mulatto, house-servant' (*ibid.*, pp. 52–3). The friendship with Francine ends on the day when Anna intrudes on the maid on her own turf, the 'horrible' kitchen where 'there was no chimney and it was always full of charcoal smoke', and knows that 'of course she disliked me too because I was white' (*ibid.*, p. 72). Anna's alienation from both black Caribbeans and white English becomes complete in the final delirious scene when she associates the faces around her with memories of the 'three days Masquerade' when black people would dress 'all colours of the rainbow' and wear grotesque pink or white masks with their tongues sticking through (*ibid.*, p. 185) in mockery of their rulers.

Like *The Years*, *Voyage in the Dark* is only indirectly a political novel. Although its picture of English culture and English people is wholly negative — the food, climate and buildings are awful; the women are racist and mean; the men contemptuously exploit women's bodies; both sexes are coldly hypocritical and the rich own everything; — the critique is made in moral and aesthetic rather than political terms. There are no satires on the class division, only a disgusted, deadpan observation of provincial towns full of 'rows of little houses . . . and smoke the same colour as the sky; and a High Street or Duke Street or Lord Street or Corporation Street where you walked about and looked at the shops' (Rhys, 1967, p. 8); no arguments about the morality of Empire, only a loyal British citizen saying 'Don't you hate foreigners?' (*ibid.*, p. 110). Yet the historical institutions of British power have, Rhys makes plain, shaped the identity of Anna and everyone she knows. The slavery which originally enriched her family has left its mark as pervasive social and racial inequality — landed wealth and leisure for the white planters, manual labour and unventilated kitchens for their black subjects. And slavery was of course enforced by the old British Empire, which still guarantees the privilege which her family has enjoyed, though the English themselves know and care little about it. The blank wall of incomprehension and dislike which Anna meets as a colonial subject is as much a product of Empire as her own memories; but history and politics are represented at the level of subject's consciousness, not as action.

Stevie Smith's autobiographical heroine, Pompey Casmilus in *Novel on Yellow Paper* (1936) and *Over My Frontier* (1938), is both more politically aware and less alienated from the institutions of British power than either Anna Morgan or the Pargiters. Convalescing in a North German castle–sanatorium from a nervous illness resulting from a broken engagement plus alienation from her boring job as a secretary to 'Sir Phoebus', the Press baron, she is recruited to the Secret Service by Tom Satterthwaite, the Intelligence officer. She rides with him over a frontier, out of her old life, into another world of war where she becomes a cleverer and more merciless spy than Tom himself. Both the journey and the frontier are of course classic 1930s motifs, familiar from the writings of Auden, Greene, Isherwood and others, which can represent the literal — and often contested — borders of nations in terms of a psychic symbolism of an unconscious self, or a political symbolism, often but not always of progress from willed passivity to revolutionary justice.[9] Stevie Smith's use of this image has a parallel in Edward Upward's novel *Journey to the Border* (1938); but whereas Upward makes his subject withdraw from a fantasy world into deliberately prosaic action by joining the Communist Party, for Stevie Smith the entry into action means consenting to the grip of a powerful, evil fantasy. Her heroine's digressive narrative is constantly preoccupied with the power of British imperialism, the power of its even nastier fascist enemies, and the relation of both to humanity's desire for cruelty. She observes that 'the parsons who write to the papers to say that England holds commission from heaven to colonize the earth must surely be dottily overlooking the Jameson Raid and the Rand Kaffir business' (Smith, 1982); she compares Italian imperialist propaganda unfavourably with English: 'when England plays that game she can play it ... more thoroughly more vilely' (Smith, 1982), and concludes, Ciceronianly, 'That [my country] is astute and on occasion equivocal, I believe. That she has conquered in greed, held in tenacity, explained in casuistry, I agree. But fools asking foolish questions have nothing to expect but folly or casuistry' (Smith, 1982, pp. 98–100). Her musings finally add up to an acceptance of the brutal *realpolitik* of imperialist capitalism, which is dramatized by her putting on a military uniform and a spy's unscrupulous, murderous identity. She circles around the ideas of power and of human cruelty, from anecdotes of wartime frenzy to a sadistically detailed highbrow dramatization of a child's death by meningitis[10] and beyond that, to the illicit *Pleasures of the Torture Chamber* (Smith, 1982, p. 60): 'the undeliberate dream that is to be endured and yet resisted, the horror of refusal with no power of refusal. Oh no, Oh no' (Smith, 1982, p. 70). These meditations on the connexions between action and dream, rational power and compulsive cruelty, lead her thought to the structures of fantasy; in all her pondered instances of cruelty — memory, textual fantasy and reverie — the common ground is the compulsive logic of sado-masochism, the 'undeliberate dream' in which that repeated, ineffective protest 'Oh no' may equally well be spoken by a powerless victim or by a victimizer unable to resist temptation.

Conclusion

This essay makes a sharp distinction between masculine case-histories which claim a representative status for their subjects' experiences, and women writing out of the margins. Of course, it is not quite that simple. It is true that the women who wrote about their own experiences in relation to history during the 1930s could not take for granted, as the men did, their own universal or representative status. Realist novelists represented a woman's relation to history mainly at the level of plot or theme, while those who did foreground female subjectivities explored the reveries and fantasies of marginal women who were subjects, though not full citizens, of an imperial nation.

It does not follow from this, however, that women autobiographers always and inevitably write from the margins.[11] Even in the 1930s, Storm Jameson and Vera Brittain did claim in their autobiographies to represent their contemporaries — and the last 20 years have seen an efflorescence of female autobiographies, both fictionalized, fragmentary and straightforward, by women born after 1940 who do appeal to the experience of a generation. The 'cradle-to-coming-of-age novel' (Isherwood, 1974, p. 74) has become a standard genre of feminist fiction both in Britain and America: Michèle Roberts (1977), Lisa Alther (1976), Rita Mae Brown (1973) and Jeanette Winterson (1985) are familiar instances. Moreover, the exemplary personal narrative often appears in feminist writing, from the brief narratives in the health book *Our Bodies, Our Selves* (Women's Health Collective, 1978) to the anthologies edited by Ursula Owen (1985) and Liz Heron (1985): the narratives of education in the latter, especially, follow a familiar case-history pattern, though the terrain is very different from 1930s memoirs. Nancy Miller's memoir 'My Father's Penis' (Miller, 1991), Valerie Walkerdine's passages of memory and psychoanalysis (Walkerdine, 1991) or Liz Stanley's inclusion of her own diaries in her study of auto-biography (Stanley, 1992) are only the most distinguished, self-reflexive instances of the common feminist emphasis: 'I've done it myself'. So if the most powerful literary representations of a feminine self in the 1930s are not of a representative identity but of a marginalized, daydreaming subjectivity, that fact is historically, not essentially determined.

Notes

1   The 1930s inspired a steady stream of post-war retrospective memoirs, which continued into the late 1980s: Crossman, 1950; Spender, 1955; Jameson, 1984; Worsley, 1966; Isherwood, 1974; Edward Upward, 1977; Ralph Glasser, 1986; Patrick Leigh-Fermour, 1977.
2   For overtly autobiographical poems, see the 'Marston' poems in Spender 1933 and 1934; Day-Lewis (1932) MacNeice (1939); Auden and MacNeice (1937), as well as the meditative poem '1929' and several lyrics (Auden, 1930 and 1936). The relationship between demanding mother and victimized son in Auden's play *Paid on Both Sides* (Auden, 1930) and in *The Ascent of F6* (Auden and Isherwood, 1939) also seems to be based on autobiographical material (Isherwood, 1971; Carpenter, 1981).
3   MacNeice was awarded a First Class degree in *Literae Humaniores* ('Lit. Hum.') in 1929 and was immediately appointed to a lectureship in classics at Birmingham University (MacNeice, 1966, p. 128).
4   It is also, presumably, a middle-class fixation (but note the absence of published evidence about the post-war psychology of working-class men born after 1900).
5   See Beatrix Campbell, 1984; also essays by B. Campbell and Deirdre Beddoe (Norris, 1984).
6   See Ken Worple (1986), Andy Crofts (1990) for sympathetic treatment of working class writing; also Kermode (1988). For women, see Batsleer *et al.*, 1985 and Alison Light, 1992.
7   Katherine Burdekin, 1892–1957, unknown until (re)discovered by Daphne Patai for the Feminist Press. She published in the 1930s under the pseudonym 'Murray Constantine'; her work includes *Swastika Night* (1936), reprinted 1941 by Left Book Club and 1989 by the Feminist Press.
8   See Brittain, 1933, Raine, 1975, and Jameson, 1932 and 1984 for accounts of their familial or economic struggle to get university educations.
9   A few classic texts about ideological journeying are Greene, 1939 (prologue), Orwell, 1937, Rex Warner, 1935, Sylvia Townsend Warner, 1936 (fiction), C. Day-Lewis, 1933 (poetry).
10 Stevie Smith is clearly referring to Huxley (1928).
11 But see Sidonie Smith (1986) for a contrary view.

References

Place of publication is London unless otherwise stated.

ALTHER, LISA (1976) *Kinflicks*, N.Y., Knopf.
AUDEN, W. H. (1930) *Poems*, Faber.
AUDEN, W. H. (1936) *Look, Stranger!*, Faber.
AUDEN, W. H. (1940) *Another Time*, Faber.
AUDEN, W. H. and ISHERWOOD, C. (1939) *The Ascent of F6*, Faber.

AUDEN, W. H. and MACNEICE, L. (1937) *Letters from Iceland*, Faber.
BATSLEER, J., DAVIES, T. and O'ROURKE, R. (1985) *ReWriting English: The Cultural Politics of Gender and Class*, Methuen.
BERGONZI, B. (1978) *Reading The Thirties*, Macmillan.
BRITTAIN, V. (1933) *Testament of Youth*, Macmillan.
BRITTAIN, V. (1936) *Honourable Estate*, Macmillan.
BROWN, R. M. (1973) *Rubyfruit Jungle*, Plainfield, Vt., Daughters, Inc.
CAMPBELL, B. (1984) *Wigan Pier Revisited: poverty and politics in the eighties*, Virago.
CARPENTER, H. (1981) *W. H. Auden: A Biography*, N.Y., Houghton Mifflin.
CONNOLLY, C. (1949) *Enemies of Promise*, Routledge. (First printed 1938.)
CROFTS, ANDY (1990) *Red Letter Days*, Lawrence and Wishart.
CROSSMAN, R. H. S. (1950) *The God That Failed: Six Studies in Communism*, N.Y., Hamilton.
CUNNINGHAM, V. (1988) *British Writers Of The Thirties*, Oxford University Press.
DAY-LEWIS, C. (1932) *From Feathers To Iron*, Faber.
DAY-LEWIS, C. (1933) *The Magnetic Mountain*, Faber.
FERMOUR, P. L. (1977) *A Time Of Gifts*, Cape.
GLASSER, R. (1986) *Growing Up In The Gorbals*, Chatto.
GREENE, G. (1934) *The Old School*, Cape.
GREENE, G. (1982) *The Lawless Roads*, Penguin. (First published 1939.)
HERON, L. (1985) (Ed.) *Truth, Dare Or Promise: Girls Growing Up In The Fifties*, Virago.
HUXLEY, A. (1928) *Point Counter Point*, N.Y., Harper.
HYNES, S. (1976) *The Auden Generation: literature and politics in the 1930s*, Faber.
ISHERWOOD, C. (1947) *Lions and Shadows*, Conn., USA, New Directions. (First published 1938.)
ISHERWOOD, C. (1971) *Kathleen and Frank*.
ISHERWOOD, C. (1974) *Christopher And His Kind*, Methuen.
JAMESON, S. (1932) *No Time Like The Present*, Cassell.
JAMESON, S. (1933) *Company Parade*, Cassell. First volume of *The Mirror in Darkness*.
JAMESON, S. (1934) *Love In Winter*, Cassell. Second volume of *The Mirror in Darkness*.
JAMESON, S. (1936) *None Turn Back*, Cassell. Third volume of *The Mirror in Darkness*.
JAMESON, S. (1945) *The Journal of Mary Hervey Russell*, Cassell.
JAMESON, S. (1984) *Journey From The North, An Autobiography*. Two volumes, Virago. (First published 1969 and 1970.)
KENNARD, J. (1989) *Vera Brittain and Winifred Holtby: A Working Partnership*, Hanover, NH, USA, University Press of New England.
KERMODE, F. (1988) *History and Value*, Oxford University Press.
LIGHT, A. (1992) *Forever England*, Routledge.
LUCAS, J. (1979) (Ed.) *The Thirties: A Challenge To Orthodoxy*, Harvester.
MACNEICE, L. (1938) *Modern Poetry*, Oxford University Press.
MACNEICE, L. (1939) *Autumn Journal*, Faber.
MACNEICE, L. (1966) *The Strings Are False*, Oxford University Press.
MILLER, NANCY K. (1991) *Getting Personal: Feminist Occasions and Other Autobiographical Acts*, N.Y., Routledge.
MONTEFIORE, J. (1987) *Feminism and Poetry: Language, Experience, Identity in Women's Writing*, Pandora.
MITCHISON, N. (1935) *We Have Been Warned*, Constable.
NORRIS, C. (1984) *Orwell: Inside The Myth*, Lawrence and Wishart.
ORWELL, G. (1983) *The Penguin Longer Non-Fiction of George Orwell*, N.Y., USA, Penguin. Includes *The Road to Wigan Pier* (first published 1936) and *Homage To Catalonia* (first published 1937).

OWEN, U. (1985) (Ed.) *Fathers: Reflections By Daughters*, Virago.
RAINE, K. (1975) *The Land Unknown*, Conn., USA, Braziller.
RHYS, J. (1967) *Voyage In The Dark*, Deutsch. (First published 1934.)
ROBERTS, M. (1977) *A Piece Of The Night*, Women's Press.
SMITH, S. (1936) *Novel On Yellow Paper*, Penguin.
SMITH, S. (1982) *Over The Frontier*, Virago. (First published 1938.)
SMITH, S. (1986) *Towards A Poetics Of Women's Autobiography*, USA, Indiana University Press.
SPENDER, S. (1933) *Poems*, Faber.
SPENDER, S. (1934) *Vienna*, Faber.
SPENDER, S. (1955) *World Within World*, Faber.
STANLEY, L. (1992) *The Auto/biographical Self*, Manchester University Press.
SYMONS, J. (1990) *The Thirties And The Nineties*, Manchester, Carcanet.
UPWARD, E. (1938) *Journey To The Border*, Hogarth.
UPWARD, E. (1977) *The Spiral Ascent*, Heinemann.
WALKERDINE, V. (1991) *Schoolgirl Fictions*, Verso.
WARNER, R. (1935) *The Wild Goose Chase*, Bodley Head.
WARNER. S. T. (1936) *Summer Will Show*, Chatto.
WINTERSON, J. (1985) *Oranges Are Not The Only Fruit*, Pandora.
WOMEN'S HEALTH COLLECTIVE (1978) *Our Bodies, Our Selves*, Penguin.
WOOLF, V. (1928) *A Room Of One's Own*, Hogarth.
WOOLF, V. (1938) *Three Guineas*, Hogarth.
WOOLF, V. (1966) *Collected Essays*, N.Y., Knopf, (4 volumes).
WOOLF, V. (1976) *Moments of Being*, N.Y., Harcourt Brace and Jovanovich.
WOOLF, V. (1990) *The Years*, N.Y., USA, Knopf. (First published 1937.)
WORPOLE, K. (1986) *Dockers And Detectives*, Verso.
WORSLEY, T. C. (1989) *Flannelled Fool: A Slice Of Life In The Thirties*. (First published 1966.)

Chapter 6

'Our War is with Words': Dora Marsden and *The Egoist*

Andrew Thacker

A magazine 'read chiefly by cranks, feminist and other': this is Hugh Kenner's judgment of *The Egoist* in *The Pound Era*, one of the key texts in the critical mapping out of the literary history of modernism (Kenner, 1972, p. 279). Recent revisions of this orthodoxy by feminist critics have focused more closely on those creative 'cranks' whose position in literary history from 1880 to 1920 and after is seemingly marginal to the conventional stories of male modernist self-creation. Sandra M. Gilbert and Susan Gubar, for example, have helped to introduce a major reconsideration of the issues of gender and modernism in their three-volume work, *The Place of the Woman Writer in the Twentieth Century*. For Gilbert and Gubar, modernism and the linguistic experiments characteristic of its avant-garde can be interpreted as products of a war or struggle between the sexes from the mid-nineteenth century onwards. It is this conflict, they argue, that underpins the creation of many of the most important works of modernism written by men: 'a reaction-formation against the rise of literary women became not just a theme in modern writing but a motive for modernism' (Gilbert and Gubar, 1988, p. 156).

In the magazine *The Egoist* (1914–19) and in its predecessors, *The Freewoman* (1911–12) and *The New Freewoman* (1913), the editorial contributions of Dora Marsden (1882–1960) raise interesting issues for how the two terms 'gender' and 'modernism' are to be associated. Marsden began her intellectual career as a staunch supporter of feminism in the form of the suffragette struggle but in the course of four years she encouraged the journal to shift its editorial focus from feminism to modernism. However, this transition from feminist discussion paper to clearing-house for modernism was not as clear-cut as the change of nomenclature suggests. By discussing Marsden's fascinating, but virtually ignored, writings in the periodical on language and feminism, I want to show how it reveals a modernist revision of suffragette feminism, rather than a simple abandonment of feminism for modernism. In particular Marsden's writings show many connections with the theories of the Imagist group,[1] poets who found a welcome journalistic space in this important 'little magazine'. A proper consideration of Marsden as a sort of 'modernist feminist' shows the complexities of analysing gender structures within the literature of this period. Marsden will not fit easily into a revisionary critical matrix which seeks to uncover the contributions of women writers obscured by the theoretical formulations of male modernists. She may exist, along with other women writers, as the implied opponent of the 'reaction-formation' of male modernism; but the structure of her philosophical egoism often displays characteristics which might, in other circumstances, be labelled as examples of 'masculine modernist' thought.

The changeover from *The New Freewoman* to *The Egoist* was not a simple androcentric coup engineered by Ezra Pound and four other men who signed a letter in 1913 calling for a less gendered appellation for the publication:

> We, the undersigned men of letters . . . venture to suggest to you that the present title of the paper causes it to be confounded with organs devoted solely to the advocacy of an unimportant reform in an obsolete political institution . . . We therefore ask . . . that you should consider the advisability of adopting another title which will mark the character of your paper as an organ of individuals of both sexes and of the individualist principle in every department of life.
>
> ('Letter', *New Freewoman*, 15.12.1913[2])

Marsden, to some extent, supported these 'men of letters' in their initiative.[3] Rebecca West, in her brief role as co-editor of *The Freewoman*, had urged Marsden to include purely literary material in the magazine in 1912, arguing: 'I don't see why a movement towards freedom of expression in literature shouldn't be associated with and inspired by your gospel' (cited Barash, 1987, p. 46). Indeed, *The Freewoman* had included poetry as early as its second issue, later adding short stories, literary reviews and discussions of contemporary art such as the Italian Futurist exhibition at the Sackville Galleries in London in 1912.

The difficulty in assessing *The New Freewoman/Egoist* from a revisionist viewpoint consists in determining whether the aesthetic material, once welcomed into the magazine, complemented or overwhelmed Marsden's 'gospel' and feminist discussion in the journal of issues such as sexual chastity, contraception, prostitution, 'uranians' (homosexuals) or paid house-work. K. K. Ruthven, for example, argues that the magazine demonstrates 'a paradigmatic instance of the subordination of women by a male-dominated modernism' (Ruthven, 1987, p. 1300).[4] A contrary interpretation understands Marsden's encouragement of Pound *et al.* as part of her own self-alienation from contemporary feminism. Opposing the dominant feminist positions of the time brought Marsden into strange consort with various tendencies within masculine versions of modernism. Marsden was therefore happy to include literary texts coinciding in orientation with her own philosophical egoism. Joyce's *A Portrait of the Artist, ur*-text of male self-creation, sits comfortably alongside Marsden's claim that

> *The New Freewoman* is not for the advancement of women, but for the empowering of individuals — men and women; it is not to set woman free but to demonstrate the fact that 'freeing' is the individual's affair and must be done first hand, and that individual power is the first step thereto.
> ('Intellect and Culture', *New Freewoman*, 1.7.1913[5])

Most of all it is Imagism, in its Poundian form,[6] which jostles with Marsden's egoism in the magazine, creating the effect of modernist collage, juxtaposing very different types of writing practice and political orientation. Egoism thus dovetailed smoothly with Imagism; poets proclaimed in their 1916 anthology to be 'Individualists' (*Some Imagist Poets* 1916, Preface). This was a description that suited publication in a magazine whose full title was *The New Freewoman: An Individualist Review*. Marsden's support for philosophical egoism derived from her interest in the anarchist ideas of the German Max Stirner, as well as from the profound influence of Nietzsche in this period in England. Stirner's *The Ego and His Own* (1884) was translated into English by a regular *Egoist* contributor, Steven Bynington, and appeared in some forty-nine editions between 1900 and 1929. Marsden called the book, 'The most powerful work that has ever emerged from a single human mind' ('Concerning the Beautiful', *New Freewoman*, 1.9.1913). Michael Levenson believes the appeal of Stirner's work stems from the collapse of liberal ideology in the years up to the war, stating that 'liberalism decomposed into egoism' (Levenson, 1984, p. 68). Such sceptical beliefs were most attractive to intellectuals and artists, among whom Levenson counts Pound and the other Imagists.

Aside from this radical subjectivism, Marsden's theoretical work also parallelled the Imagist campaign to cleanse poetic language of abstraction. Her welcome of the titular alteration of *The New Freewoman* to *The Egoist* demonstrates just such a belief in linguistic reform. Marsden declares one important strategy for the emancipation of the individual to be a war against the inherent abstraction of linguistic structures. Here I disagree with Les Garner who, in his excellent recent biography of Dora Marsden, doubts the existence of any real theoretical overlap with Imagism (Garner, 1990, p. 3). At a time when T. E. Hulme's critique of linguistic abstraction was producing a profound influence upon Imagist thought, resulting in a poetry attentive to 'small, dry things' (Hulme, 1924, p. 131), Marsden introduced a critique of suffragette arguments for their concern with words rather than things. Imagist texts, imbued with Hulme's theories, thus found a welcome home in a journal whose editor perceived the poets to be engaged in a campaign similar to her own. Formally, then, Imagism resembles Marsden's feminism; in terms of content, their difference is quite marked.

Marsden, after studying philosophy at Manchester University, joined the Pankhurst-led Women's Social and Political Union (WSPU) in 1908 in Southport. In March 1909 she was arrested for a 'Women's Parliament' demonstration in London and served a six month jail sentence. She became a paid organizer for the WSPU in 1909 and staged a protest at one of Winston Churchill's public addresses by hanging from a hole in the ceiling of Southport's Empire Hall. Throughout 1910, however, Marsden came into conflict with the WSPU leadership, mainly because they were unhappy with her ideas for public demonstrations. In January 1911 she resigned from the organization and set up *The Freewoman* with co-editor and fellow WSPU-dissident Mary Gawthorpe. The magazine was intended partly as a feminist forum for a critique of suffrage in the WSPU mode and, indeed, by the second issue was openly critical of the Pankhursts, incurring many angry responses from readers worried by Marsden's apparent sectarianism. Millicent Fawcett is said to have read one issue and then to have torn up the paper in disgust (Garner, 1990, p. 60). Garner argues that Marsden's disillusion with the WSPU was partly due to the autocratic leadership exercised by Christabel Pankhurst and her mother (Garner, 1984, p. 47). Theoretical objections also influenced Marsden's separation from the

WSPU. The critical emphasis of *The Freewoman* and its successor was upon the myopia perceived in the suffragette concentration upon 'the vote': 'feminism is the whole issue, political enfranchisement a branch issue and the methods, militant or otherwise, are merely accidentals' ('Bondwomen', *The Freewoman*, 23.11.1911). The new journal, as initial publicity declared, was to be 'essentially a thinking organ and will afford expression for all phases of feminism — not being politically inclined merely' (cited Barash, 1987, p. 40). Marsden's critique pursued the language and arguments deployed by suffragism for displaying 'an unthought out and nebulous feminism' ('The New Morality', *The Freewoman*, 14.12.1911). Marsden thus detected the same error, a 'nebulous' lack of clarity, that Imagism detected in much contemporary poetry.

The Freewoman continued until the distributors, W. H. Smith, boycotted the paper in September 1912 due to 'the nature of certain articles which... render the paper unsuitable to be exposed on the bookstalls for general sale' (cited Hanscombe and Smyers, 1987, p. 165). This refers to the full and prescient discussion of issues surrounding men, women and sexuality in the magazine. Within the journal's pages Marsden attacked monogamy, suggested a national system of nurseries, and debated the importance of free advice upon contraception. Stella Browne wrote frankly about 'auto-eroticism' in a letter in 1912, and there were several pieces on homosexuality by followers of Edward Carpenter. 'Freewoman Discussion Circles' were started to continue the debate stimulated by the paper. Open to both sexes, and very popular, the circles maintained a similarly controversial choice of topics (Garner, 1990, p. 73). However, as a result of the economic difficulties introduced by W. H. Smith's boycott, *The Freewoman* announced its last issue in October. Marsden revived the paper in the following year with the financial assistance of Harriet Shaw Weaver and the editorial help of Rebecca West.

The first issue of *The New Freewoman* in June 1913 found Marsden keen to distinguish her position from that of the suffrage 'cause'. A publicity flyer for the magazine boasted that it was the 'only journal of recognized standing espousing a doctrine of philosophic individualism'. Its editorial policy, the leaflet continued, 'will endeavour to lay bare the individualist basis of all that is most significant in modern movements including feminism' (Shaw Weaver, undated). Marsden employs this individualistic method of analysis in her initial editorial article. The style is typical of her 500 or so contributions to the magazine from 1913 to 1919. 'Views and Comments' commences with a close reading of the rhetoric of Mrs. Pankhurst's message, 'The Cause is the "Vote" ' (*New Freewoman*, 15.6.1913). To Marsden this phrase is inaccurate and should be translated into its proper egoistic formulation: 'I want the vote given to myself.' Pankhurst, argues Marsden, has neglected individual desires and abandoned her politics to discursive generalization:

> She has pinioned herself with words — words — words, and these, not her own. She ventured into the maze of the symbolists, whose vulturous progeny — the empty concepts — got her! She began to 'lead a Cause,' and imperceptibly the Cause became Leader — leading where all causes tend — to self-annihilation. Mrs. Pankhurst may die and great is the Cause. What cause? the Cause of the empty concept — the fount of all insincerity: the Cause of the Symbol — the Nothing worked upon by the Dithyramb (*ibid.*).

For Marsden, 'empty concepts', offspring of a too boisterous symbolist aesthetic, are represented by any form of abstract word — freedom, cause, or woman itself: 'Accurately speaking there is no "Woman Movement". "Woman" is doing nothing — she has, indeed, no existence' (*ibid.*). Words produce 'empty concepts' and these then capture the individual, driving her away from egoistic impulses.

Criticizing the 'Cause of the Symbol' showed Marsden's divergence from the suffragette strategy of symbolic public martyrdom, activities for which Marsden herself had earlier been imprisoned and possibly force-fed (Garner, 1990, pp. 35–6; Clarke, 1985, p. 30). Theoretically this critique demonstrates Marsden's affinity with Imagism which, jettisoning the symbolic, called famously for a 'Direct treatment of the "thing", whether subjective or objective' (Pound, 1913a) and endorsed Pound's claim that 'Language is made out of concrete things' (Pound, 1950, p. 49). For both Marsden and the Imagists a surer realm of 'things' existed beneath language. 'The Verbal Age', as Marsden described the contemporary period, would be routed if 'we recognise that there exists nothing save things and the relations between things' ('Views and Comments', *New Freewoman*, 15.10.1913). Rejecting words as mere symbols in favour of things recalls Pound's insistence in the same year, in 'A Few Don'ts by An Imagiste', that 'the natural object is always the *adequate* symbol' (Pound, 1913b).

Marsden's analysis of Pankhurst in the earlier article continues by subjecting another suffragette call for 'woman's freedom' to similar scrutiny. She discovers it consists of three elements: 'two notions and an atmosphere' ('Views and Comments', *New Freewoman*, 15.6.1913). One notion is of force, one of a barrier through which the force pushes, and the atmosphere is 'half swoon, half thrill. It is the essence of sensation'. Freedom is a 'vague symbolic indefinable thing', distinct from the individual effort implied by the force of 'getting free'. Thus it is the exercise of force by the individual which identifies the true definition of 'freedom'. Anyone espousing the 'Cause of Freedom' is actually calling for 'one long course of banalities and mis-statements' (*ibid.*). 'Freedom' as an abstract symbol of political aspiration must be displaced by the more robust action of freeing the self.[7]

Marsden's dislike of any linguistic abstraction chimes with Pound's dictum in 'A Few Don'ts by an Imagiste': 'Go in fear of abstractions' (Pound, 1913b). This theme persists as a phobia in Pound's imagination, culminating in the 1934 claim that 'The disease of the last century and a half has been "abstraction" ' (Pound, 1954, p. 59). Pound cites changes in the meaning of the concept 'liberty' as an example of a term with a precise sense in the eighteenth century, but which had now lapsed 'into meaning mere irresponsibility' (Pound, 1954, p. 59). Guiding Marsden's critique of abstract political rhetoric is a distinction found in the philosopher Bergson between the solidity of intuition and the insipid nature of the intellect. This is a distinction that was influential in Imagist circles, and which resonates throughout modernist writing (see Schwartz, 1985; Ellmann, 1987). Marsden offers a long list of abstract nouns or 'empty concepts' which have 'gangrened all culture' — noting, like Pound, 'liberty', but also adding 'equality, fraternity, truth, unity, and humanity' — and then provides her definition of a proper concept:

> A true concept is the framework which the intellect puts round something *felt*: feeling experienced either directly in the Soul, or indirectly through the perceptions of sense. An intellectual concept is not, strictly speaking, a concept at all: it represents the giving of a 'local habitation and a name' to a Nothing.
> ('Views and Comments', *New Freewoman*, 15.6.1913)

Marsden's political critique depends very much on this familiar opposition of sense versus concept, Bergsonian intuition over intellect. Suffragette thought erred precisely in being thought rather than sensation. Suffragette politics would undoubtedly fail because its 'intellectual concepts' formed 'a poison diet' for its believers. 'A virile people turns to thought', notes Marsden, evoking the muscular language of a T. E. Hulme, and 'creates a culture which promptly turns upon it to encompass its destruction' (*ibid*.). Marsden's arguments thus revolve around the same set of binary terms often found in conventional modernist literary theory.

Marsden's analysis identifies two related errors of suffragette feminism. First, it believes in language which, in an intrinsic manner, is linked to intellectual and 'empty concepts'. Second, suffragettes foolishly produce a collective political discourse which, in its advocacy of generalized concepts, inevitably smothers individual particularity. The rhetorical use of the term 'woman', for example, is a thoroughly empty and pernicious notion, as Marsden argues later: 'Woman, spelt with a capital, woman-as-type, has no existence ... it is an empty concept and should be banished from language' ('Intellect and Culture', *New Freewoman*, 1.7.1913). It must be exiled because it glosses over the individualist basis of life and language: 'Accurately, every sentence begins with "I" ' ('I AM', *Egoist*, 1.1.1915). Neglect of this egoistic doctrine results in that most abhorrent of Imagist sins, abstraction from the particular. The specific sensuous desires of the individual are thus the true basis for a feminist politics, not the conceptual abstractions of the suffragettes. Marsden concludes her critique with the statement that individuals cannot be 'lumped together into a class, a sex, or a "movement" ' ('Views and Comments', *New Freewoman*, 15.6.1913). Individual satisfactions are the basis of action since 'The centre of the Universe lies in the desire of the individual, and the Universe for the individual has no meaning apart from their individual satisfactions.' Women following this rather isolating allegiance are to be recognized as 'Egoists', for whom 'intensive satisfaction of Self is ... the one goal in life' (*ibid*.).

Marsden's October 1914 *Egoist* article, 'Women's Rights', signals the end of the political concerns of *The Freewoman* with a gesture to the arrival of World War One: 'The War ... has brought the wordy contest about Women's Rights to an abrupt finish, and only a few sympathetic words remain to be spoken over the feminist corpse' ('Women's Rights', *Egoist*, 1.10.1914). 'Rights' is another bogus term and feminist struggle for them is misdirected: 'The confusion has arisen out of an assumption that ultimate authority lies in words.' Compared with the 'exercise of force' displayed in the war, feminist demands are feeble: their 'words have the value — and no more — of the detonation of the combatants' guns: they have effects which impress the timid and the simple' (*ibid*.). Symbolic action is judged once more to be inferior if contrasted with an Imagist-like 'directness'. Women's position will only improve by 'an effectual assertion of physical force', an assertion that could make 'Englishwomen . . . as good a fighting force as the Japanese' (*ibid*.). In other words, feminism is a mere set of signifiers, lacking the solid meanings of signifieds necessary to effect real change. Once again Marsden's modernist sympathies are evident, shown in her suspicion that language is not adequate to convey the truth of a situation or sensation.

By January 1915 Marsden's references to the suffragettes or to feminist questions have all but disappeared. *The Egoist* now has Richard Aldington as Assistant Editor (replacing Rebecca West), and is publishing Joyce's *Portrait* and running Pound's series of articles upon Renaissance drama. Its role as a key magazine for the emergent avant-garde was established, perhaps its only serious rival being Margaret Anderson's *Little Review* in America. Reviewing the role of small literary periodicals in 1934 Pound stresses the importance of *The Egoist* in publishing material that *The New Age*, another English rival, refused to print (Pound, 1950, p. 259).[8] Marsden's attack upon linguistic abstraction in the columns of the paper was now echoed in the rhetoric of Imagism. Early in 1914 she had written that abstract terms were 'choking the frail tentacles of perception' ('Views and Comments', *Egoist*, 16.2.1914). Imagism's promise to restore a sensual experience of the concrete via the clarity of the poetic 'image' parallels Marsden's argument that literary discourse relies upon the production of images. In the course of a critique of H. G. Wells, pet hate of many a modernist, Marsden notes:

> The growth of literature in the increasingly precise outlining in words of images felt clearly enough to make their features definite for the one who feels them. A poor writer is one who writes before his images are clear — before he knows in fact.
>
> ('Views and Comments', *Egoist*, 1.6.1914)

Images are therefore not ideas, but emotions understood sensually. Hulme too had argued: 'All emotion depends on real solid vision . . . it is physical' (Hulme, 1955, p. 78). In the Imagist issue of *The Egoist* in May 1915 Marsden echoes this view: 'Things are feelings' ('Truth and Reality', *Egoist*, 1.5.1915). It was to become an important component of Imagist theory that images were akin to emotions not ideas, thereby transforming feelings into solid phenomena. Marsden, of course, had been insisting since 1913 that ideas were to be distrusted: 'A thought i.e. an idea, is not a real thing, its existence is verbal like that of a dragon or snark . . . to think is to hesitate; awaiting the verification of a fact'

('Views and Comments', *New Freewoman*, 15.10.1913). Later Pound echoed Marsden when, writing in *The Egoist* in 1919, he claimed that an 'idea is only an imperfect induction from fact' (Pound, 1919, p. 7), or as William Carlos Williams was famously to state: 'no ideas but in things' (Carlos Williams, 1967, p. 390). Imagism, with its perspicacious presentation of 'things', appeared to Marsden a discourse impatient with pure thought, aiming for a concrete realm to which she thought feminism should also aspire.

Marsden's first piece in 1915, *I AM*, illustrates her intellectual journey out of a critique of feminism and into a liaison with a certain strand of linguistic argument within Imagism. *The Egoist*, she notes, has 'unique work' to achieve. It must attempt 'to blast the stupefactions of — The Word. Our war is with words and in their every aspect: grammar, accidence, syntax: body, blood, and bone' ('I AM', *Egoist*, 1.1.1915). Marsden then produces the almost ritual denunciation of the 'dangerous fungus' of language and proposes using psychology to reduce the verbal basis of philosophical problems. In a mood which would later be called Logical Positivist, Marsden notes that 'grammatical form reduced to maniable limits by psychology will entail as a first consequence the scrapping of the verbal conundrums which constitute existing philosophy' (*ibid*.). Once this task is accomplished, and language and thought clarified, then work will be able to turn to the 'definite images' which form the true basis of thought. The human brain 'is at home only in that aura of images which is thrown off from the living "I" ' (*ibid*.). In terms of epistemology, therefore, this philosophical egoism is closely related to Hulme's argument that 'thought is prior to language and consists in the simultaneous presentation to the mind of two different images' (Hulme, 1955, p. 84).

Marsden continues the article 'I AM' by noting the contemporary 'wide-spread dissatisfaction with the grammatical structure in this form or that', and mentions the Futurist Marinetti and the Imagists as examples ('I AM', *Egoist*, 1.1.1915). In one of the few explicit references to those she called 'Our friends, the "Imagists" ' (*ibid*.), Marsden describes the Imagist attack upon adjectives as an important but superficial reform of language. The more pressing task is to recognize the individualist basis of the world: 'Our worlds? We each grow our own!' (*ibid*.). The difficulty for certain women of 'growing' their own subjectivity does not seem to have troubled Marsden. Creation of self-identity for Marsden is a Nietzschean effort: strenuous, solitary and distinct from any sense of community, female or otherwise.[9] Language only stifles the individual ego, male or female, preventing self-realization. Raymond Williams has argued that this position, where language is perceived as 'blocking or making difficulties for authentic consciousness' (Williams, 1989, p. 77), is one of two attitudes towards language that are widespread in modernism. Marsden's war against the political terminology employed by the suffragettes thus develops into a more general, and emphatically modernist, critique of all words.

As Marsden's magazine became home to Imagist writers in the wartime years, so her articles restate the case against suffragette discourse in terms increasingly akin to Imagist thought. Marsden's quarrel came to be more with words and 'empty concepts' than with patriarchal society. It is, however, difficult to judge how far Marsden's philosophical and political development can be attributed to other tendencies within modernism. Isolated from the London coterie surrounding *The Egoist* because she lived in Southport tending to her sick mother, Marsden's correspondence with managing editor Harriet Shaw Weaver (from June 15, 1914) shows her to be suspicious of the takeover threat from groups associated respectively with Pound and Aldington. Marsden confided to Weaver that she had a 'genuine distrust of Pound' (Shaw Weaver, 31.1.1916) and that he was a 'schemer' (Shaw Weaver, 16.5.1917). Marsden was, however, keen to keep the interest of Pound and his associates, perhaps more so than of the group around Aldington. Pound's presence in the paper was viewed as a guarantee of sales (a meagre 200 was an average figure from 1916 to 1919) and as a means to elicit good contributors (Shaw Weaver, 6.5.1917). Marsden was an astute enough editor to realize how important 'the exploitation of personalities' (Shaw Weaver, Oct. 1915) was for a successful literary journal. Marsden's fears of Pound's machinations were well-founded: in 1917 she discovered with annoyance that Pound had been paying contributors (in this case T. S. Eliot) directly, without the knowledge of the two women editors. To Marsden this confirmed a bogus 'proprietary position' (Shaw Weaver, 20.5.1917) on Pound.[10]

But if Marsden spent a lot of time pondering how to keep unruly male modernists under her proprietorial thumb, the relation of her own ideas to theirs is not consciously discussed in her correspondence with Weaver. The absent editor certainly read a great deal of the literary material prior to publication. Marsden commented that Wyndam Lewis's *Tarr* was 'a conglomeration of smart views' and though being 'half-baked' in parts, would be 'provocative' (Shaw Weaver, 12.1.1916) and useful for sales because of this. Joyce's *Portrait* was a 'tip-top' (Shaw Weaver, Feb. 1917) novel but the 'Proteus' section of *Ulysses* produced a more negative judgment: 'I have just re-read episode III of

"Ulysses". My dear editor go down on your knees and thank your stars for possessing *one* writer of metaphysics who is *CLEAR*! That's *ME*!! Joyce is — my word! He's appalling!' (Shaw Weaver, 10.4.1918). Subsequent literary history has reversed the values of the comparison, but Marsden's opinion on Eliot's *Prufrock* volume, published by the Egoist Press, has become more accepted: 'I've just read some of Eliot's poems through again: the sense of freshness is even stronger. "The Portrait of a Lady" I liked particularly. The book is good' (Shaw Weaver, 16.5.1917). In her support — however qualified — for these writers Marsden not only shows herself to be a good editor; her awareness of the importance of experimentation with form and language in modernist literature develops from her own critical feminist perspective upon language.

Marsden's main written contributions to the magazine from 1916 consisted of a series, 'Lingual Psychology', which ran from July until *The Egoist* closed in 1919. Feminism became even more displaced and, paradoxically, Marsden continued building grand philosophical systems that avow egoistic particularism. With Harriet Shaw Weaver's assistance she published three large and unwieldy works upon metaphysics and the philosophy of religion after *The Egoist* closed: *The Definition of the Godhead* (Marsden, 1928); *The Mysteries of Christianity* (Marsden, 1930); and the posthumous *The Philosophy of Time* (Marsden, 1955). Apart from proclaiming that the most important lesson of the previous 300 years of philosophy is a 'need for precision of speech' (Marsden, 1928, p. 55), these works bear little resemblance to her earlier work on women and language.

How then are we to judge Marsden as a modernist woman? In her transition from feminism to modernism it is difficult to view Marsden as part of any alternative tradition of female modernists. Her theories have clear associations with male modernist rhetoric. On the other hand, drawing out such connections provides no evidence that she was either influenced and/or overwhelmed by ideas deriving from the Imagists. Indeed, arguments can be made for her influence upon the philosophical basis of Pound's Imagism (Clarke, 1992; Bush, 1990). Her philosophical egoism, replete with modernist motifs of surface versus depth and abstract versus concrete, is an assertion of the need for women to articulate themselves emphatically as individuals. Marsden, however, appears unaware that she employs conceptual categories such as abstract versus concrete, words and things, which are open to a gendered interpretation where women are placed on the side of the 'inferior' term. Pound, for example, repeatedly distinguishes between 'hard' and 'soft' forms of aesthetic practice, praising Vorticism for its evasion of 'flaccidity' (Pound, 1970, p. 88) and condemning symbolism for its 'Soft mushy edges' (Pound, 1950, p. 90). With hindsight it is clear that such gendered binary terms form an important axis around which our received notions of modernism operate. To find a writer like Marsden using them as part of a feminist critique obviously complicates any easy assumptions about how gender structures work within and across modernism. One argument might be that Marsden is attempting to appropriate and reaccentuate conceptual categories — solidity, clarity, and hardness, for example — which have so often been structured as 'other' relative to the styles of women writers.

However, Marsden's attack on suffragette discourse for its own form of 'flaccidity' may derive from the feminist perspective she evolved while engaged in suffragette action. The self-empowering of women was a wider and more problematic project, she perceived, than could be accomplished by the simple possession of the vote. Part of this larger project involved Marsden in an investigation into the relation of women to language and representation, an exploration typical of female modernists. From the point of view of style, Marsden's own prose veers repeatedly towards abstraction, eschewing the concrete and direct style endorsed by both herself and the Imagists. This inability to match form and content in her own expression may point to the difficulties facing a woman appropriating a masculine rhetoric of 'hardness'. In another sense, these contradictions might be what makes Marsden a modernist writer, if we accept Marianne DeKoven's recent argument that 'unresolved contradiction' (DeKoven, 1991, p. 24) is one of the principles constituting literary modernism. Marsden's rhetorical style, in its complex syntactic patterns and profuse use of punctuation, seems to have distinct resemblances with other contemporary female writers. Marsden, however, is not a Woolf nor a Richardson. She advocates a feminist revolution *against* rather than *of* the word. In this respect Marsden's critique of language might reinforce Julia Kristeva's argument about the nature of the symbolic order, a system which must remain 'foreign' (Kristeva, 1986, p. 204) and other to women's selfhood. Marsden's apocalyptic assault on language, her war with words, illustrates Kristeva's point that women will 'invest' in the 'machine of terrorism' (Kristeva, 1986, pp. 204–5) and violence as a reaction to the frustrations offered to women by the symbolic order. Kristeva herself, in this essay and elsewhere, seems to echo Marsden's linguistic critique of the 'Woman Movement' for its neglect of individual subjectivity: 'having started with the idea of difference, feminism will be able to break free of its belief in Woman, Her power, Her writing, so as to channel this demand for difference into each and every element of the female whole, and finally, to bring out the singularity of each woman' (Kristeva, 1986, p. 208).

Juxtaposing Kristeva and Marsden in this way is not intended to assign easily theoretical value to the latter. Rather, it tries to display the problematic insights into feminism, language and the individual that both provide. Early on, her friend Mary Gawthorpe criticized Marsden's Individualism for its tendency to verge on elitism: 'Intellectually you have signed on as a member of the coming aristocracy' (cited Garner, 1990, p. 83). In this respect Marsden resembled, once more, the ideas of Ezra Pound who, in the pages of *The Egoist*, had produced a rallying-call for an 'aristocracy of the arts' (Pound, 1914, p. 67). Isolation of the self from others in this political configuration always has the potential for a practical selfishness.

But perhaps it is most productive to consider Marsden's work as a fascinating — and politically ambiguous — linguistic analysis of the relations between feminism and modernism. Some sixty years before Kristeva's *Women's Time* queried the linguistic collectivity of 'women', Marsden raised a similar scepticism:

> 'Woman Movement' forsooth. Why does not someone start a 'straight nose movement' or a 'mole movement' or any other movement based upon some accidental physical contouration? Woman? Is there such a thing as woman sensed from the inside?
> ('Intellect and Culture', *New Freewoman*, 1.7.1913)

What such a sense of self would be, freed from the wounding otherness of the symbolic and able to respect individuality, without blandly eulogizing it, is still today an open and crucial question for interpretations of women in modernism. Marsden's proprietorship of *The New Freewoman* and *The Egoist* helped propel English literature towards an acceptance of modernism. The similarities between Marsden and Imagism point to a congruence of ideas. Arguments over the direction in which influence operated, however, are ultimately not as interesting as discussions which analyse the connections between ideas from different discourses — political, philosophical or aesthetic — within the modernist period. A fuller understanding of what we call 'modernism' requires attention to debates within turn-of-the-century feminism. Dora Marsden's 'war with words' is one such important conjuncture of the terms 'gender' and 'modernism'. Analysing one woman's war with words helps illuminate the larger work of grasping how categories of gender organize the whole range of practices we now describe as modernism.

Notes

1   The Imagist group, one of the most important movements in Anglo-American modernist poetry, published five anthologies from 1914 to 1930. Key members of the group included Richard Aldington, Hilda Doolittle (H.D.), John Gould Fletcher, F. S. Flint, Amy Lowell and Ezra Pound.

2   Reference to Marsden's articles in *The Freewoman*, *The New Freewoman* and *The Egoist* will be given in the main text in the following way: article title, magazine title and date. A slightly different version of this chapter first appeared in *English Literature in Transition* 36:2, 1993.

3   Les Garner shows that the change of name was agreed by Marsden, along with others, at a Directors Meeting for the paper on the 25th November 1913. Garner claims that 'it would be extremely fanciful to see the change of name as a male plot against feminism' (Garner, 1990, p. 118). Part of the origin for this simplified version of events is Harriet Shaw Weaver's typed manuscript history of the paper, dating from sometime after the closure of the magazine and held in the British Library. Weaver writes: 'The new masculine element which had allied itself with the paper, before long raised objections to the title... and, as Miss Marsden... was also in favour of a new name, on January 1st 1914 the title was changed to *The Egoist*' (Shaw Weaver, undated).

4   Other critics have taken a similar view of these events. James Longenbach offers a similar reading, arguing that 'Pound persuaded Dora Marsden to change its *The New Freewoman* title' (Longenbach, 1989, p. 100). Alan Durant argues that for Pound, the change of title demonstrates how 'the challenge of political liberation for women is replaced by the assurance of the ego's self-possession' (Durant, 1981, p. 107). See also Benstock (1987, p. 364).

5   I disagree somewhat with MacKendrick's view that it was only 'coincidence' (MacKendrick, 1972, p. 187) that Joyce's *Portrait* was anticipated by some of Marsden's points on egoism and identity. Though there is no clear evidence of literary influence, similarities can be noted in terms of the common ideas and practices which we have subsequently learnt to call modernist.

6   By Pound's version of Imagism I mean those writers that Pound encouraged to contribute to *The Egoist* and other modernist little magazines, specifically Aldington and H.D. After publication of the first anthology Pound fell out with John Gould Fletcher and Amy Lowell. Lowell went on to support the publication of the next three anthologies without contributions from Pound. Lowell very rarely contributed to *The Egoist*, and concentrated upon publicizing Imagism, as she understood it, in America. In retrospect it seems that Pound's definition of Imagist theory does not quite capture the various practices of all of the other members of the group.

7   Marsden's espousal of force or energy recalls certain theories of the Vorticist group. Longenbach argues that male modernists such as Pound sought to re-direct the energy displayed by the suffragettes into the modernist war against staid contemporary English culture (Longenbach, 1989, pp. 99–100). Certainly the message to the suffragettes in *BLAST* praised their expression of energy, if only in the context of asking them to leave art alone:

'WE MAKE YOU A PRESENT OF OUR VOTES. ONLY LEAVE ART

ALONE...WE ADMIRE YOUR ENERGY. YOU AND ARTISTS ARE THE ONLY THINGS (YOU DON'T MIND BEING CALLED THINGS?) LEFT IN ENGLAND WITH A LITTLE LIFE IN THEM'.

BLAST, 1914, p. 151

8   For further discussion of the publication of the magazine, see Lidderdale and Nicholson (1970). For discussion of *The New Age*, see Martin (1967).

9   Barash comments that 'Marsden seems at times to have taken women's communities for granted, and had little sense of their importance to so many of her feminist contemporaries' (Barash, 1987, p. 37). Clarke defends Marsden's political belief in egoism in the following manner: 'Marsden's anarchism develops directly out of the feminist perspective on servility and defencelessness and is then generalized to all power arrangements. If her egoism is reactionary, it is so first and foremost from the tyrannies of self-sacrifice which thwart the individual power motive' (Clarke, 1985, p. 37).

10 For another account of Pound's plotting in relation to *The New Freewoman* see Fletcher (1937, p. 62, 127). Pound used money that Fletcher received for poems published in *Poetry* to pay Pound's own contributors in *The Egoist*.

References

BARASH, C. (1987) 'Dora Marsden's Feminism, *The Freewoman*, and the Gender Politics of Early Modernism', *Princeton University Library Chronicle*, Winter.

BENSTOCK, S. (1987) *Women of the Left Bank*, London, Virago.

BLAST (1914) **1**, June, London.

BUSH, R. (1990) 'Introduction to Ezra Pound', in KIME SCOTT, B. (Ed.), *The Gender of Modernism: A Critical Anthology*, Bloomington, Indiana University Press.

CARLOS WILLIAMS, W. (1967) *Autobiography*, New York, New Directions.

CLARKE, B. (1985) Dora Marsden's Egoism and Modern Letters: West, Weaver, Joyce, Pound, Lawrence, Williams, Eliot, *Works and Days*, **2**, 2.

CLARKE, B. (1992) 'Dora Marsden and Ezra Pound: *The New Freewoman* and "The Serious Artist" ', *Contemporary Literature*, **33**, 1.

DEKOVEN, M. (1991) *Rich and Strange: Gender, History, Modernism*, New Jersey, Princeton University Press.

DURANT, A. (1981) *Ezra Pound, Identity in Crisis: A Fundamental Reassessment of the Poet and His Work*, Brighton, Harvester Press.

ELLMANN, M. (1987) *The Poetics of Impersonality: T. S. Eliot and Ezra Pound*, Brighton, Harvester Press.

FLETCHER, J. G. (1937) *Life is My Song*, New York and Toronto, Farrar and Rinehart.

GARNER, L. (1984) *Stepping Stones to Women's Liberty Feminist Ideas in the Women's Suffrage Movement 1900–1918*, London, Heinemann.

GARNER, L. (1990) *A Brave and Beautiful Spirit: Dora Marsden 1882–1960*, Avebury, Gower Publishing.

GILBERT, S. G. and GUBAR, S. (1988) *No Man's Land: The Place of the Woman Writer in the Twentieth Century*, New Haven and London, Yale University Press.

HANSCOMBE, G. and SMYERS, V. (1987) *Writing for their Lives: The Modernist Woman*, London, Women's Press.

HULME, T. E. (1924) in READ, H. (Ed.) *Speculations: Essays on Humanism and the Philosophy of Art*, London, Routledge and Kegan Paul.

HULME, T. E. (1955) in HYNES, S. (Ed.) *Further Speculations*, Minneapolis, University of Minnesota Press.

KENNER, H. (1972) *The Pound Era: The Age of Ezra Pound, T. S. Eliot, James Joyce and Wyndham Lewis*, London, Faber.

KIME SCOTT, B. (Ed.) (1990) *The Gender of Modernism: A Critical Anthology*, Bloomington, Indiana University Press.

KRISTEVA, J. (1986) 'Women's Time' in MOI, T. (Ed.), *The Kristeva Reader*, Oxford, Blackwell.

LEVENSON, M. (1984) *A Genealogy of Modernism: A Study of English Literary Doctrine*, Cambridge, Cambridge University Presss.

LIDDERDALE, J. and NICHOLSON, M. (1970) *Dear Miss Weaver: Harriet Shaw Weaver 1876-1961*, London, Faber.

LONGENBACH, J. (1989) 'The Women and Men of 1914' in COOPER, H. M., AUSLANDER MUNICH, A. and MERRILL SQUIER, S. (Eds) *Arms and the Woman War, Gender, and Literary Representation*, Chapel Hill and London, University of Carolina Press.

MACKENDRICK, L. K. (1972) '*The New Freewoman*: A Short Story of Literary Journalism', *English Literature in Transition 1880-1920*, **15**, 3.

MARSDEN, D. (1928) *The Definition of the Godhead*, London, Egoist Press.

MARSDEN, D. (1930) *The Mysteries of Christianity*, London, Egoist Press.

MARSDEN, D. (1955) *The Philosophy of Time*, Oxford, Holywell Press.

MARSDEN, D. (Ed.) (1913) *The New Freewoman: An Individualist Review*, 1 volume, London.

MARSDEN, D. and GAWTHORPE, M. (Eds) (1911-12) *The Freewoman: A Weekly Feminist Review*, 2 volumes, London.

MARSDEN, D. and SHAW WEAVER, M. (Eds) (1914-19) *The Egoist: An Individualistic Review*, 2 volumes, London.

MARTIN, W. (1967) *'The New Age' Under Orage: Chapters in English Cultural History*, Manchester, Manchester University Press.

POUND, E. (1913a) 'Imagisme', *Poetry*, March, reprinted in JONES, P. (Ed.) (1972), *Imagist Poetry*, Harmondsworth, Penguin.

POUND, E. (1913b) 'A Few Don'ts By an Imagiste', *Poetry*, March, reprinted in JONES, P. (Ed.) (1972).

POUND, E. (1914) 'The New Sculpture', *The Egoist*, 16th Feb.

POUND, E. (1919) 'Aeschylus', *The Egoist*, Jan/Feb.

POUND, E. (1950) in PAIGE, D. D. (Ed.) *Selected Letters of Ezra Pound 1909-1941*, London, Faber.

POUND, E. (1954) 'The Teacher's Mission' in ELIOT, T. S. (Ed.) *Literary Essays*, London, Faber.

POUND, E. (1970) 'Vorticism', *Fortnightly Review*, Sept. 1914, reprinted in *Gaudier-Brzeska: A Memoir*, New York, New Directions.

RUTHVEN, K. (1987) 'Ezra's Appropriations', *TLS*, Nov. 20-26.

SCHWARTZ, S. (1985) *The Matrix of Modernism: Pound, Eliot and Early Twentieth Century Thought*, New Jersey, Princeton University Press.

SHAW WEAVER, H., *Harriet Shaw Weaver Papers*, London, British Library.

Some Imagist Poets 1916 An Annual Anthology, (1916), Boston and New York, Houghton Mifflin.

WILLIAMS, R. (1989) *The Politics of Modernism: Against the New Conformists*, (Ed.) TONY PINKNEY, London and New York, Verso.

Chapter 7

Becoming as Being:
Leonora Carrington's Writings and
Paintings 1937–40

Gabriele Griffin

After due reflection, I said to myself that it was easy to see this
horse wasn't just an ordinary horse.

(*The House of Fear*, Carrington, 1989b, p. 28)

If I hadn't known that it was Lucretia, I would have sworn that
it was a horse. She was beautiful, a blinding white all over, with
four legs as fine as needles and a mane which fell around her
long face like water.

(*The Oval Lady*, Carrington, 1989b, p. 41)

Issues of Identification

Femme et Oiseau (Figure 7.1), a painting by Leonora Carrington dating
from *c*. 1937, presents the portrait of a creature, described in the title of
this painting as a *woman*, whose image merges the contours of a horse's
head and neck with the facial features of a human being, androgyne[1]
rather than specifically feminine.[2] The woman/horse's head is framed
by a window, seemingly cut into thick stone, on the inside sill of which a
magpie is sitting.[3] The woman/horse is looking in from the outside,
regarding the bird which appears to be simultaneously returning the
woman/horse's gaze and looking at a further creature, mandrake-like
emerging out of the stone frame on the inside of the window.

The painting represents the viewer with multiple ambiguities, not
only concerning the identity of the woman/horse whose (sexual) self is

Figure 7.1 *Femme et Oiseau* (1937)

indeterminate but also in terms of the dynamics of the gazes relative to the spatial position of the figures, and their significance. The woman/horse, outside, is looking in, her flowing mane suggesting the possibility of movement and freedom which, both in terms of the inward gaze and the rather sad expression on her face, seems not to be mirrored by a sense of liberation in the woman/horse. The bird, though not constrained by a window pane or bars from flying off, crouches on the window sill, not obviously ready to leave. Both woman/horse and bird are not spatially confined but seem caught in a hermeneutic exchange of gazing, the circularity of which appears to actualize a psychological rather than a material constraint. I shall return to the issues of confinement and flight represented here.

Another striking aspect of the portrait is the degree to which a merging of human and equine features is achieved in the painting: here is no juxtaposition of opposites, nor a sense of the incongruous conjoining of inalienably separate or separable bits. To call the creature 'woman/horse' or 'horse/woman' is thus to draw attention to the inadequacy of the English language to (re)present such imaged merging accurately, to index the specificity of categorization demanded in language and refused in this painting which requires the invention of a new word to describe the being portrayed here.

As the quotations at the beginning of this chapter indicate, the merged figure of the woman/horse is found not only in Leonora Carrington's paintings; it also occurs in her writings, particularly in the phase between 1937–40 during which time she painted *Femme et Oiseau* (1937). This merged figure — the conjoined animal/woman — and its significance in Carrington's work and life provides the starting-point for this chapter, in a context of exploring constructions of one female self in the modernist period.

Carrington's work, like that of many women artists of the modernist period, has suffered a silencing,[4] broken, in Britain, only in 1989, when Virago published two collections of her short stories and again in 1991, when a major one-woman retrospective exhibition of her paintings was mounted by Andrea Schlieker at the Serpentine Gallery in London. Until the late 1980s Carrington's work was thus virtually unknown to a wider public in Britain although she was born in Lancashire in 1917, lived in Britain until she was 19, and has been a writer and painter since the late 1930s. Her work has been subject to dis-/misplacement. In this it is, of course, not singular; the displacement signalled by her gender[5] which Carrington externalizes and enacts at the level of language (writing predominantly in French) and of geography (living outside Britain since 1936, when she eloped with the Surrealist painter Max Ernst to France), is a condition she shares with many women artists not only of the modernist period. The exiled self,[6] negotiating its position from a point of awareness of that marginality and alienation, thus becomes a prominent focus of Carrington's work and, in part, explains the construction of her merged female figures, half animal, half human.

Half Animal, Half Human

All the merged figures of Carrington's writings of the period 1937–40 share the trait of conjoining a *female* human being with an animal. In one of her early stories, *The Debutante*, (Carrington, 1989b, pp. 44–8) a young girl befriends a hyena. At a ball given in the girl's honour the hyena masquerades as the girl.[7] Her disguise is effected by the hyena wearing the girl's clothes and by her using, as a mask, the face of the girl's maid whom the hyena kills for that purpose. The disguise is discovered because of the hyena's smell. In this story, the first person narrator, the young girl, and the animal remain discrete entities but are presented as potentially interchangeable (only to be distinguished by their smell) and as joined by a sense of mutual support. In another story, *The Oval Lady*, (*ibid*. 37–43) the eponymous heroine, also known as Lucretia, has a rocking horse, Tartar, with whom she plays: 'Let's make believe that we're all horses'. In the course of playing, Lucretia appears to acquire the features of a horse and simultaneously, the wooden horse seems to come to life. When her father threatens to burn the wooden horse, Lucretia pleads for the animal, tears running from her 'great horse's eyes' (p. 42). As he goes to burn the horse, 'the most frightful neighing sounded from above, as if an animal were suffering extreme torture' (p. 43). This sentence with which the story ends creates an intra-textually unresolved ambiguity concerning who/what precisely is making the noise and who/what is suffering here, Lucretia or the wooden horse.

In *As they rode along the edge* (Carrington, 1989a) a similar ambiguity concerning the precise identity of the protagonist is constructed: Virginia Fur, the central character, has 'a mane of hair yards long and enormous hands with dirty nails'; she acts in such a way that 'one couldn't really be altogether sure that she was a human being. Her smell alone threw doubt on it — a mixture of spices and game, the stables, fur and grasses' (p. 3). The question of precisely what identity the female figure has is also raised in *The Sisters* (Carrington, 1989a) in which one of the protagonists, Juniper — who, vampire-like, appears to exist on blood — is described thus: 'Her body was white and naked, feathers grew from her shoulders and round her breasts.[8] Her white arms were neither wings nor arms' (p. 44). Carrington's stories thus feature protagonists framed in transgressive terms, resisting the boundaries and categorizations which determine what is human, animal, lifeless or animated. But what do the specificities of these transgressions signify?

Resistance to Social Strictures and Institutionalized Power

The focus in Carrington's stories tends to be on a small number of individuals whose relations with one another become the subject of scrutiny (one might argue that *Femme et Oiseau* presents the same scenario) in the course of the story — a focus typical for fairy tales,[9] with which Carrington's stories share some traits. Noticeable in all the stories is that they project a protagonist who is presented as a predominantly solitary figure, existing outside a wider social frame, indeed rejecting society. Thus the debutante's friendship with the hyena is constructed as a function of the debutante's rejection of other human beings: '[I] knew the animals better than I knew the girls of my own age. Indeed it was in order to get away from people that I found myself at the zoo every day' (Carrington, 1989b, p. 44). The debutante appeals to the hyena to take her place at the ball by declaring the latter to be '[her] only friend' (p. 45). Presenting herself as socially isolated, the debutante thus acts in multiply transgressive fashion: she befriends an animal not usually considered an appropriate pet for a young girl as it is undomesticated and associated with cadavers/death; she rejects the social imperative which demands interaction with other human beings, and, finally, she rejects the imposition of social expectations which demand that she mark her *rite de passage* from childhood to adulthood by coming out at a ball in her honour. These refusals are heightened by the debutante's relatively casual and unsentimental condoning of the hyena killing her maid as part of the masquerade.

The hyena's and the debutante's situation are constructed as similar. Both are en-caged, trapped to be exhibited to a gaping public, the one in a zoo, the other in the confines of an upper-middle class home. The debutante is at a point of transition from childhood to adulthood, signalled by her designation 'debutante' and by the ball which is meant to index the end of her childhood and the beginning of her adulthood, supposedly the point of her integration into society as an adult, potentially however the ultimate moment of entrapment for a woman. The debutante resists, the hyena flees — both movements positioning them outside the conventional; but the question of where this resistance leads them remains unanswered.

Virginia Fur in *As they rode along the edge* lives 'in a village long abandoned by human beings' (Carrington, 1989a, p. 4). Her relationship with the boar Igname, itself — because an act of bestiary — transgressive, is destroyed through the intervention of a human being, Saint Alexander, who encourages the killing of the boar as a way of punishing Virginia Fur for refusing to join his Church and believe in his visions. Virginia in turn avenges the boar by having the saint killed by other animals.

Both Virginia Fur and the debutante live their lives apart from human society which is presented as threatening to the mode of living these female protagonists have evolved. Both are propelled into violent action by proxy, enlisting animals on their behalf, to defend the status quo congenial to their sense of self which is threatened by the intervention of a human being who is presented as authoritative as well as supported by institutional power. In the debutante's case, the mother's demands are underwritten by social convention; in the case of Virginia Fur, Saint Alexander's attempts at enticement are sustained by the institution of the Church (here presented as a means of male self-aggrandizement).[10] Authoritative persons in Carrington's stories, generally represented as male, wholly human and unsympathetic to the animal world (as opposed to the female protagonists who are either half animal/half human or who, at least, side with the animal rather than the human), are constructed as bound by conventions, as opposing the protagonist's lifestyle and as attempting to impose upon the protagonist a particular mode of living which is a form of entrapment for that person and posits a moment of choice. What the self has to face is 'the hostility of Conformism' as Carrington describes it (Carrington, 1989b, p. 163).

Family Romances and the Refusal of the Father

As briefly suggested, this 'hostility of Conformism' presents itself in the guise of predominantly male authority figures seeking to intervene in the life of the young fe/male protagonist. In *The Oval Lady* Lucretia's playing with the rocking horse is presented as a resistance to the father who desires Lucretia to act as an adult. This entails no longer playing with the rocking horse. Given that girls' attraction to horses is associated with autoeroticism and masturbatory fantasies, one might argue that Lucretia, in refusing to give up the horse, is refusing to move from a state of — as Freud would have it — infantile sexuality and narcissism (the latter indexed in the story by her resemblance to the horse) to an adult female sexuality, focused on heterosex and submission to the law of the father. Lucretia bonds with the horse precisely because, as she puts it, it 'loathes my father' (Carrington, 1989b, p. 40). But the father is positioned as irresistible in this story — his act of destruction cannot be prevented by Lucretia, in the same way that Virginia Fur is unable to prevent the male authority figure, Saint Alexander, in *As they rode along the edge*, from killing her love, the boar. But whereas Virginia subsequently orchestrates her revenge on male authority by having the saint killed, Lucretia seems left bereft or, possibly, herself destroyed.

The problematic of the relationship between male authority figures and the young female self figures recurrently in Carrington's biography and (biographical) writings. In 1936 when she eloped with Max Ernst she was 19, he 46 — a male authority and father figure both as regards their age difference and as regards their position in the artistic world in which she was the *femme-enfant*[11] and he very much the *seigneur*. The aesthetic context of the Surrealist art movement which promoted the retention of the female child self on the one hand, and the social context of her relationship with Ernst which led to her associating with people — *his* friends and acquaintances — much older than herself, enabled Carrington to retain the childhood self that had been threatened by the demand to grow up made on her at home in England. This retention of the childhood self is encoded in *Little Francis* (1937-8), interpreted by Marina Warner as a *roman à clef* about Carrington's relationship with Ernst and 'revealing in the devotion and passivity of the boy Francis (Carrington's *alter ego* in the story), the tutelage in which Ernst and other masters held their *femmes-enfants* . . . (Carrington, 1989b, p. 10). Little Francis is portrayed as a victim who has to suffer the moves Uncle Umbriaco makes. Unable to assert his emotional needs successfully, he has a breakdown on being abandoned by the uncle, a psychosomatic manifestation of his perception of powerlessness *vis-à-vis* Uncle Umbriaco.

In *Down Below*, (Carrington, 1989b) Carrington's account of her breakdown in the wake of Ernst's internment by the occupying Nazi forces in France, male authority figures again operate as the points of reference and definition for the young female self; humiliated and desecrated, that self is constructed literally as at the mercy of plural intersecting worlds (the nation state, the police, the asylum, international conglomerates) ruled and determined by men. Thus the first person narrator's attempts to leave France for Spain are met by 'gendarmes, totally indifferent and uninterested' (p. 166) who refuse to give her a travelling permit to cross the relevant borders. Through the interventions of a curé, the protagonist's father, and 'a very dirty piece of paper, coming from I know not what agent of my father's business connection, ICI (Imperial Chemicals)' (p. 170), a move is finally effected. In the asylum, the narrator is subjected to the authority of male doctors, one of whom she describes as 'my brother, who has come to liberate me from the *fathers*' (p. 174):

> In truth, I believe he was attracted to me, all the more so as he was aware of the power of Papa Carrington and his millions, as represented in Madrid by the ICI.

In these homosocial configurations[12] in which the female protagonist experiences herself as at the mercy of various males, all more powerful than her by virtue of their material/professional/social status, the loss of the 'good' father (Max Ernst) leads to the young female's desolation and her finding herself at the mercy of a series of 'bad' fathers. She attempts to counteract this by a bonding with nature (e.g. p. 169), against the forces of the 'bad' fathers from whom she seeks to escape. In this reaction against a sense of disempowerment, the protagonist of *Down Below* at once reinvests herself with significance, achieved through an androgynous merging[13] with the natural environment and the cosmos, which enables the woman (i.e. that which is powerless) through a fusion with the male (i.e. that which is powerful) 'to struggle against the invisible powers that were striving to detain me' (p. 197). These invisible forces are aligned with various male figures in *Down Below*, among them Van Ghent: 'To me Van Ghent was my father, my enemy, and the enemy of mankind; I was the only one who could vanquish him' (p. 173). The father, both as a symbolic and as a literal entity, is thus overtly presented as 'the enemy'.

What finally appears to liberate the protagonist of *Down Below* from her state of broken-down-ness is the doctor telling her 'not to return to [her] parents': 'At that moment I regained my lucidity' (p. 208).[14] The text here seems to suggest that the protagonist's return to self is predicated upon a successful resistance to the parents.

In her postscript to *Down Below*, Carrington makes clear that she resented her parents' failure to come to her rescue in person when she was incarcerated in the asylum in Spain:

> One would have thought they would have come themselves to

Santander. But you know, they didn't. Nanny was sent. You can imagine how much Spanish Nanny talked. It's a wonder she ever got there. What is terrible is that one's anger is stifled. I never saw my father again (p. 214).

The shift from 'one' to 'I' in this passage is significant. I would suggest that the emotion underlying Carrington's sense of her parents having failed her in not coming to her rescue in person is negotiated through a dissociation expressed in the use of 'one' instead of 'I'. The question of why Carrington never saw her father again remains unanswered — the very starkness of the final statement an indication of the unresolved problematic of that relationship.

Carrington utilizes other distantiating devices in the stories in which she replays family relations such as *The Oval Lady*, *The Royal Summons* (1989b), or *The Sisters* (1989a). In the first two of these, the first person narrator is constructed as an outsider to the family scene who bears witness, without being able to alter the course of the terrrible scenes that take place and in which the narrator becomes implicated. In the third story, a third person narrator is invoked, thus overtly severing the link between author/first person narrator problematically and commonly assumed.[15] In *The Sisters*, Drusille embodies the self which submits to the paternal law preparing everything for the arrival of the king (= the father), while Juniper, the bird/woman, represents resistance to the father, the self which is kept chained, hidden, but which surfaces and ultimately triumphs at the point when Juniper escapes and eats the maid (as the hyena had eaten the maid in *The Debutante*) and Drusille, simultaneously, treats the king like a feast, ready to be eaten.[16]

Transgresssion and Transformation

Carrington's characters resist conformity and convention. Her stories of the 1937–40 period in particular offer family romances in which 'bad fathers' battle with recalcitrant fe/male children who do not wish to submit to their law. Through their allegiance to the natural, specifically, the animal world, the female children encode and enact their resistance. But the effectiveness of this resistance is questionable: Lucretia cannot prevent the father's retribution against her rocking horse; the debutante's hyena is unmasked; Drusille cannot keep her vampiric bird/sister cooped up forever; Little Francis cannot make Uncle

Umbriaco stay. And: the first person narrator only ever manages to escape from anywhere with the help of others.

Carrington's stories thus document two things: the desire of the young fe/male to escape from social strictures and the paternal law, *and* the inability of the protagonist to achieve this unequivocally and effectively. One might argue that the latter is a function of how the protagonist seeks to bring about her liberation. Exchanging one father figure for another, for example, does not facilitate the change in status of the child *as child*. Similarly, the allegiance to and fusion with animal figures does not alter the sense of otherness which it is meant to alleviate. Carrington's characters are, by their very construction, forever being pulled back into a world of conflicting claims and demands on the self, made both by that self and by others. As a result they remain in a state of transition.

Demands on the protagonists to conform are met by the protagonists' resistance which is then reacted to by the (quasi-)parental figures in authority, resulting either in the protagonist's defeat or in a state of suspense whereby an ambiguity concerning what will happen next remains. Will Drusille eat the king? And where will having done so leave her? This ambiguity reflects an ambiguity in the whole of Carrington's oeuvre concerning the nature of transformation and change. As Renee Riese Hubert rightly maintains: '[Carrington] always emphasizes evolution and change' (p. 722). But, I would argue, rather than evolution and change leading to liberation, that is, rather than the desire for transformation resulting in a linear progressive triumphalist narrative of change successfully effected and evidenced in the achievement of a specific and specifiable goal, what Carrington's work documents instead is the psychological effects which the desire for trans-formation has.

This is particularly noticeable in her two portraits, *The Inn of the Dawn Horse [Self-Portrait]* (Figure 7.2) and *Portrait of Max Ernst* (Schlieker, 1991, pp. 50–1). In both portraits there is an encoding of movement, which is, of course, a prerequisite for change and liberation. In *The Inn of the Dawn Horse* (and note that the word 'dawn' is both about 'beginning' and 'awakening realization'), the rocking horse and the white horse featured in the background seen through a window are in flight; the woman is sitting on the edge of her seat as if about to get up, and the hyena is lifting one of her front legs as she might in motion. In *Portrait of Max Ernst*, the figure of Ernst appears to be walking along. But, and this 'but' applies to both these images as well as referring back to the opening remarks on *Femme et Oiseau*, what is

Figure 7.2 *The Inn of the Dawn Horse* (1936–7)

really striking about both portraits is the — with reference to *Portrait of Max Ernst* literal — frozenness, and consequent stylization of the movement portrayed. In the *Portrait of Max Ernst*, the horse, Carrington's supposed *alter ego*,[17] exists in two versions: as a frozen ice sculpture and as a galloping image, caught in the globe of the lamp the Ernst figure is carrying. Carrington's *alter ego* here is trapped,[18] frozen and this is not changed by being carried away by the Ernst figure. Similarly, in *The Inn of the Dawn Horse*, though the Carrington figure stares at the viewer, this could be in defiance and/or in terror, and though everything is portrayed as if either in motion or about to move, the fact that the Carrington figure is turned towards the interior of the house rather than looking out, that the motion of the horses — out of the room and away from the house — is not mirrored by any motion in the draperies (the curtain and the valance of the chair), suggests resistance but not *purpose* to a potential flight. The Carrington figure and the hyena are presented as *striking a pose*; the wildish hair of the Carrington figure seems to indicate terror (hair standing on end) rather than liberation and movement; all appear frozen in a moment of unrealized possibilities with no clear sense of what, if anything, will happen next. That is also the sense one gets in reading Carrington's stories from the 1937–40 period with their indeterminate endings.

In *Speaking with Forked Tongues: 'Male' Discourse in 'Female' Surrealism?* (in Caws *et al.*, 1991), R. J. Belton maintains, *à propos* of *The Inn of the Dawn Horse* that:

> this *femme-enfant*'s toys provide a clear escape from the enclosing walls only by a transformation begun by a man: . . . the implication is that without the intervention of this male element, the central figure would remain trapped . . . she seems to have concluded that she was genuinely creative, but chiefly because her ability to regress had been awakened by Ernst. (pp. 53–4)

I would argue, on the contrary, that Carrington's work from the 1937–40 period documents the problematic of achieving transformation and the fact that, far from being *only* liberating, the intervention of male elements function as a form of traumatizing containment encoded in her work, which set the scene for Carrington's life-long preoccupation with the state of change, with the process of transformation.[19]

Carrington created *Femme et Oiseau* at a time of sustained disruption and change in her life. Having eloped to France with Ernst in 1936, she spent the following four years in various locations in France and Spain, negotiating the transition from a privileged, materially secure, sheltered lifestyle and teenage rebelliousness to the uncertainties of an adult bohemian existence, living in a foreign country the language of which she at least initially spoke only imperfectly, in an alien and occasionally hostile context, without immediate recourse to the social and other resources she could expect to take for granted in her parental home. The period 1936–40 thus constitutes a phase for Carrington which was both a *rite de passage* and formed the basis of a pattern which appears to govern her life to this day: the establishment of the self as living at a remove from its immediate surroundings, as being permanently alienated and a concomitant concern with transition/transformation.

Created by a someone who at the beginning of that period was a teenager still, who, possibly in pursuit of the ideal parent, had exchanged one father figure for another, Carrington's work reveals the Janus face of the transition from childhood to adulthood, figured as a psychological, non-material form of entrapment whereby the backward gaze falls upon the nursery toys that have to be left behind as part of the move away from childhood but the forward gaze seems to have no clear object or purpose. The adolescent is thus trapped in the pre-social and pre-socialized world of the child in which animals seem closer to the self than human beings and toys may offer the sympathy lacking in adults. The rocking-horse, representing motion in stasis (not going anywhere), here becomes the emblem of a desire for movement and change which lacks an object and thus turns into a state of being rather than indicating a process of becoming. Movement becomes an end in itself, reflecting the permanence of destabilization which is the foundational moment of Carrington's art.

Notes

1   The possibility of androgyny as an answer to the 'war of the sexes' was discussed by a number of women engaged in cultural production during the modernist period. Examples can be found in Virginia Woolf's famous passage in *A Room of One's Own*, in her *Orlando*, in the writings of Radclyffe Hall, H.D., and Djuna Barnes. See also R. J. Belton's *Androgyny: Interview with Meret Oppenheim* in Caws *et al.*, 1991.

2   Carrington's questioning of conventional femininity is evident not only in the transgressive behaviour of her female protagonists but is also indicated in Whitney Chadwick's discussion of the female quest for autonomy in the context of the Surrealist movement with specific reference to Leonor Fini and Leonora Carrington's friendship, and Fini's portrait of Carrington dressed as a warrior in plated armour (Chadwick, 1985, pp. 80–7).

3   Carrington's story *The Oval Lady* offers a parallel narrative to *Femme et Oiseau*; its protagonist Lucretia appears to look like a horse as she plays with her rocking-horse Tartar and has a pet magpie, Matilda.

4   Women's cultural marginalization has been the subject of sustained discussion within feminism. See, for example, Tillie Olsen's *Silences*; Rich, 1980; Pollock, 1988; Chadwick, 1991; bell hooks' *Feminist theory: from margin to center*, or Bonnie Scott's introduction to *The Gender of Modernism*.

5   See Hanscombe and Smyers' (1987) first chapter and Benstock's, 'Expatriate Modernism: Writing on the Cultural Rim', in Broe and Ingram (Eds), 1989.

6   The exiled self is explicitly discussed in Broe and Ingram (Eds), Shari Benstock's *Women of the Left Bank*, or for a theoretical framing, Julia Kristeva's *Strangers to Ourselves*.

7   The possibility of 'womanliness as masquerade', i.e. as role rather than essence, is raised in an essay by the same title which, though written in 1929, predates in its comment: 'The reader may now ask how I define womanliness and the "masquerade". My suggestion is not, however, that there is any such difference; whether radical or superficial, they are the same thing.' (Riviere, 1929, p. 38) current debates about constructions of femininity as discussed in texts such as Judith Butler's *Gender Trouble*. Dressing up, or putting on a role, was a favourite pastime of many artists of the early twentieth century. Its transformative quality suited Modernist preoccupations with the relationship between surface/appearance and interior/unconscious.

8   A figure similar to Juniper the birdwoman is presented in Carrington's story 'Pigeon, Fly!' (p. 26) where, however, that figure is a man. An interesting photo of the Surrealist artist Leonor Fini (a friend of Carrington's during the 1937–40 period) as a birdwoman is reproduced in Chadwick, 1985, p. 109.

9   Perhaps the best known exposition of the fairy tale as a site for working out family conflicts and relational structures is Bettelheim, 1976.

10   A similar position is adopted in *Little Francis* where the disempowered figure of Francis fantasizes about dressing up as a bishop, thus instilling fear in the villagers of Maze. One might argue that this fantasy was intended to counteract the hostility with which Carrington was apparently met by the villagers of St. Martin d'Ardeche where she and Ernst had eloped to. (Chadwick, 1985, p. 84)

11   See Chadwick, 1985, especially p. 74, for some pertinent comments on Carrington as *femme-enfant* and its problematic.

12   The notion of woman as object of exchange between men whose homosocial relations are organized through this exchange has been discussed in Sedgwick, 1985.

13   The relevant passage reads: 'I felt that, through the agency of the Sun, I was an androgyne, the Moon, the Holy Ghost, a gypsy, an acrobat, Leonora Carrington, and a woman. I was also destined to be, later, Elizabeth of England. I was she who revealed religions and bore on her shoulders the freedom and the sins of the earth changed into Knowledge, the union of Man and Woman with God and the Cosmos, all equal between them' (Carrington, 1989b, p. 195).

14   The idea of resistance to the parents as a movement towards autonomy, mental health and adulthood has been encoded in a variety of texts by women which offer a triumphalist narrative of breakdown as breakthrough to a 'more authentic' self (e.g. H.D.'s *Her*, Sylvia Plath's *The Bell Jar*).

15   The relationship between author and narrator has been subject to much debate in the context of feminist theory/criticism. For a theoretical discussion of the relationship between the two see Rimmon-Kennan, 1983, pp. 86–105.

16   Occurring repeatedly in Carrington's stories are sumptuous quasi-baroque meals during which taboos regarding what is 'fit for consumption' are transgressed. Virginia Fur in *As they rode along the edge*, for example, consumes all her offspring bar one from her relationship with the boar, Igname, as part of the funeral feast for him (Carrington, 1989a, p. 10). I am reminded of Peter Greenaway's film *The Cook, The Thief, His Wife and Her Lover* which features similar scenes of breaking taboo in feasting. The relationship between orality, the establishment of boundaries and food taboos is discussed in Julia Kristeva's *Powers of Horror*.

17   The horse has been variously identified as Carrington's *alter ego*: see Chadwick, 1985, pp. 78–9; Colvile in Caws *et al.*, 1991, pp. 159–81.

18   As Warner suggests in Schlieker, 1991: 'Her portrait of Ernst captures the ambivalence of her feelings of love and liberation, as well as owning up to the emotional captivity their liaison also represented to her' (p. 14).

19   This would be one explanation for Carrington's interest in alchemy as discussed in Choucha, 1991 and in Chadwick, 1991.

References

BELTON, R. J. 'Androgyny: Interview with Meret Oppenheim' in CAWS, M. L. *et al.* (Eds) (1991) *Surrealism and Women*, Cambridge, Mass: MIT Press, pp. 63–75.

BELTON, R. J. 'Speaking with Forked Tongue: "Male" Discourse in "Female"

Surrealism' in CAWS, M.L. *et al.* (Eds) (1991) *Surrealism and Women*, Cambridge, Mass: MIT Presss, pp. 50–62.

BENSTOCK, S. 'Expatriate Modernism: Writing on the Cultural Rim' in BROE, M.L. and INGRAM, A. (Eds) (1989) *Women's Writing in Exile*, Chapel Hill, University of North Carolina Press, pp. 19–40.

BENSTOCK, S. (1987) *Women of the Left Bank*, London, Virago.

BETTELHEIM, B. (1976) *The Uses of Enchantment*, London, Thames and Hudson.

BROE, M.L. and INGRAM, A. (Eds) (1989) *Women's Writing in Exile*, Chapel Hill, University of North Carolina Press.

BUTLER, J. (1990) *Gender Trouble: Feminism and the Subversion of Identity*, London, Routledge.

CARRINGTON, L. (1937–40, reprinted 1989a) 'As they rode along the edge' in *The Seventh Horse and Other Tales*, London, Virago, pp. 3–15.

CARRINGTON, L. (1937–8, reprinted 1989b) 'The Debutante' in *The House of Fear*, London, Virago, pp. 44–8.

CARRINGTON, L. (1943, reprinted 1989b) 'Down Below' in *The House of Fear*, London, Virago, pp. 163–214.

CARRINGTON, L. (1989b) *The House of Fear*, London, Virago.

CARRINGTON, L. (1937–8, reprinted 1989b) 'Little Francis' in *The House of Fear*, London, Virago, pp. 69–148.

CARRINGTON, L. (1937–8, reprinted 1989b) 'The Oval Lady' in *The House of Fear*, London, Virago, pp. 37–43.

CARRINGTON, L.(1937–40, reprinted 1989a) 'Pigeon, Fly!' in *The Seventh Horse and Other Tales*, London, Virago, pp. 19–29.

CARRINGTON, L. (1937–8, reprinted 1989b) 'The Royal Summons' in *The House of Fear*, London, Virago, pp. 49–54.

CARRINGTON, L. (1989a) *The Seventh Horse and Other Tales*, London, Virago.

CARRINGTON, L.(1939, reprinted 1989a) 'The Sisters' in *The Seventh Horse and Other Tales*, London, Virago, pp. 42–9.

CAWS, M.A. *et al.*, (Eds) (1991) *Surrealism and Women*, Cambridge, Mass: MIT Press.

CHADWICK, W. (1991) 'Pilgrimage to the Starts: Leonora Carrington and the Occult Tradition' in SCHLIEKER, A. (Ed.) (1991) *Leonora Carrington: Paintings, Drawings and Sculpture 1940–1990*, London, Serpentine Gallery, pp. 24–34.

CHADWICK, W. (1990) *Women, Art, and Society*, London, Thames and Hudson.

CHADWICK, W. (1985) *Women Artists and the Surrealist Movement*, London, Thames and Hudson.

CHOUCHA, N. (1991) 'Max Ernst and Leonora Carrington: Alchemy, Shamanism and Psychoanalysis' in CHOUCHA, N. (1991) *Surrealism and the Occult*, Oxford, Mandrake, pp. 105–21.

HANSCOMBE, G. and SMYERS, V.L. (1987) *Writing for their Lives: The Modernist Women 1910–1940*, London, Women's Press.

H.D. (1927, reprinted 1984) *Her*, London, Virago.

HOOKS, B. (1984) *Feminist theory: from margin to center*, Boston, Ma, South End Press.

KRISTEVA, J. (1982) *Powers of Horror: An Essay on Abjection*, New York, Columbia University Press.

KRISTEVA, J. (1991) *Strangers to Ourselves*, London, Harvester/Wheatsheaf.

OLSEN, T. (1965, reprinted 1980) *Silences*, London, Virago.

PLATH, S. (1963, reprinted 1980) *The Bell Jar*, London, Faber and Faber.

POLLOCK, G. (1988) *Vision and Difference: Femininity, Feminism and the Histories of Art*, London, Routledge.

RICH, A. (1972, reprinted 1980) 'When We Dead Awaken: Writing as Revision' in RICH, A. (1980) *On Lies, Secrets, Silence,* London, Virago, pp. 33–49.

RIESE HUBERT, R. (1991) 'Leonora Carrington and Max Ernst: Artistic Partnership and Feminist Liberation' in *New Literary History*, **22**, pp. 715-45.

RIVIERE, J. (1929, reprinted 1986) 'Womanliness as Masquerade' in BURGIN, V. *et al.* (Eds) *Formations of Fantasy*, London, Methuen, pp. 35-44.

SCHLIEKER, A. (Ed) (1991) *Leonora Carrington: Paintings, Drawings and Sculptures 1940-1990*, London, Serpentine Gallery.

SCOTT, B. (1990) *The Gender of Modernism*, Bloomington, Indiana University Press.

SEDGWICK, E. K. (1985) *Between Men: English Literature and Male Homosocial Desire*, New York, Columbia University Press.

SULEIMAN, S. R. (1990) 'Feminist Intertextuality and the Laugh of the Medusa' in SULEIMAN, S. R. (1990) *Subversive Intent: Gender Politics and the Avant-Garde*, Cambridge, Mass: Harvard University Press, pp. 141-80.

WARNER, M. (1991) 'Leonora Carrington's Spirit Bestiary: or the Art of Playing Make-Belief' in SCHLIEKER, A. (Ed.) (1991) *Leonora Carrington: Paintings, Drawings and Sculptures 1940-1990*, London, Serpentine Gallery, pp. 10-23.

Chapter 8

Susan Hiller, Automatic Writing and Images of Self

Penelope Kenrick

Preamble

Susan Hiller is an artist whose work stems from the 1970s when alternative media were used to question traditional assumptions about art production and when 'conceptual' art had a political edge in opening up debates about representation and meaning.[1] Hiller has a particular interest in language and its relation to gender. She explores the hidden meanings of the written and manufactured signs that we produce in our culture which she sees as manifestations of secret desires and fears. She is fascinated by the repetition of archetypes which to her signal a collective unconscious repressed or explained away by convention and ritual behaviour. She wishes to investigate the interconnections between the rational and irrational worlds. In all these issues she sees gender used as the basis for interpretation and she questions these gendered assumptions.

I wish to trace a thread through Hiller's work which is related to the theme of the Other as Self. The notion of a portrait of the Self or of an Other is explored by Hiller in ways that are unexpected. She uses body parts, casual photobooth images and automatic writing[2] to suggest alternatives to conventional portrait representations of individuals.

Hiller's training as an anthropologist before she became an artist is significant. In *The Myth of Primitivism* (1991, p. 2) she describes her shifting relationship with anthropology and art, pointing out their similarities of approach particularly in relation to their representation of Others. And she is interested, throughout her work, in setting what is thought to be 'scientific' knowledge next to the conventions assumed for 'artistic' expression. She uses automatic writing, for example, as one of the artifacts she collects (along with photographs, wallpaper, postcards and so on) as evidence to be deciphered, interpreted and questioned. Her work fits into the Modernist context of Surrealism and Abstract Expressionism[3] which she both draws from and criticizes. Within Surrealism and Abstract Expressionism there is an interest in automatism (automatic writing and painting, sometimes produced in a state of trance), chance effects and irrational juxtapositions. Artists such as the Surrealist Matta, and the Abstract Expressionist Pollock, use brush marks in an open and expressive way which are supposed to reveal the individual or collective unconscious workings of their minds. Both are interested in using dream and the irrational as keys to understanding reality or being. The gender bias of their interpretations is one thing Hiller criticizes. Another aspect she undermines is assumptions about the purely personal artist's mark which in Abstract Expressionist painting and other more recent Neo-expressionist work she sees as 'reactionary, self-aggrandising gesturalism' (Brett, Parker and Roberts, 1984, p. 22). She not only questions her relation to the work as its producer but wants to involve us in the debate, make us active participants.

I hope to demonstrate, using selected examples of her work, that Susan Hiller develops an increasingly complex interpretation of the relation between Other and Self. She wishes to break down the notion of their polarized difference and propose a fluid inter-relation, a relation in fact in which perhaps we cannot distinguish between the two. Such oscillation occurs, she would argue, in every-day experience but also, in particular, in the imaginative realms, on the edge of consciousness (Brett, Parker and Roberts, 1984, p. 25).

The concerns in Hiller's work could be seen as developing in parallel to those expressed in feminist debates during the last two decades. The works *The Sisters of Menon* (1972) and *10 Months* (1977) (Figure 8.1) reveal the awkwardness and discomfort of her position as a woman artist in the 1970s and parallel texts discussing gendered assumptions about creativity published at that time, such as Linda Nochlin's seminal article *Why have there been no great women artists?* (in Baker and Hess, 1973). Her use of automatic writing as a metaphor for women's marginalized position and the possibility that the writing might represent a feminine bodily language are suggestive of links between her work and feminist discourse of the 1970s, stemming from essays such as *The Laugh of the Medusa* by Hélène Cixous (in Marks and de Courtivron, 1981). Hiller's sympathy for conceptions of Collectivity, her rejection of an autonomous Self, is indexed in her photomat portraits. Her lack of interest in Freudian/Lacanian analysis (with its emphasis on individual subjectivity) and her concern to question the idea of the polarized, binary difference between Other and Self, parallels recent feminist theoretical writing of the late 1980s, like that in *Gender Trouble* (Butler, 1990). Further, she not only wishes to re-evaluate the notion of Self and Otherness in visual images, but also to break down the separation between spectator and artist's product (subject and object) through a mode of story-telling which allows meanings to shift and change in each telling and by which the spectator becomes an active participant in the art work (Fisher, 1990, p. 2). Hiller thus moves from questioning the representation of her individual self to a story-telling around collective experience.

10 Months (1977)

Susan Hiller is white, middle-class, heterosexual, Jewish. Brought up in America, she works and lives in Britain. However, her works are not concerned with analysing these specifics of her position in any direct way, unlike the work of some of her feminist contemporaries.[4]

In Western society a woman who is a producer of cultural images is in an awkward position. As a producer, she assumes a subject position but in dominant culture she is always seen as the object, always represented as the Other. Given this contradiction, how does she represent herself and how does she define her relationship with others?

Take, for example, Hiller's *10 Months* (Figure 8.1) where we see a so-called impersonal record, month by month, of the expanded stomach of a pregnant woman. It seems to be the equivalent of the nineteenth and twentieth century medical records which categorize human types and diseases. But it also suggests a record of ancient burial mounds, the earth as womb (Lippard, 1983, p. 61). These seemingly simple images are bound into an extremely complex system of signification. The images invite the spectator's speculation about mysterious areas of knowledge and collective fantasy about women's bodily potential and power, beyond the rational. The repetition (with variations of tone) increases the impact and the potential for multiple meanings.

The simplicity of the images and their presentation both reinforce and are an ironic comment on purified and reduced Modernist art production, such as the sculpture of Brancusi or the Minimalist art of the 1960s.[5] In the Western Modernist art world an emphasis has been placed on reducing imagery to its ultimate essence. The simpler the form, the purer, the more profound and universal it is assumed to be.

Figure 8.1 '*10 Months*' month six

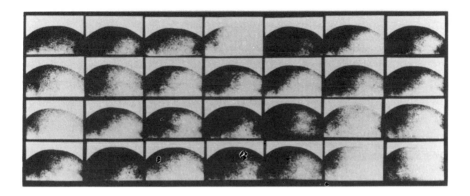

SIX/ She speaks (as a woman) about everything, although they wish her to speak only about women's things. They like her to speak about everything only if she does not speak "as a woman", only if she will agree in advance to play the artist's role as neutral (neuter) observer.

She does not speak (as a woman) about anything, although they want her to. There is nothing she can speak of "as a woman". As a woman, she can not speak.

Hiller is critical of this notion of universality when it in fact refers to white, middle class, male assumptions. But on the other hand she is deeply interested in collective memory and history. In *10 Months* the Modernist emphasis on beautiful material and immaculate technique is satirized in the mechanical, aesthetically casual reproductions. The repeated images of the stomach echo her male contemporaries' serial work and play with the notion of the impersonal, but whereas theirs invite comparison with mass industrial production and the grand scale of modern technological structures, hers is using technology (the camera) to capture the fleeting, unstable changes of her individual body.

Each section of *10 Months* has an accompanying text recording anxieties and theoretical speculations, in marked contrast to the seeming coolness of the images. The text could be seen as extracts from a personal diary, but by being written in the third person, Hiller distances herself from intimate speculations and presents a public commentary. And even though the photographs represent an actual trace of her body, the spectator is unaware of a particular identity. The fragmentary parts increase the sense of alienation from the individual.

'Self betrayal spoils the work of so many women artists . . . my own predilections and talents lie in working with emotional material, but I had to educate my emotions so that when I made a gesture I was not betraying myself as a woman' (Brett, Parker and Roberts, 1984, p. 30). This rather contradictory remark by Hiller displays a fear of revealing herself and of not being taken seriously because of being associated with 'female emotions'. It represents one of the difficulties for women artists and it relates to the undervaluing of female emotional expression and personal experience as 'women's nonsense' or hysterical reaction. This contrasts with the common expectation that male artists are valued more highly when they are as emotionally expressive and personal as possible. In the twentieth century, the popular image of the male artist has been of an individual who allows his emotions free reign. He is ideally the *enfant terrible* or the 'noble savage' who does not allow rational, intellectual thought to control and repress his creative, intuitive potential. This image is most typically exemplified in the figures of Picasso and Jackson Pollock.[6] (A paradox is that their genius was seen as the product of Nature, whereas woman's closeness to Nature excluded her from being a creative genius.)

The contradictions between being pregnant (a creative activity which excluded women from the public sphere) and being a creative artist (which propelled one into the public sphere despite being a woman) are presented in the text and the images (all body and no head, as natural as the hills, and so on). Hiller's comments revolve around her shifting, unstable sense of who she is in relation to others.

> *Month Three:* ... their 'we' will soon be extended, her 'I' will be altered, enlarged or annihilated ... this is the terror hidden in bliss ...
> *Month Five:* ... it is her voice, her body. It is painful being inside and outside simultaneously ...
> *Month Ten:* ... her discovery of a way out through truth-telling — acknowledging contradictions, expressing inconsistencies, double talk, ambiguity. She writes she is no longer confused.
>
> (Hiller, 1980, p. 28)

This ends the sequence and gives it a measure of narrative completion. It could be interpreted as an optimistic resolution of the previous uncertainties and conflicts in both public and private spheres. But it could also be interpreted as deeply ironic; she is no longer confused!

One central issue, then, in this portrait *10 Months* is that of the creative woman, social expectations and the woman artist's own mixed feelings about various kinds of creativity and the role she is expected to play. Conventional attitudes about the creative genius of an artist and the gendered limitations of its definition are now well known (Parker and Pollock, 1981, p. 7). The assumption that men are artists and women can only be artists if they are surrogate males can induce conflict and guilt in women who wish to create art and express their experiences 'as a woman' (whatever that means) within the conventions of society. In *Gender and Genius*, Battersby outlines recent Western philosophical discussion of the male artist's creativity in relation to female creativity and the feminine. She suggests that one construction of male artistic genius revolves around the notion of the male adopting the feminine in order to be complete or to be more than an ordinary male. Thus she cites C. G. Jung's statement that 'the great artist is the feminine male' (Battersby, 1989, p. 7).

The French Surrealist, André Breton, also pursues this point:

It rests with the [male] artist to make visible everything that is part of the feminine as opposed to the masculine system of the world. It is the artist who must rely exclusively on the woman's power to exalt, or better still, to jealously appropriate to himself everything that distinguishes woman from man.

(Chadwick, 1985, p. 65)

Here the commentators accept feminine qualities in the male artistic self but would not go further and propose the reverse in female artists as they are seen as aberrations.[7] The male artist should create like a woman, using aspects associated with the feminine such as intuition, flexibility, naturalness, emotion, irrationality. And his artistic creativity necessarily equates him with the position of the Outsider. A clear distinction is assumed between the Outsider and the Other. Others because of the paradigm of normal humanity are those who are not quite human (because of their race or sex, for example). Outsiders, on the other hand, are fully human but not normal, such as shamanistic males or the avant-garde male artist. Thus the marginality attributed to the male artist has quite a different status from that of the woman constructed as Other (Battersby, 1989, p. 138).

The conflict for the woman practising as an artist manifests itself in the woman simultaneously maintaining at least two positions — personal identification in the work as maker and subject and at the same time distancing herself from the activity (which the male artist has no need to do). She creates in the context of male individuality and female Otherness, both of which she resists from another position. Battersby writes, 'in order to create at all, women have had to adopt a double perspective on themselves. But this fissured ego is by no means the same as the egolessness celebrated by [the Modernists] and the Lacanians' (Battersby, 1989, p. 148). She insists that there is an active place from which the female artist works which she distinguishes from that of the feminine Other enshrined in *L'écriture Féminine*,[8] in which, she maintains, there is a blurring between creating **like** a woman and **as** a woman. Battersby argues that the peculiarity of the female artist's position, being neither of the male nor of the female convention but Another Other, can produce a distinctive genre.

This is raised directly in *10 Months*. Hiller as mother, the strange, mysterious, natural body, the object of our perusal, is Other; and simultaneously, as creative artist and intellectual coordinator, in authority, outside looking in (as she notes, pregnant with thought, giving birth to an idea, the work as her brainchild) we observe her as a strange aberration, Another Other (because society dictates that she cannot hold the same position as the male artist). Her text raises the difficulty of these different positions. The seemingly random feminine diary-like jottings accompanying her images include incisive statements and questions grounded in a knowledge of feminist cultural theory.

> *Month Six:* . . . they like her to speak about everything only if she does not speak 'as a woman', only if she will agree in advance to play the artist's role as 'neutral observer' . . . [and] . . . she does not speak (as a woman) about anything, although they want her to. There is nothing she can speak of 'as a woman'. As a woman she cannot speak . . .
>
> (Hiller, 1980, p. 28)

This last statement is mirrored in an interesting way in an incident which occurred in 1972. Hiller was conducting a joint drawing project with other artists. They were all to draw at the same moment each day (even though they were living in different places) and later they would share the result to see what communality they may have manifested. (A similar group approach was adopted in her project *Dream Mapping*, 1974.) (Brett, Parker and Roberts, 1984, p. 7)

The frequent use of collectivity, metaphorical or actual, in the work of women artists (particularly in the 1970s) has been noted as perhaps the denial of creation as a solitary act, and that this is the expression of women's need to create group solidarity in the face of an absence of female cultural history and the overwhelming presence of male masterpieces in visual art (Chicago, 1975, p. 112, see her account of the

Womenhouse project). Hiller reflects this in her comment:

> I always had avoided self-portraiture in my work [in the 1970s] refusing to make a statement in the traditional way that male artists do, as if the first person was speaking. I would instead set up situations where I was collaborating with other people, or using some device that enabled me to speak on behalf of or along with a number of anonymous others, while attempting to raise that kind of anonymity to social visibility.
>
> (Brett, Parker and Roberts, 1984, p. 31)

Sisters of Menon 1972–1979

In 1972 Hiller had, for her, a unique, mediumistic experience. 'The pencil seemed to have a mind of its own and wrote page after page of text in an unfamiliar style' (Hiller, 1983, Note 1). Most of the words were distinguishable and Hiller believed the Sisters of Menon, women from Thebes, were speaking through her. 'I am the sister of Menon . . . we three sisters are your sister . . . I live in the water, I live on the air . . . the riddle is the sister of zero . . . we are the mother of men . . . last night we were three sisters now we are four sisters . . . ' (Hiller, 1983).

The pages were published in facsimile as documentary material to be analysed, not as a creation of the artist. But the writing was transcribed by Hiller and 'rationalized'. Hiller would now acknowledge that her mediumistic experience was embedded in the cultural attitudes of the time. The relationship between Nature and Ancient Greek oracular women was a popular concept within the Women's Movement of the early 1970s. For seven years the scripts were 'lost'. Interestingly they resurfaced in 1979, just after the Dada and Surrealism Reviewed exhibition at the Hayward Gallery and its accompanying publications, which included discussion and exhibition of automatic work from the 1920s, and these perhaps reminded the artist that her automatic material had a legitimate artistic context.

Although Hiller had been aware of the use of Automatism by the Surrealists and writers such as W. B. Yeats and C. G. Jung, she did not at first realize the potential of her own scripts. Perhaps it needed a near decade of feminist activity and publications to give artists such as Hiller the confidence to value such an event and use it to advantage in the public realm. In contrast, Bréton, after his earliest automatic experiences, immediately had the idea to use them as material for poetic construction (Bréton, 1969, p. 22). This highlights the different relationship to Automatism conventionally assigned to men and women in the West. Hiller points to this difference in her notes to *Sisters of Menon*. The male use of Automatism was seen as respectably scientific, poetic, artistic, whereas the female use was associated with mediumship (women as mechanical channels) and with patients and lunatics under care. Hence perhaps Hiller's understandable reluctance at first to use her experience in the public sphere of art.

In the *Sisters of Menon* script, the deciphered messages imply a collective solidarity amongst women and a questioning of autonomous identity. The artist notes the peculiarity of her own position 'simultaneously participant and spectator, author and reader, singular and plural' (Hiller, 1983, Note 4). (This echoes the double perspective already mentioned in relation to *10 Months*.)

Hiller physically made the marks but in an alienated way and the Other voices conveyed messages through her. It made her question more closely the state of being expressed in Rimbaud's oft-quoted remark 'I is another' (Fowlie, W., 1946, p. 10). The distinct separation between Self and Other breaks down. Who is she in this context? In relation to this work Hiller states: 'It's a new starting point. Identity is a collaboration, the self is multiple, "I" am a location, a focus' (Brett, Parker and Roberts, 1984, p. 19). She later turns this experience into a more general manifestation: 'Everyone knows, when you draw or write, there is a sense in which you are "being written"' (Hiller, 1989). Hiller mentions the Surrealists, Yeats and Jung as preceding her with an interest in Automatism. They each, however, interpreted it in differing ways although all associated it closely with male creativity. Thus Yeats saw his wife as a mere passive channel for the Communicators, coming to inspire *his* creative imagination. (The control that George in fact had over what was produced is explored by Harper (1987) in *The Making of Yeats's 'A Vision'*.) In contrast, Bréton in 1933 presents automatic writing in a much wider context of creativity. It is 'nothing to do with the supernatural and is for each and everyone the very vehicle of revelation' (Rosemont, 1978, p. 106). The automatic works are presented as fully realized poetic exchanges but he notes that their chief characteristic is one of 'immediate absurdity'. (Interestingly he calls them 'magnetic fields', thus relating them to scientific phenomena.) Most of the Surrealist automatic events are presented as dialogues.[9] The more bizarre the imagery the more it delighted them. The chance bringing together of words, phrases, images is considered as producing a disruptive effect which should trigger the unconscious and offer insights into other worlds. Further, Bréton believed Automatism would unite conscious and unconscious to produce a new state of absolute liberty, an awareness of the flexibility and scope of the human condition. The term automatic was applied to a range of activity from utterances in a trance-like state to chance mixing of cut-out words on the table and to uninhibited doodling, a wider application of methods than Hiller uses. A clear distinction is made between the poetic inventions of verbal exchanges which are privileged by Bréton, and automatic techniques adopted by the Surrealist painters, in other words, a distinction is made between the semantic 'word games' of the Surrealist poets and the abstract marks made by the chance or unconscious action of the painter's hand. In contrast, Hiller is more concerned with the unifying character of the drawing and writing (which she sees developed by Henry Michaux in the 1960s). Her automatic marks are simultaneously writing (although indecipherable by the rational mind) and drawing.

Bréton assumes a distinction between male poetic creativity (his type of Automatism) and female, passive, mediumistic experience, which he describes as mechanical although more authentic. Women, in his view, have a natural ability to loosen repressed thoughts and allow hidden areas of the mind to emerge, whereas his male colleagues require alcohol or drugs as stimulants. 'Their hand, anaesthetized, behaves as if it were guided by another hand' (Rosemont, 1978, p. 102). Visually this gender division is represented in the image *Automatic Writing* in the Surrealist magazine *Révolution Surréaliste* of 1927. It is a photograph of a seductive young school-girl (the *femme-enfant*),[10] pen poised as though about to write a mediumistic message. As Chadwick notes, she is 'caught in a moment of sexual ambiguity' and passively awaits revelation by men (Chadwick, 1985, p. 33).

Hiller gives us her own account of the significance of Bréton's use of Automatism and emphasises those aspects which are closest to her own interests:

Bréton's writings on automatism were part of his endeavour to reconcile Marxism and Psychoanalysis. He felt that a grasp of the implications of automatism would eventually erode all notions of personal property rights and individual authorship of works . . . the early automatic pieces produced by the Surrealists were collective and anonymous. An involvement with spontaneous gesture and utterance erodes notions of personal authorship because everyone can do it . . . no minimal standards ... particularly since it's unpredictable and seems to be outside any kind of individual control (Brett, Parker and Roberts, 1984, p. 23).[11]

The paradox of Automatism is that it is presumed to eliminate the subject and effect anonymity, yet is admired for being the original and eccentric product of the artist, unique and personal to him, as shown particularly in Abstract Expressionist work such as that of Jackson Pollock. This conflictual relation between the individual and the collective was developed in particular during the Modernist period and best exemplified in the Surrealist movement (Hiller, 1991, p. 33). Hiller, herself, plays a fine line between the use of the personal mark and the impersonal, collective utterance. But rather than accept these as given, she questions and makes us question the value and the interpretation attributed to them.

Bréton notes that mediums lose their capacity for 'directed Automatism' over a period of time (Rosemont, 1978, p. 105). Their later efforts are more conscious. This, in fact, parallels the shift in Hiller's production of automatic writing/drawing. She increasingly uses it as a metaphor for gender politics and an alternative awareness of the 'reality of self': 'Incoherent insights at the margins of society and at the edge of consciousness stand as signs of what cannot be repressed or alienated, signs of that which is always and already destroying the kingdom of law' (Hiller, 1985, p. 4). This can be seen in her work of the early 1980s and I want now to focus on Self Portrait.

Self Portrait 1983

Is the title of *Self-Portrait* (Figure 8.2) ironic? How does this image function as a portrait? The centre, where the body should be, is empty and the rhythmic script, the automatic message from the *other* side, holds the margins. It substitutes for the self. It could be interpreted, bleakly, as her negation of her self. Blank and empty Hiller remains as woman artist, simply the channel for an Other being, or the mirror surface on which the spectator projects her/his own desires. More positively, could this be a *tabula rasa* (like Malevich's *Black Square*, c. 1915) already beginning to teem with new life? It could represent an enlarged, changed conception of self, beyond external appearances. The scale could be cosmic. Further it could be seen as a confirmation of collective dreaming and creative potential (the script as a collective

Figure 8.2 *Self Portrait* 1983

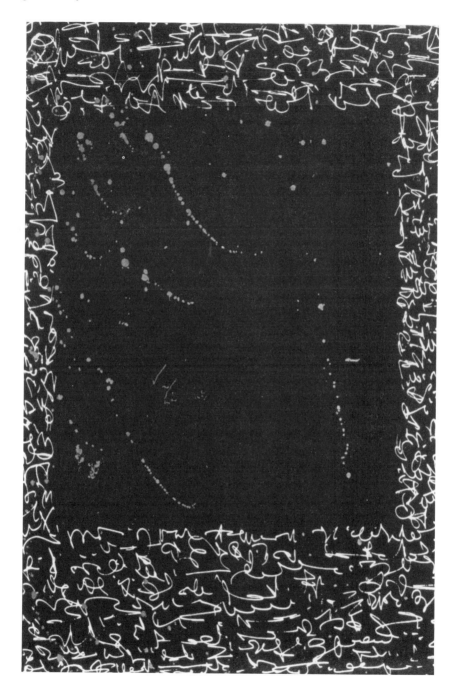

utterance), a new verbal/visual representation free from existing stereotypes. As Hiller says:

> I realised I couldn't present my face in the literal sense because that's not how one experiences it from the inside... I'd like to make a distinction between lacking an authoritative first-person voice, which isn't a problem, and the undermining of authentic self-presentation through being forced to exist in a world structured by the language of the Other, which is.
>
> (Brett, Parker and Roberts, 1984, p. 31)

The illumination of the white script and the gold drips of paint function as a pun for Hiller's own illumination, her increased understanding. (The drips of paint also make an ironic reference to the authentic personal artist's mark seen in Pollock's drip paintings.) 'I want to show how one can claim a position of speaking from the side of darkness, the side of the unknown, while not reducing oneself to darkness and the unknowable...' (*ibid.*, p. 26)

Hiller believes there is no distinction between reading images and reading text, and in *10 Months* she uses image and text as equivalents but she notes that these are constructed intermediaries separating her (and us) from lived experience. However, automatic writing/drawing she sees as more closely integrated with body and mind, 'because the marks go on and on in a rhythm like breathing and walking, they relate to internalised rhythms which are neither aestheticized nor distanced from us physically' (*ibid.*, p. 23). There is present here a utopian desire for unity and harmony between expression and experience, which might leave behind the conflicts and uncertainties of Hiller's position as artist and woman. The automatic script might represent a more authentic integrated Self, eliminating an alien Other.

In the early 1980s, in works such as *Alphabet* (1983) Hiller saw the script as an alternative language from the edge of consciousness, from the margins, which could not yet be read.

> When I began to work in this way 10 years ago, theory had not yet begun to link up... the analytic and the ecstatic... what I hope for now is that these works... are taken seriously as a form of patterned utterances... I'd like to see a full phonemic study some day.
>
> (Brett, Parker and Roberts, 1984, p. 21)

There are obvious parallels with the proposal for an *écriture féminine*, closely related to ecstatic bodily experience (Marks and de Courtivron, 1981, p. 245). But if the irrational and the incoherent are associated with the feminine in opposition to the masculine, this would not be a helpful opposition for Hiller to emphasize (Felski, 1989, p. 69). In fact, Hiller thinks that automatic writing/drawing is 'an area of experience which is universal but which is pushed to the margins.' (Hiller, 1985, p. 5). In other words, it is not gender specific and in particular it is not elitist, not confined to select ecstatics but open to everyone. However, because of women's position in modern Western society she believes they are more willing to explore these areas of consciousness or are allowed more easily this type of expression.

In *Self-Portrait* the automatic script acts as a metaphor to question the clear distinctions made in Western society between past and present, collectivity and individuality, Self and Other. Hiller has always been more interested in a collective unconscious and its relation to social structures than in Freudian/Lacanian analyses of individual subjectivity. She states: 'I take it then that consciousness refers to shared subjectivity. In this sense there is no gap between the individual and society . . . the individual is an abstraction' (Hiller, 1981, p. 10).

Through the 1980s Hiller's preferences could be seen as unpopular among cultural theorists and feminists who might have viewed them as lacking in concern for the discourses re-evaluating the formation of the female subjective self.[12] However, her representations of being, the emphasis on the ambivalence of lived experience, her blurring of the differences between Self and Other, have echoes in more recent feminist writing, such as Judith Butler's *Gender Trouble* (1990). Freudian and Lacanian psychoanalysis assumes that identity is only formed in relation to an Other (Lacan, 1982, p. 172). It is through the response of the Other that we measure and define ourselves but in that very response we become the Other (Hiller, 1991, p. 248). There is a continuous oscillation between two positions, each can only be identified in relation to its opposite. Butler argues that the distinction between Self and Other needs to be broken down as it mimics the polarization between masculine and feminine, male and female which excludes a range and variety of different identities which may themselves constantly be changing (Butler, 1990, p. 67). As Hiller writes: 'It is past time to relinquish the quest for one totalising seemingly authoritative perspective in favour of a more complex, fragmented evocation, that allows contradictions to emerge as spaces where new understandings can form themselves' (Hiller, 1991, p. 6).

Photomat Portraits

In this context Hiller's Photomat images (Figure 8.3), such as *Midnight Baker Street* and *Lucid Dreams* (both of 1983), are not self-portraits in any conventional sense. Photomat portraits are associated with

Figure 8.3 *Photomat Portrait* 1982

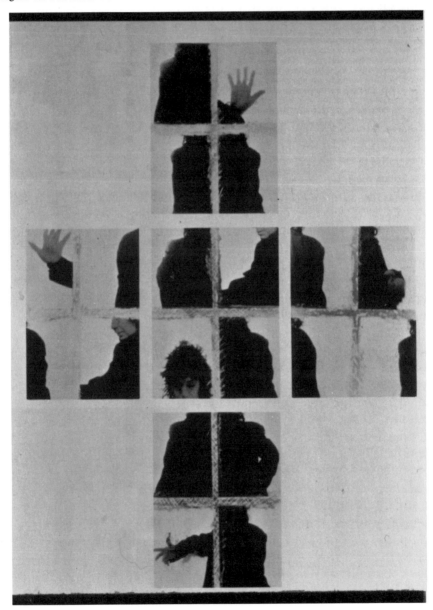

institutions, the power of external authorities to identify individuals in order to regulate them. The external appearance of her face, thus, is a liability, is alien and Hiller interrupts the identificatory fixing by overlaying the body with automatic writing/drawing. This script could be seen as violent, scratching over the image like street graffiti, or it could be caressing, gently moving over the body. Is the script the authentic Self surfacing and overwriting the distant culturally bound image? Or is the alternative 'voice' from the outside smothering the authentic 'I'? Do both these modes of representation denote Others and is there therefore no Self? Hiller comments: 'It is an attempt to show the inside on the outside' (Hiller, 1991, p. 152). But what does this inside and outside connote? The images remain deliberately suggestive, ambiguous and unresolved.

> My adoption of primitivist devices is a deliberate one, with reference to the female self as a cultural site of mystery, otherness, etc. As an artist I flow between this constructed self and an anterior/interior self. Any artist of female gender in our society . . . must deal with this, representation is not value free.
>
> (Hiller, 1991, p. 152)

In some of her images Hiller withdraws from the viewer by closing her eyes or turning away (*Gatwick Suite*, 1983) (Figure 8.4). This is reminiscent of the Surrealist group portrait in *Révolution Surréaliste* (no. 12, 1929) where the closed eyes signify an alternative revelatory 'seeing' in dream or trance, although comparison also highlights interesting differences. Hiller's image is multiple, fragmentary, casually caught and scattered with automatic writing/drawing. In *Lucid Dreams* she exposes only parts of her body. The hand of the artist takes on an equal importance to the head or the shoulder. Why need one part of the body be privileged over another in the issue of identity? 'She breaks identities into fragments and wants nothing less than to alter the order of speech and the mechanisms of social symbolism' (Hiller, 1981, p. 11).

The multiplication of the images reinforces the sense of dissolving any stable identification. (There may be an interesting link here with the analysis of women's autobiography which Felski (1989, p. 105) discusses as a mode of self-denial.) Placed in quadrants the Margins become Central and if the automatic script is seen as graffiti it could represent an anarchic act by a outsider defacing the high realm and certainties of the art establishment.

On the one hand Hiller denies the viewer the voyeuristic pleasure of

Figure 8.4 *Gatwick Suite* 1983

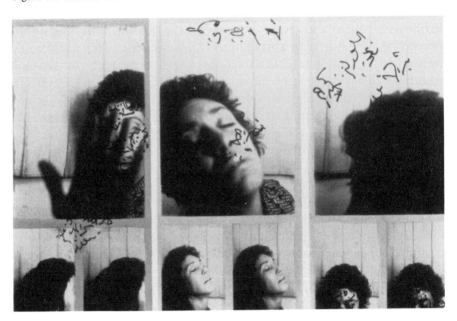

gazing at an image of a masquerading Other, a seamlessly constructed type, but on the other she wants to invite commonality with the spectator. 'I try to enable people to have an actual physical identification with the fragmented body image I'm using' (Brett, Parker and Roberts, 1984, p. 30). She invites the spectator to transform the Otherness of the image into an identificatory mirror for the spectator's own self, to recall suppressed desires or fears that might surface in dreams. 'Art functions as a kind of mirror to show people, including the artist, what they don't know that they know' (Nairne, 1987, p. 121).

As Jean Fisher has pointed out, these images do not represent the mirrored body or self of Hiller 'but are an embodiment of those acts by which the self continually re-invents itself' (Fisher, 1989, p. 46) through the act of seeing, speaking, making, writing, listening, sharing. The images do not present a reassuring narcissistic fantasy in which the reflection is of an individual self-hood. They do not represent a stable world of self-contained appearances. The fragments do not display a particular gendered type; they are free from the limitations of a polarized binary masculine/feminine or self/other.

However, it could be argued that such generalized images also contain the danger of not engaging directly with any spectator, because they become too remote, too removed from the personal experience of sexuality and politics. It may be argued that the feminist agenda has to be so consciously exercised in the viewing of the images that the spectator's passionate engagement is lost. However, Hiller attempts to keep a delicate balance between intellectual critique and emotional absorption. She is not interested in the presentation of the artist's personal experience or in self expression, she wishes to expose the mechanisms, the assumptions by which visual images are interpreted but at the same time she does not wish to lose the magic of engagement with the image. She hopes to retain that moment of fascination, that moment of loss of self, when the spectator becomes fused with the image, however momentarily. This absorption can be initiated as much by a sense of unease as anything else. The unease is due to the blurring of boundaries, typical also of Surrealist imagery which was defined in the first *Manifesto* (1924) as the bringing together of two more or less separate realities (Bréton, 1969, p. 14), and similar also to Freud's *The Uncanny* (Freud, 1955, p. 219), which he describes as that image which excites dread and induces uncertainty, a fearful reminder of something else that has been long suppressed.[13]

A portrait conventionally presents a reassuring illusion of coherent individualism and is a record which negates the sitter's death. Hiller's images, on the other hand, are particularly disturbing because of the lack of focus, the sense that the figure is slipping out of view and because the skin is overlaid with dark, energetic writing. Roberts notes that 'the writing gives Hiller's portraits the exoticism of an ethnographic specimen' (Brett, Parker and Roberts, 1984, p. 42). In other words, they are removed from the safe boundaries of Western culture to places where specimens have mysterious powers. The shadowy forms in these images have the presence of a death mask. The apparition of Death is the ultimate Other and several of Hiller's works explore the fear and fascination with Death, for example *Monument* (1981) and *An Entertainment* (1990). She uses voices, script, images as though from beyond the grave. Because hallucinations or eruptions of unconscious feelings do not correspond to the rational world we have learnt to live with, Hiller states: 'We invariably locate the source of such images outside the subjects who experience them' (Fisher, 1990, p. 27). In these images the apparition of Death is fused/confused with the present body.

Postscript

Hiller's confidence in the manipulation of signs, automatic writing/drawing, and alluring images in order to question any neat, conventional separation between Self and Other (for both herself and the spectator) is fully realized in the series *Secrets of Sunset Beach* (1989). This work is different from her earlier deliberately awkward representations in *10 Months* and *Sisters of Menon* where there is also the sense that she functioned through others. Hiller could be understood to have moved from the confessional work of *10 Months* to the story-telling mode of *Secrets of Sunset Beach*, from questioning the existence of an individual Self to a story about collective experience and fantasy. In this work, the automatic writing, shone as light, has a rich, transformative character which fuses with the exotic artifacts in the interior of a flat. It was constructed by the owners to represent a fantasy and Hiller appropriated it as a surface on which to project the illuminating marks, making the space more suggestive and dreamlike. The images are metamorphic and invite numerous interpretations. The presentation as a sequence (there are ten photographic images in all) enhances the sense of story-telling.

Story-telling here is taken as being distinct from mainstream narrative writing, if we take the definition from Deleuze that 'story-telling is not an impersonal myth, neither is it a personal fiction, it is a speech act through which the character continuously crosses the boundary which would separate his/her private business from politics and which itself produces collective utterances' (Deleuze, 1989, p. 222). Story-telling is a participatory event, between teller/artist and the listener/viewer. It is in the relation between these two that the story is invented. It has no finite form; it is based on collective experience and popular memory and will constantly change with the telling.

Hiller summarizes this in another way:

> What I am trying to do, I suppose, is to bring into view those areas which are repressed socially and culturally, those areas which we do in fact share, and to retrieve for all of us . . . a sense of ourselves as part of a collective, to insert a notion of ourselves as the active makers [of meaning] rather than the passive recipients of a culture.
>
> (Hiller, 1985, p. 5)

Notes

1   See Lucy Lippard (1973), for an introduction to Conceptual Art and the issues it raises. Hiller's place within feminist art production is shown in two essays, *Fifteen years of feminist action* and *Feminism and Modernism* in Parker and Pollock (1987).

2   Automatism can be in the form of writing, drawing, painting or speech. The primary characteristic is the absence of conscious control by the producer. It represents, to many, the eruption of the unconscious into the realm of the conscious and so the automatic marks or sounds are believed to reveal thoughts, feelings and an understanding which otherwise would be repressed or hidden. Because of this, Automatism has been associated with 'free' expression or a more 'truthful' expression and a rebellion against conformity. Automatism is also linked with spiritualism when voices from beyond the grave communicate through an individual, a medium. The interpretation and uses of Automatism vary according to who is using it and in what circumstances. André Bréton explores several constructions and its use for Surrealiam in his essay *The Automatic Message*, 1933 (in Rosemont, 1978, p. 97).

3   This is demonstrated through the formal arrangements she adopts in presenting her work but also in the meanings she explores. Her sympathies lie more with Surrealism than Abstract Expressionism, but they have in common an interest in the artist's painterly mark, its link with the unconscious and notions of male creativity. Hiller and her contemporaries of the 1970s were conscious of the domination of Abstract Expressionism in the art world at that time and this fuelled their critique. Rubin, W. (1969) is a useful introduction to that work, and Shapiro, D. and Shapiro C. (1990) set out some of the debates.

4   Several women artists are concerned with analyzing their identity in relation to class and age (e.g. Jo Spence); sexuality (e.g. Rachael Field); ethnicity (e.g. Sonia Boyce, Sutapa Biswas); disability (e.g. Jacqui Duckworth).

5   See Shanes (1989) for an introduction to Brancusi's work. Battcock (1968) presents the issues discussed about Minimalism at that time.

6   This mythic identity is explored by Berger (1989). The noble savage image of Jackson Pollock is displayed, for example, in *Pollock Painting* (Rose, 1980).

7   In contrast, a contemporary of Bréton's, Käthe Kollwitz, identified that it was both masculine and feminine aspects combined that gave her the strength to produce her work and she goes further to say that this combination is necessary for all artists, male and female (Kearns, 1976, p. 58). And recent feminist criticism has reiterated this more even-handed representation, an intrinsic bi-sexuality, for example Cixous in her essay *The Laugh of the Medusa* (Marks and de Courtivron, 1981, p. 245).

8   *L'écriture Féminine* is unfolded in the essay by Hélène Cixous called *The Laugh of the Medusa*, found in Marks and de Courtivron (1981, p. 245).

9   An example of one of these dialogues is found in Levy (1936, p. 45).

What is day?
A woman bathing nude at nightfall.
What is absence?
Calm, limpid water, a moving mirror.

The Surrealists published these automatic verbal exchanges in their journal *La Révolution Surréaliste*. See Ades and Sylvester, 1978, p. 203. Examples of automatic poems can be found in Read (1936, p. 216).

10   As Chadwick explains, the *femme-enfant* or child-woman was an image that
     dominated Bréton's vision in the 1930s. For him she embodied a naiveté and
     purity that allowed a more direct and free connection with her unconscious, but
     her sexuality and her passivity often predominates in the Surrealists' fantasy. The
     child-woman was completely dependent on the male to use her gifts.
11   Hiller's emphasis on collectivity can be seen to parallel C. G. Jung's interpretation
     of Automatism as representing the common, universal activity of the mind, that it
     reveals core concepts and images and is the source of the collective self. See Wehr
     (1988) for an exploration of his work.
12   Artists involved in this examination include Mary Kelly and Victor Burgin. See
     Kelly (1983) and Burgin (1986).
13   Bréton, in his 1924 essay defining the characteristics of Surrealism, emphasizes all
     those aspects that might destabilize the certainties of rational thought, including
     dream images, strange juxtapositions, the extravagant, excessive and fearful.
     Freud's essay on *The Uncanny* (1919) attempts to interpret the mechanisms that
     trigger the metaphysical shudder of dread and pleasure that the uncanny
     provokes. He relates it to the collapse of the distinction between fantasy and
     reality and to, among other things, animism, a primitive belief in magic. This is
     discussed in relation to Surrealist Photography in Krauss (1986, p. 85).

References

ADES, D. and SYLVESTER, D. (1978) *Dada and Surrealism Reviewed*, London, Arts
     Council.
BAKER, E. and HESS, T. (Eds) (1973) *Art and Sexual Politics*, New York, Macmillan.
BATTCOCK, G. (Ed.) (1968) *Minimal Art: A Critical Anthology*, London, Studio Vista.
BATTERSBY, C. (1989) *Gender and Genius: Towards a Feminist Aesthetic*, London,
     Women's Press.
BERGER, J. (1989) *Success and Failure of Picasso*, London, Granta Books.
BRÉTON, A. (1969) *André Bréton: Manifestoes of Surrealism*, Michigan, University of
     Michigan Press.
BRETT, G., PARKER, R. and ROBERTS, J. (1984) *Susan Hiller: The Muse my Sister*,
     Glasgow, Third Eye, Londonderry Orchard Gallery and London, Gimpel Fils.
BURGIN, V. (1986) *Between*, Oxford, Basil Blackwell.
BUTLER, J. (1990) *Gender Trouble: Feminism and the Subversion of Identity*, London
     and New York, Routledge.
CHADWICK, W. (1985) *Women Artists and the Surrealist Movement*, London, Thames
     and Hudson.
CHICAGO, J. (1975) *Through the Flower*, London, Women's Press.
DELEUZE, G. (1989) *Cinema 2: The Time Image*, London, Athlone Press.
FELSKI, R. (1989) *Beyond a Feminist Aesthetics*, London, Hutchinson.
FISHER, J. (1989) *Lifelines*, Liverpool, Tate Gallery.
FISHER, J. (1990) *Revenants of Time*, London, Matts Gallery.
FOWLIE, W. (1946) *Rimbaud: myth of childhood*, London, Dobson.
FREUD, S. (1955) *Sigmund Freud: the Standard Edition*, **17**, London, Hogarth Press.
HARPER, J. (1987) *The Making of Yeats's 'A Vision'*, London, Macmillan.
HILLER, S. (1980) '10 Months', *Block*, **3**, London.
HILLER, S. (1981) *Monument*, Birmingham, Ikon Gallery.
HILLER, S. (1983) *Sisters of Menon*, (facsimile) London, Coracle Press.
HILLER, S. (1985) *Belshazzar's Feast*, London, Tate Gallery.
HILLER, S. (1989) *Kettles Yard Lecture*, unpublished.

HILLER, S. (Ed.) (1991) *Myth of Primitivism*, London, Routledge.
KEARNS, M. (1976) *Kathe Kollwitz*, New York, Feminist Press.
KELLY, M. (1983) *Post-Partum Document*, London, Routledge.
KRAUSS, R. (1986) *L'Amour Fou: Photography and Surrealism*, London, Arts Council.
LACAN, J. (1982) *Écrits:A selection*, London, Tavistock Press.
LEVY, J. (1936) *Surrealism*, New York, Black Sun Press.
LIPPARD, L. (1973) *Six Years: Dematerialisation of the Art Object*, London, Studio Vista.
LIPPARD, L. (1983) *Overlay: Contemporary Art and the Art of Pre-history*, New York, Pantheon.
MARKS, E. and DE COURTIVRON, I. (Eds) (1981) *New French Feminisms*, Brighton, Harvester.
NAIRNE, S. (1987) *State of the Art: Ideas and Images of the 1980s*, London, Chatto and Windus.
PARKER, R. and POLLOCK, G. (1981) *Old Mistresses*, London, Pandora.
PARKER, R. and POLLOCK, G. (1987) *Framing Feminism: Art and the Women's Movement*, 1970–1985, London, Pandora.
READ, H. (Ed.) (1936) *Surrealism*, London, Faber and Faber.
ROSE, B. (Ed.) (1980) *Pollock Painting*, New York, Agrinde Publications.
ROSEMONT, F. (Ed.) (1978) *André Bréton: What is Surrealism?*, London, Pluto.
RUBIN, W. (1969) *Dada and Surrealism*, London, Thames and Hudson.
SHANES, E. (1989) *Brancusi*, New York, Abbeville Press.
SHAPIRO, D. and SHAPIRO, C. (Eds) (1990) *Abstract Expressionisn: A Critical Record*, Cambridge University Press.
WEHR, D. (1988) *Jung and Feminism: Liberating Archetypes*, London, Routledge.

Chapter 9

Lee Krasner : Mrs Jackson Pollock

Sue Wragg

A photograph taken in Jackson Pollock's studio during the 1950s shows the absorbed artist standing upright looking at his work, whilst, sitting at his feet, Lee Krasner (Mrs Jackson Pollock) looks up at him (Naifeh and White Smith, 1992, p. 156). One might use such an image in conjunction with others as a means to suggest some of the difficulties inherent in trying to find a context in which to look at Krasner's work since her identity as a woman producer has been variously confused with or compromised by her identity as Mrs Jackson Pollock. One might further site such an image alongside others done by women producers dealing with imagery traditionally encoded as female; works by Mary Cassatt for example, particularly those on the theme of mother and child, and Mary Kelly's *Post-Partum Document* (1974–9), which is an investigation into the social construction of both mother and child. While matters of gender are an overt issue in the subject-matter of Mary Cassatt (1844–1926) and Mary Kelly, in the case of Pollock and Krasner gender would seem to be harder to read in works which are both abstract and to do with process.

To invoke the work of Mary Cassatt is not coincidental. When Lee Krasner was arrested during a demonstration in the 1930s, she apparently told the police that her name was Mary Cassatt (Munro, 1979, p. 108). Cassatt's work offered to Krasner — as it does to us — an example of the ways in which a woman producer might find the means to picture modernity, means which would inevitably mediate the specificity of her experiences. Such picturings are not only determined by subject-matter, but are also achieved through the particular ways in which Cassatt utilizes and creates pictorial conventions which she then applies to what Griselda Pollock has called 'the spaces of femininity' (Pollock, 1988, p. 90).

Such spaces are clearly defined on both class and gender lines. In the studio, woman has a very specific role: she was seen as model/muse/mistress for the male producer. By the nineteenth century the studio model for the nude was likely to be working class and therefore to occupy an ambiguous class position, since her depiction would usually fail to acknowledge this fact. Interestingly, Cassatt might model fully clothed for Degas in the Louvre or the milliner's shop, but as his social equal she would not take off her clothes for him in the studio.

The relationship between artist and model in the studio is re-enacted in western painting with great regularity from Vermeer to Courbet (Hess and Baker, 1971, p. 82), with the active role being assigned to the male artist. For example, Renoir's notorious statement 'I paint with my prick' was re-cast by Lawrence Gowing in 1985 as 'An artist's brush had hardly been so completely an organ of physical pleasure and so little of anything else as it was in Renoir's hand. Its sensate tip, an inseparable part of him seemed positively to please itself. In the forms it caressed it awakened the life of feeling' (House *et al.*, 1985, p. 31).

Scenes of Pollock at work photographed by Namuth and others confirm his status as a creative artist by catching him *in flagrante*, so to speak. In these depictions Krasner appears either as an indistinct blur, the background to male creativity, or in focus as a frank admirer of Pollock, absorbed in his work. Obviously then, it is *his* work which matters here, and thus a link is forged between these images and those earlier studios, where the gendered nature of working and viewing has become so apparent. My point is that issues of class in nineteenth century painting are re-worked in the imaging of Pollock and Krasner, despite the fact that Pollock and Krasner occupied the same social 'space'. Class then, can be read palimpsestically in these images even where it is not explicit as such.

The issue of the relationship between gender, class and the studio has recently been updated by Sally Swain's *Great Housewives of Art* series (1988-91) in which the putative wives of selected canonical painters are shown in the style of that painter, struggling with the housework while he (present only through the style of the drawing) gets on with the creative bit. As a humorous piece of populism these books are no doubt intended to answer the question raised by Linda Nochlin in *Art and Sexual Politics* (Hess and Baker, 1971, pp. 1–43), as long ago as 1971 — why have there been no great women artists? — as well as taking on the issue of housework. The difficulty is that such an ahistorical perspective merely re-inscribes the myth: if we take *Mrs Degas vacuums the floor* at face value (this shows a Degas-style ballet dancer wielding a hoover) we are obliged to forget that there *was* no Mrs Degas, and if there had been, her class would have precluded her from being either dancer or model — *and* from doing the housework.

In this context, then, how can the question of the Abstract Expressionist painter's wife, who is also herself a painter, be addressed? Is it the 'either' of being hidden from history and awaiting reclamation by feminists for an extended male canon, or the 'or' of the wholesale re-writing of that selective tradition, which, as even Francis Frascina has pointed out, was largely the creation of a small number of male critics and the Museum of Modern Art in New York? (Here, it should be noted, the canonical view of a specifically abstract modernism in the writings of Clement Greenberg, together with the 'action painting' identified by Harold Rosenberg, has been considered formative in the construction of a macho modernism centred on the person, as well as the work, of Jackson Pollock.[1]) For such male critics the spaces of femininity hardly exist, and even where they are acknowledged they are cast as superficial supplements to the important business of painting (male) myth. This explains some of the responses to Mary Kelly's much discussed *Post-Partum Document*. Even before its completion Laura Mulvey had invoked Mary Cassatt in comparison as being one of the few 'artists' (the scare-quotes are Mulvey's) to have used the theme of mother and child — 'the despised domestic' in her words — as a major theme in her work (Parker and Pollock, 1987, p. 203). But Mulvey deals implicitly with what has become one of the central concerns of feminist visual art: that is, the use of non-traditional art materials, or what has resulted in a rejection of the phallic brush. Painting in Kelly's *Post-Partum Document* made an absent entrance in the form of the now notorious soiled nappy liner, recalling the nineteenth century German critic who rounded on Turner's work with the comment 'crapped is not painted' (Gage, 1987, p. 8). Kelly's work also employs the distantiating device of writing described by her as the 'scripto-visual' (Parker and Pollock, 1987, p. 310). Her text often consists of layers of words, some indecipherable because they are the hieroglyphs of her son's struggle to enter the symbolic order (with all its Lacanian connotations); others are excerpts from various existing writings — overlaid with con*text*ualizations by Kelly herself. She takes the Kristevan view that:

> because of the co-incidence of language and patriarchy the 'feminine' is (metaphorically) set on the side of the heterogeneous, the unnameable, the unsaid, and that in so far as

the feminine is said or articulated in language, it is profoundly subversive'

(*ibid.*, p. 310)

I take this to mean that Kelly's work attempts to undermine the dominant discourse of painting, and offers a way out of the closures of Greenbergian modernism. I want to argue that it is productive to see Krasner as situated between Cassatt and Kelly.

At this point some biographical information becomes relevant. Krasner's experience as the daughter of Jewish immigrants (the first of their children to be born in America) gave her concrete insights into the available spaces of femininity and into the importance of the Word as Law. The synagogue (which she attended) segregated male worshippers from women and the ten commandments expressly forbade the making of graven images. By the time she was nineteen she had enrolled at the National Academy of Design, changed her name from Lenore Krassner to the more obviously American, and more gender-ambiguous, Lee Krasner, and stopped believing in God. Her experiences of art teaching also brought the question of her gender to the fore. Areas of the art school were forbidden to women. Ironically for Krasner (given that working on still life themes had always been considered a suitably feminine or harmless activity) one of these was the still life room because of its unsuitable or dangerous location in a dark basement. It should be remembered here that the nineteenth century had excluded women from much more central activities, particularly life drawing, for ostensibly moral reasons — looking at the body, male or female but especially male, was considered a form of empowerment which was regarded as an exclusively masculine preserve. Tamar Garb has recently drawn attention to the ways in which female looking was either contained or ridiculed at this time (Garb, 1993, p. 241, and Adler and Pointon, 1993, p. 33ff.). Krasner's first test piece self-portrait (1930) was initially rejected by her art teachers because it was assumed to be faked and later, in the studio of the avant-garde emigré Hans Hoffman, her work was praised with the comment 'this is so good you could not know it was done by a woman' (Rose, 1983, p. 13). Ironically, it was the Depression which gave hitherto marginalized groups of American society, such as women and blacks, temporary opportunities to work on equal terms with white men and Krasner, under the auspices of federal work schemes, was able to give up her work as a model and waitress and work full time as an artist.

By 1942, when Krasner was 34, she and Pollock were sharing a studio and living together. In 1945 they got married — a church wedding at his insistence and one of the only two times in her adult life when she reverted to her original name. From then on she became (when seen at all) a part of the Pollock myth. Even in David and Cécile Shapiro's *Abstract Expressionism: A Critical Record* published in 1990 she appears in the index as 'Lee Krasner (Mrs Jackson Pollock)'. This has a doubly marginalizing effect. Through the work of Clement Greenberg and others, Jackson Pollock has been written up as the logical American consequence of European modernism figured by Cubism, and thus as the figure standing at the end of art history. Harold Rosenberg's theory of 'action painting' helped create the myth of Pollock as frontiersman /loner/man on the edge, the rugged individual, but such an ideology did not easily fit the more prosaic fact of his marriage to a woman who was also an artist. Even without the complication of being married to Pollock, Krasner was simply an absence when she failed to be present at a photo-call taken by the so-called Irascibles — the group which formed the basis of Irving Sandler's view of what constituted the triumph of American painting.

Further photographic evidence came to embody Abstract Expressionism itself: I refer, of course, to those photographs taken by Hans Namuth of 'Jack the Dripper' at work, where a vivid demonstration of the act of painting called attention to his insistence on procreation, whilst providing the public with an easy way of coding the modernist extremist who was one of their own. Krasner, on the other hand, was rarely photographed in the act of painting; the effect is that of disengagement and subservience, a mere footnote to the great man's charisma. Even well after Pollock's death, the association of Namuth's photographs with some essentially male process appears to haunt writers on art. Francis V. O'Connor (1967, p. 66), concerned by the inadequacy of 'Jack the Dripper', tried to replace 'drip' with 'pour', using the OED definition of 'to emit a stream . . . to discharge' — here the gendering of painting remains intact as we move from violence to sex. John Berger, (1989) reviewing a joint Krasner/Pollock exhibition in 1989, goes as far as to suggest that Pollock was responsible for 'the suicide of art'. His work is, so we are told, 'metaphysical in aim and violent . . . He paints an explosion; she, using almost identical elements, constructs a kind of consolation' (Berger, 1989). In other words, their work constitutes evidence of the age-old relationship between man the destroyer and woman the nurturer. This despite Berger's admission that at points their work becomes so close as to be interchangeable: 'In 1953', he writes, 'Pollock produced a canvas called *Easter and the Totem* which anybody might mistake for a Krasner' (*ibid.*).

But I think that the partnership of Krasner and Pollock signifies more than yet another case of a female artist lost in the shadows of an artist husband. Hitherto histories of Abstract Expressionism have placed Pollock (both the personality and the oeuvre) at the centre of the movement while Krasner has remained in every sense on the margins. My argument is that for both Pollock and Krasner the artistic relationship should be read as central and productive. Although there is no need to read their work as a single venture I suggest that their explorations of media and their particular kinds of abstraction represent a clear move away from the frequently aggressive and even patriarchal concerns of much canonical modernism, and that for both of them these concerns coincided with their living together.

Both Krasner and Pollock used oil paint and a variety of collaged materials in their work. Both were influenced early in their careers by two strands of European modernism — she by Mondrian and Cubism, he by Surrealism and Picasso's *post*-Cubist work. Both painters also began to introduce hieroglyphic or calligraphic forms into their work during the 1940s. In Pollock's case the effect can resemble a kind of graffiti as though the image is being erased or superseded by writing. Thus, in *Stenographic Figure* of 1942 Pollock painted a reclining female figure with the flat areas of colour, strong black outlines and distorted features associated with his assimilation of Picasso; the figure is overlaid with a series of scrawled crosses and letters.

Krasner's work at this time (she and Pollock had just started living together) is reduced to that almost catatonic state of flat grey surfaces, unstructured slabs which she scraped down to begin again. What eventually surfaces is a series of works which are known as the 'Little Image' paintings — 'little' because of their scale. Whilst these fall into three distinct groups (Rose (1983) has called them 'mosaic', 'webbed', and 'grid'), what they have in common are shapes and forms which resemble writing. Letter forms are suggested, as is a stress on surface, but reading, or meaning, is blocked. At the same time these works reject pictorial interpretation — there are no figurative elements. Their small scale, their insistence on pattern and detail, suggest the exact opposite of Robert Motherwell's description of what artists of the period were doing: 'a modern Stonehenge, with a sense of the sublime and the tragic' (Brookeman, 1984, p. 199) which would replace the despised intimate and domestic that he saw in some European work.

Krasner's acknowledgment of, and pleasure in, detail at this time, and the terms in which Motherwell defines the parameters of Abstract Expressionism, is reminiscent of the argument which brackets the feminine with detail in both literary and art criticism from the sixteenth century onwards. This feminine can be contained by the domestic but if allowed to get out of hand threatens to overwhelm with chaos. This fear is clearly seen in a passage by Baudelaire, quoted by Naomi Schor (1987) (I follow the quote with her gloss):

> The more our artist turns an imperial eye on detail, the greater is the state of anarchy. Whether he be long-sighted or short-sighted, all hierarchy and all subordination vanishes.

Baudelaire's troping of the detail as revolutionary mob [as occurs earlier in the passage] overtly politicizes the aesthetic; the peril posed by succumbing to the invasion of the barbaric and feminine upstart detail — the crowd and the female are on the same continuum in the nineteenth century male imaginary — is nothing less than the end of civilization itself (Schor, 1987, p. 21).

This threat of chaos is something which became increasingly associated with Jackson Pollock's work, no doubt because chaos represents the end of civilization. Indeed, an article in *Time* magazine in November 1950 was actually headed *Chaos Damn It* (O'Connor, 1967, p. 56). If Schor's assertion regarding the barbaric as a feminine 'other' is to be taken seriously, then it is Pollock's work, with its high public profile during the 1950s, which was ringing alarm bells because of his drip-technique, which was seen as lacking any structure. However, the interesting fact is not that both Pollock and Krasner worked mainly in oil paint, but that both also used a variety of collaged materials. With few exceptions, such use of collage reinforces texture. Occasionally elements in both artists' works appear to refer to parts of the body or other organic forms, but such references are oblique.

More recently, the ways in which the work of such painters as Avis Newman and Thèrese Oulton appear to reject closure has brought into focus the possibility of a *peinture feminine* as suggested in the following description of Newman's work:

> Rejecting the Renaissance perspectival tradition for the heterogeneous spaces of the palimpsest Newman's paintings release pictorial space for women from the tyranny of logic.
>
> (Roberts, 1990, p. 168)

Invoking Irigary and Kristeva, John Roberts continues:

A number of women artists have sought a female 'visual economy' based upon the rejection of women into the post Oedipal circuit of symbolic exchange. By refusing the descriptive or demonstrative as forms of representation which stabilize this circuit of exchange, woman's self-representation is located within a pre-Oedipal register of *indirect* representations. Embracing the fugitive and ambiguous as a poetic discourse of female nay-saying, 'non-representation' . . . takes on a would be radical, delegitimizing function.

(ibid., p. 174)

As can be seen from the words 'would be', Roberts is unhappy with this type of work, arguing that 'in pushing modernism's critique of representation into a critique of representation *as such*, the social referent disappears in its fear of its complicity with the dominant culture' *(ibid.*, p. 180). This seems a rather literalist interpretation of the social referent, but it serves as a useful reminder that much canonical modernism uses its critique of representation to parody or celebrate forms of mechanization in a variety of styles which may reject Renaissance perspectival conventions, but which do not reject the enclosing frame. The work of the Abstract Expressionists, it is true, generally eschews the theme of mechanization. However, for most of the New York based artists, such as Barnet Newman and Franz Kline, the desire for monumentality and the sublime, or the continuation of the traditional subject-matter of western art (as in de Kooning's paintings of women) does little more than extend the language of patriarchy inherent in western painting and canonical modernism.

I do not think it without significance, therefore, that Krasner and Pollock moved out of New York and into a rural setting. The city had become both the emblem of modernity *and* modernism, its spaces an exclusive stage for the continuation and rationalization of modernism itself. Pollock had already identified himself with nature rather than culture with his (in)famous comment to Hoffman: 'I *am* nature', where nature is culture's other.

The Namuth photographs which have done so much to etch Pollock into the public imagination as the lonely and tormented genius acquire another significance in this context, since they can be read to suggest that Pollock is making magic like the Navaho sand painters whom he admired — in other words that his 'workings' can be read as shamanic. The 'magic' element in Pollock can be understood in terms of a specifically artistic, rather than communal, context. Thus we read in

Reynolds' description of Gainsborough's paintings: 'all those odd scratches and marks . . . which appear rather the effect of accident than design; this chaos, this uncouth and shapeless appearance, by a kind of magick [sic], at a certain distance assumes form' (Reynolds, 1961, p. 226). I am suggesting here that the tradition of relating painting to magic is part of the history of western art. A more recent comment on this tradition can be found in the art work of Joseph Beuys — for example, in *How to Explain Paintings to a Dead Hare* (1965) where Beuys presented himself as a shamanic figure. Yet in introducing the theme of shamanism I do not necessarily want to shift my discussion into the anthropological domain; rather I want to hang on to the idea of gender in relation to a psychology of the creative process. One of the characteristics of the shaman is its gender instability — it can be trans or bi sexual.

I want to develop this point with reference to a further element common to Krasner's and Pollock's work. Collage is a form which Krasner developed with great refinement, using her own past work, recycling previous paintings and drawings which no longer satisfied her, and doing the same with some of Pollock's discarded or unfinished pieces. This method of working suggests a number of themes. Perhaps the most obvious is that the use of collage makes it difficult to read Krasner's career as one of linear progression. 'Traditional' art history creates a narrative from the works done by artists; indeed Picasso is said to have claimed that he dated all his works to enable *his*tory to be clearly understood. Krasner's very working method subverts this reading; as she said: 'My own image of my work is that I no sooner settle into something than a break occurs. These breaks are always painful and depressing . . . All my work keeps going like a pendulum; it seems to swing back to something I was involved with earlier' (Rose, 1983, p. 139).

This collaging of material from her own past might perhaps be compared with the nineteenth century art of quilt making; it also re-uses materials in order to create abstract forms. Supposedly anonymous quilts were in fact designed and made by one person — indeed she would often sign her work — and despite being termed 'quilts', few were used for warmth. This, together with the processes already described — hieroglyphics, collage, particular uses of oil paint — can further be paralleled with what Jo Anna Isaak describes in the work of Gertrude Stein. Narrative without end, or circular narrative undermines narrative:

[Stein's] entire work can be seen as an attempt to circumvent the end, the closure implied in the capitulation to the 'law of the Father'. 'What is the use of being a little boy if you are to be a man what is the use' she whimsically asks.

(Isaak, 1986, p. 122)

Krasner's work resists closure through its re-use of its actual material. Pollock used other means to achieve a similar goal. He said 'There was a reviewer a while back who wrote that my picture didn't have any beginning or any end. He didn't mean it as a compliment, but it was. It was a fine compliment' (Interview for *The New Yorker*, quoted O'Connor, 1967, p. 51). Thus far separate mythologies have grown up around Krasner and Pollock; their biographies and their work are used by different groups for their own ends. I would argue that Krasner's other, her role as Mrs Jackson Pollock, should not be read as muse nor as submissive wife, but neither should it be read as irrelevant: what emerged from this relationship was surely the possibility of a *peinture feminine* for both Krasner *and* Pollock. The phrase *peinture feminine* makes deliberate reference to the concerns of Hélène Cixous with production and gender which reject the idea that the 'sex' of an author is a necessary guide to the 'sex' of what is produced. For Cixous spoken and written language carry overtones of patriarchal exclusion; like Krasner's, Cixous' origins are Jewish, and like Krasner, the language she learned to speak — her mother tongue — was not her mother's tongue. As Krasner later complained: 'any member of my family could always break out in a language I couldn't understand' (Naifeh and White Smith, 1992, p. 368). I have already cited ways in which certain aspects of visual culture (collage and quilting) may be seen as challenges to the closures of a (male) constructed narrative; for Cixous this can be extended to include the act of painting. For her, the painter transcends the fear which is associated with the act of writing and in doing so *devient femme* [becomes woman] (Cixous, 1986, p. 181). This is an argument which can easily become reductive and I have no wish to apply it in any universalizing way. But even the recent biography of Jackson Pollock by Steven Naifeh and Gregory White Smith, which is deeply hostile to Lee Krasner, acknowledges a mutuality of influence. It is surely the denial of this mutuality which reinscribes the closures which exist in the too well policed feminist art histories, relying for their efficacy on the demonization of 'patriarchy'. In saying this I do not want to be understood to be saying that feminist art histories which draw attention to the closures of patriarchy are mistaken or wrong-headed. What I am saying is that the recuperation of the situation of Krasner and Pollock can help to problematize the over-indulgences of both camps.

Note

1 There is no space in this essay to consider the much-discussed situation of Clement Greenberg, although I am aware that his presence in my argument requires further theorization. In terms of the basic issues one might begin with the essay *Modernist Painting* in Frascina and Harrison (1982, pp. 5–10). So much ink has been spilt on the theory of autotelic modernism that any further recommendations are bound to be arbitrary. For a flavour of the issues at stake, especially where Greenbergian modernism runs up against 'the social history of art', one obvious port of call is Frascina (1985). See also the *American Studies Journal*, Winter 1991, which refers to this and other publications on this subject.

References

ADLER, K. and POINTON, M. (Eds) (1993) *The Body Imaged. The Human Form and Visual Culture since the Renaissance*, Cambridge, Cambridge University Press.

American Studies Journal, 'Over Here', Nottingham, Winter 1991.

BERGER, J. (1989) 'The Suicide of Art', *Guardian Review*, 23rd November, London.

BRACH, P. (1982) 'Tandem Paint: Krasner/Pollock', *Art in America*, **70**, 3, pp. 92–5.

BROOKEMAN, C. (1984) *American Culture and Society since the 1930s*, London, Macmillan.

BROUDE, N. and GARRARD, M. D. (Eds) (1982) *Feminism and Art History. Questioning the Litany*, New York, Harper and Row.

CANNELL, M. (1984) 'An Interview with Lee Krasner', *Arts Magazine*, **59**, 1, pp. 87–9.

CAVALIERE, B. (1980) 'An Interview with Lee Krasner', *Flash Art* (Italy), **94–5**, pp. 14–16.

CHADWICK, W. (1990) *Women, Art, and Society*, London, Thames and Hudson.

CIXOUS, H. (1986) 'Le Dernier Tableaux ou le portrait de Dieu', in *Entre l'Ecriture*, Paris, des Femmes.

FRASCINA, F. and HARRISON, C. (Eds) (1982) *Modern Art and Modernism. A Critical Anthology*, London, Harper and Row.

FRASCINA, F. (Ed.) (1985) *Pollock and After. The Critical Debate*, London, Harper and Row.

GAGE, J. (1987) *J. M. W. Turner 'A Wonderful Range of Mind'*, New Haven, Yale University Press.

GARB, T. (1993) 'Gender and Representation' in GARB, T., FRASCINA, F., FER, B., HARRISON, C. and BLAKE, N., *Modernity and Modernism. French Painting in the Nineteenth Century*, London, Yale University Press in association with the Open University.

GLUECK, G. (1981) 'Scenes From a Marriage. Krasner and Pollock', *Art News* (USA), **80**, 10, pp. 57–61.

HESS, T. B. and BAKER, E. C. (Eds) (1971) *Art and Sexual Politics*, New York, Collier.

HOUSE, JOHN, et al. (Contributors) (1985) *Renoir*, New York, Harry N. Abrams, London Exhibition Catalogue.

ISAAK, J. A. (1986) *The Ruin of Representation in Modernist Art and Texts*, Ann Arbor, UMI Research Press.

KRASNER, L. (1986), *Lee Krasner Collages*, Exhibition Catalogue, New York, Robert Miller Gallery.

LANDAU, E. G. (1981) 'Lee Krasner's Early Career, Part 2: The 1940s', *Arts Magazine* (USA), **56**, 3, pp. 80-9.

LANDAU, E. G. (1984) 'Lee Krasner's Past Continuous', *Art News* (USA), **83**, 2, pp. 68-76.

MUNRO, E. (1979) *Originals, American Women Artists*, New York, Simon and Schuster.

MYERS, J. B. (1984) 'Naming Pictures. Conversations Between Lee Krasner and John Bernard Myers', *Artforum*, **23**, 3, pp. 69-73.

NAIFEH, S. and WHITE SMITH, G. (1992) *Jackson Pollock An American Saga*, London, Pimlico.

NEMSER, C. (1975) 'Conversations with 12 Women Artists, *Art Talk*, New York, Scribner's.

NEMSER, C. (1973) 'A Conversation with Lee Krasner', *Arts Magazine* (USA), **47**, 6, pp. 43-8.

O'CONNOR, F. V. (Ed.) (1967) *Jackson Pollock*, New York, MOMA Exhibition Catalogue.

O'CONNOR, F. V. and THAW, E. (1978) *Jackson Pollock Catalogue Raisonné*, New Haven, Yale University Press.

PARKER, R. and POLLOCK, G. (Eds) (1987) *Framing Feminism. Art and the Women's Movement 1970-85*, London, Pandora.

POLLOCK, G. (1988) *Vision and Difference, Femininity, Feminism and the Histories of Art*, London, Routledge.

REYNOLDS, J. (1961) *Discourses on Art*, New York, Collier Books.

ROBERTS, J. (1990) *Postmodernism, Politics and Art*, Manchester University Press.

ROBERTSON, B. (1973) 'The Nature of Lee Krasner', *Art in America*, **61**, 6, pp. 83-7.

ROSE, B. (1983) *Lee Krasner: A Retrospective*, Houston, Museum of Fine Arts and New York, Museum of Modern Art.

ROSE, B. (1985) Life On The Project, *Partisan Review*, **LII**, 2, pp. 74-86.

SHAPIRO, D. and SHAPIRO, C. (1990) *Abstract Expressionism. A Critical Record*, Cambridge, Cambridge University Press.

SCHOR, N. (1987) *Reading in Detail. Aesthetics and the Feminine*, London, Methuen.

SWAIN, S. (1988-91) *Great Housewives of Art*, London, Grafton Books.

VETROCQ, M. E. (1984) 'An Independent Tack: Lee Krasner', *Art in America*, **72**, 5, pp. 137-46.

WOLFF, J. (1990) *Feminine Sentences. Essays on Women and Culture*, Cambridge, Polity Press.

Chapter 10

The Pioneer Players:
Plays of/with Identity

Katharine Cockin

The crisis in and of representation with which novelists and poets were struggling in the early twentieth century was shared by dramatists and practitioners in the theatre. As Raymond Williams has said, the crisis in the theatre had, since the late nineteenth century, been marked by experiments in naturalism and in reactions against the commercial theatre (Williams, 1983, p. 171). These experiments manifested themselves in what has become known as the European free theatre movement, typified by Andre Antoine's *Théâtre Libre* founded in 1887. The *Théâtre Libre* was a play-producing subscription society, a form of organization typical of the free theatre movement. Societies such as the *Théâtre Libre* produced plays privately for their membership at hired or borrowed theatres, thus avoiding both the overheads of a permanent theatre building and the regulation of theatre managers and licences for public performances. Avant-garde theatre societies in London tended to be formed with similar aims: campaigning against censorship and regulation of the stage; pressing for the establishment of a National Theatre and for the improvement of a so-called national drama; and attempting to raise the status of theatre from theatre as business, to theatre as Art.[1]

The Pioneer Players, a London-based play-producing subscription society active between 1911 and 1925, shared these general aims to some extent but was, in addition, breaking new ground regarding the position of women in avant-garde theatre. As a theatre subscription society, the Pioneer Players was different from its predecessors and contemporaries in having a majority of women at all levels of membership and in the many plays by women which it produced. However, men were included in its membership and the society performed plays written by men, such as Nikolai Evreinov's (1915) *The Theatre of the Soul* which will be discussed in this chapter. The society's performance of this particular play signals a partial shift in the Pioneer Players' agenda as well as a sustained interest in exploring gender identities.

The Pioneer Players, unlike the earlier play-producing subscription societies, cannot be identified with the production of one dramatic form. The Pioneer Players resisted categorization, as the advertisement for the society in the programme for the charity production of Evreinov's play states:

> In their choice of plays the Society have always tried to avoid limiting their field of action to any particular school, and have refrained from proclaiming that revolutionary aesthetic formulae, as such, have any value. What they ask of any play which they produce is some dramatic quality, and they attempt to give it a *mise-en-scène* which shall create a dramatic atmosphere by means of colour, form and lighting.

This advertisement shows that the society was redefining its agenda which hitherto had been described as performances of 'the play of ideas'. The production of Evreinov's play therefore signals a shift to some extent for the society as a whole. However, several members of the Pioneer Players had been interested in forms other than naturalism before the society was founded. Edith Craig's earlier attempt to form a play-producing subscription society, which in some ways could be seen as a proto-type for the Pioneer Players, was not successful. In 1903 Craig, together with W. B. Yeats and others, formed a society called The Masquers which announced a symbolist repertoire.[2] Pamela Colman Smith, the symbolist artist who designed the programme for the Pioneer Players' production of *The Theatre of the Soul*, was to have been librarian for The Masquers.[3]

The Pioneer Players, like The Masquers, was formed in reaction to the much larger, male-dominated Stage Society formed in 1899, with which Edith Craig had been involved. Craig's experience in the Stage Society may be taken as typical of the position of women in the male-dominated subscription society, illustrating the importance of the Pioneer Players in defining a space in which women might be free to experiment. Although she was a member of the Stage Society's management council and helped W. B. Yeats by getting his play *Where There is Nothing* produced by this society in 1904, (Schuchard, 1978, p. 444) she is credited in its annual reports only for her work as 'honorary wardrobe mistress'. Unlike Harley Granville Barker whose career took off after his involvement with the Stage Society, Edith Craig was given few opportunities by the Stage Society and was forced to create her own space outside it.

The Masquers failed and in its failure emerges a conflict between the professional theatreworkers and the amateurs, between the men involved, such as Gilbert Murray and the women, keen to experiment with new ideas for performing. Stella Campbell, known as Mrs Patrick Campbell, had innovative ideas for instance about make-up and performance style for staging Murray's translation of *Hippolytus* which Murray found threatening.[4] After The Masquers collapsed, Edith Craig came into her own, in her work as producer and pageant director in the women's suffrage movement. Her mother's lecture on *Shakespeare's Triumphant Women* performed for the Pioneer Players, provides some indication of the problems facing women which the Pioneer Players sought to address. Ellen Terry, an emblematic woman cited as an inspiration for *The Freewoman* in the first issue, noted the institutional constraints experienced by women in the theatre; even at the Lyceum Theatre she found it difficult to get her ideas for performing put into practice:

> I reflected that for one thing I did not like doing at the Lyceum, there would probably be a hundred things I should dislike doing in another theatre. So I agreed to do what Henry wished, under protest. I have played Beatrice hundreds of times, but not once as I know she ought to be played.
>
> (Terry, 1932, p. 97)

As Christopher St. John says in her introduction to Terry's lectures, Terry's comments on Juliet, Desdemona and Cordelia '... should do much to destroy the accepted notions of these characters, and induce actresses to abandon the traditional way of playing them' (Terry, 1932, p. 17). Terry's own performance of the lectures supported the idea that pauses, the non-verbal and the visual, were techniques available to the female performer: 'Her asides and impromptus were as pregnant with intention as her set speeches' (Terry, 1932, p. 19). In *The Theatre of the Soul*, the visual is the very means whereby the patriarchal text could be re-written.[5]

The Pioneer Players developed from the theatre of the women's suffrage movement, specifically from Edith Craig's involvement in the Actresses' Franchise League and her freelance directing of *A Pageant of Great Women* which Craig devised with Cicely Hamilton. The early years of the Pioneer Players showed a commitment to producing plays written by women and those which presented a critique of patriarchal values. Most of the society's plays were directed by Edith Craig (1869–1947), an important theatre director whose work has been neglected.[6] Working as a woman in the field of theatre direction she faced some opposition as Christopher St. John has suggested (St. John, 1949, p. 25). As the daughter of Ellen Terry who was the president of the Pioneer Players, and as the sister of Edward Gordon Craig, Edith Craig sometimes benefited from, and sometimes bore the burden of, belonging to a theatrical dynasty, her work usually acknowledged only in relation to one or other of her relatives. As a lesbian, Craig seems to have been marginalized; she was offered no permanent position in the commercial theatre in spite of her experience and excellent work. Craig's direction of a play by Evreinov in 1915 exemplifies her pioneering productions; it predates Copeau's direction of Evreinov's *A Merry Death* in Paris in 1922 and Pirandello's productions of Evreinov's drama in Rome (Carnicke, 1989, p. 22). The Pioneer Players' production of *The Theatre of the Soul* in 1915 was important in Craig's career as a director. It was important also as an example of the Pioneer Players' many translated plays new to a British stage. The society produced, for example, the first British productions of plays by Paul Claudel, Torahiko Kori and Chekhov, which were not associated with women's suffrage. The society performed plays for women's suffrage events, for other societies and organizations to raise funds, but Evreinov's *The Theatre of the Soul* was one of several plays performed by the society for charities.

The Pioneer Players' pre-war repertoire, largely supportive of women's suffrage, revealed the inequalities in women's position in the workplace and in (and out of) marriage; it assumed a shared experience with the audience, a philosophical position typical of realism. After the outbreak of war, although the Pioneer Players maintained its majority of women members, the society's constituency changed. This was reflected in the Pioneer Players' developing interest in innovative form as it tried to foster an audience supportive of Art Theatre. By 1920, five years after the society's performance of Evreinov's play, the Pioneer Players had cultivated a very different image. Their production of *The Higher Court* by M. E. M. Young was reviewed in the *New Statesman* by Virginia Woolf, summing up what an audience had, by 1920, come to expect from a performance by the society:

Pioneers — a subscription performance — Sunday evening — the very name of the play — all conspire to colour one's preconceptions. We are not going to enjoy ourselves comfortably all over (that is the shade of it); we are going to be wrought into a sharp nervous point. How queer the Strand will look when we come out; how sharp and strange will be our contact with our fellows for the whole of Monday morning and a considerable part of the afternoon! In short, we are going to be scraped and harrowed and precipitated into some surprising outburst of bitterness against — probably the Divorce Laws. On the other hand, there is the new Bastardy Bill, and Dr. Freud may very well have discovered something entirely new and completely devastating about children's toys. What, when you come to think of it, is a Teddy bear?

(*New Statesman*, 17 April 1920)

We might then assume that watching a Pioneer Players' performance was an uncomfortable experience, a relationship between audience and stage which is typical of experimental theatre. Although Woolf's impression of the Pioneer Players' agenda was supported by the production of Evreinov's play and the society was changing its agenda and constituency, there are some continuities in the Pioneer Players' theatrical practice in that the society sustained its critique of rigid gender roles even in Evreinov's play which seems to offer little for a feminist reading.

The society's production of *The Theatre of the Soul*, translated by the lesbian writer Christopher St. John (Christabel Marshall) and Marie Potapenko, was one of many plays translated for the society by women demonstrating the Pioneer Players' commitment to making women's work visible. *The Theatre of the Soul* was first performed on 14 October 1912 at the Crooked Mirror Theatre in Moscow, a cabaret theatre favouring parody, of which Evreinov was director from 1910–17 (Carnicke, 1989, p. 19). Between 1915 and 1931, Edith Craig directed *The Theatre of the Soul* at least four times.[7] She directed the play for the Pioneer Players' membership at the Little Theatre on 7 March 1915, and at the Shaftesbury Theatre on 3 December 1915 as part of the programme of events organized by Lady Randolph Churchill for a charity matinee, at which J. M. Barrie's play *The Fatal Typist* (more of which later) was also performed. Both plays are comedies which examine identity but I shall argue that the Pioneer Players transformed Evreinov's play in performance by means of casting to offer a critique of conventional gender roles.

The plot of *The Theatre of the Soul* is similar in some respects to an earlier Pioneer Players' drama, Harcourt Williams' dramatisation of a Maupassant short story, *The Duel*. In *The Duel* a man preparing for a duel is shown to be in despair, struggling with the pressures of a masculinity which promises to destroy him. In *The Theatre of the Soul* the male self is revealed and then commits suicide. The play is a monodrama: the action takes place over 18 seconds, set inside the body of a man who has to decide whether to stay with his wife or to leave her for his mistress who is a dancer. Space becomes gendered and politicized, the site for struggle. The Male Self in this play is comprised of an Unconscious, seen asleep at the edge of the stage, and the Emotional and the Rational selves, represented by two actors, who are in conflict. The Rational Self, disagreeing with the Emotional Self, argues that the man should remain with the wife. The female characters are thoughts or concepts of the male self, figured on stage by two female performers. These different concepts do not merely take on verbal existence, but are embodied materially by two actors who physically fight. The wife is at times seen as maternal and pure and the dancer as bald, with false teeth. Once the Concept of the Dancer has won, with her foot on the Concept of the Wife, the apparently victorious Emotional Self kills the Rational Self. The Emotional Self then discovers that his Concept of the Dancer does not really love him, and by means of the telephone (signifying the nervous system) he instructs the man to kill himself. The play shows ironically that the Emotional Self is not completely in control of his Concept of the Dancer and that the choice is not his alone. His contemplation of Woman as Subject, as independent decision-maker and not merely as his Concept, kills him. The male self cannot see himself as Object and remain alive.

This play may seem to be a strange choice for a theatre society such as the Pioneer Players which had been very vocal in its support of women's independence; it could be regarded as a drastic divergence from the society's earlier agenda of producing the 'play of ideas', calling for social reforms, including women's emancipation. The author of this play, Nikolai Evreinov, was a Russian playwright whose plays found little favour after the Revolution, and as Sharon Carnicke has said in her study of Evreinov, his plays offer little for the feminist in their representation of woman as destroyer. Evreinov's concepts of women were ironically little different from those presented in this play. In the light of the history and constituency of the Pioneer Players, the production of the play may have been used to parody masculine notions of dangerous women and their dangerous ideas, thus turning Evreinov's crooked mirror on himself. Several of the Pioneer Players' plays dealt with the psychological disintegration of men as a result of thinking patriarchy, or thinking chivalry, reminding us that the society's play of ideas was a feminist play of ideas.[8]

I would suggest that the Pioneer Players' production of this play, rather than subscribing to Evreinov's views of woman as destroyer, questioned what was destructive and needed to be challenged: the Pioneer Players was exploring alternatives to the conventional roles available to women at this time. As the society had seen in their 1912 production of Jess Dorynne's play *The Surprise of His Life*, women could choose to be single mothers in spite of society's expectations to the contrary. This was an argument produced not only by the play text, but also reinforced by the audience's awareness that Jess Dorynne had been abandoned when pregnant by Edward Gordon Craig, Edith Craig's brother. The Pioneer Players' stage then became the arena and space in which the destructive effects of patriarchal thinking were put on trial.

The extent to which casting is significant for a particular performance is, in the context of a play-producing subscription society, an important question. In Evreinov's play, the male selves' concepts of women are crude, as St. John said in the preface to her translation of the play. They are dependent on binary oppositions, in crisis because the selves are bound to a monologic view of life.[9] This was made clear in the Pioneer Players' performance by the casting of the characters: the concepts of the dancer were played by women who were dancers, such as Eleanor Elder, Ethel Levey and Margaret Morris.[10] This fulfilled the need for casting a woman sufficiently skilled in dancing to present a convincing performance. It also offered a means by which the sign of 'woman as performer' could be used to foreground women, both as characters and as individuals with their own histories, in a particular play (Aston and Savona, 1991, p. 103). Ethel Levey for instance was famous for bringing Ragtime music to Britain. The casting of such prominent women in the roles of mere concepts of a masculine mind served to undercut the patriarchal thrust of the play by foregrounding the tension between role and real life.

Margaret Morris's performance of the dancer in particular offered an opportunity for further public criticism of specific men, suggested by Morris's own account of her affair with John Galsworthy published long after the event (Morris, 1967). It seems that Galsworthy, unlike the Emotional Self in Evreinov's play, chose to stay with his wife and rejected the dancer. However, Galsworthy subsidized Margaret Morris's theatre, opened in 1911, which enabled Morris to develop her ideas of dance and to devise an international language, similar to shorthand and significantly non-verbal, for transcribing visual body movements (Morris, 1928). Morris had been trained by Raymond Duncan and was acclaimed for her performance in Maeterlinck's *The Blue Bird*, (Morris, 1967) but her theatre was not only concerned with symbolist and gestural dance; it was also the venue for naturalist drama, such as Halcott Glover's play *Pressure*, which investigated the very material effects on women of a patriarchal culture: a young woman's experience of sexual harrassment at work. Morris, like the Pioneer Players, may have eschewed the constraints of categorization, in favour of a playing with various dramatic forms.

Similar to modernist prose writers and symbolist dramatists, (Esslin, 1991, p. 534, p. 553) Evreinov was concerned with representing subjective impressions and showing that the external world exists only in so far as the observer or protagonist perceives it. In his monodramas, of which *The Theatre of the Soul* is one example, the entire scene and other characters are presented as the protagonist sees them. The audience sees only what the protagonist sees, fusing with the character. Thus the female characters in *The Theatre of the Soul* are always presented from the point of view of either the Emotional or the Rational male selves. Evreinov wanted the audience to become involved in the play, something with which Edith Craig agreed, and which in the early days of the Pioneer Players was underwritten by the society's commitment to the women's suffrage campaign. Later in her career Craig was to lecture on the need to challenge the passivity and apathy of both actor and audience.[11]

Evreinov's attempts to control the audience in this monodrama are ultimately thwarted by the nature of theatre which is at odds with the notion of a single self (even if presented as fragmented and comprised of several conflicting components) (Faulkner, 1990, p. 22). Any performance is open to other transgressive selves in the forms of the audience, the backstage workers, the theatre building and even the rebellious scenery. In spite of this, the Pioneer Players, including Miles Malleson who experimented with the monodrama form,[12] recuperated from Evreinov an interest in transformation, and in relativizing concepts of normality.

At the same programme of events as the Pioneer Players' production of *The Theatre of the Soul* at the Shaftesbury Theatre, J. M. Barrie's one-act play, *The Fatal Typist* was performed by Gladys Cooper and Gerald du Maurier. Although it was not performed by the Pioneer Players, it shares the society's interest in playing with gender, in ironically juxtaposing the visual with the verbal. In *The Fatal Typist* it seems that words as well as thoughts can get out of hand. The fatal typist of the title is a man, who has replaced the theatre's usual female typist, taken by munitions work. The play begins with du Maurier directly addressing the audience and warning them that Cooper is distraught. The typist's fatal mistake is to have given Cooper the man's lines and du Maurier the woman's lines to learn. Du Maurier announces that, as professionals, they must continue. The two then, in full evening dress, perform their confused parts: Gladys Cooper as the man, in an evening dress, and Gerald du Maurier as the woman, in top hat and tails. It is a comedy of verbal cross-dressing which relies on the conflict between costume, gesture and verbal text.

The stage directions indicate the comedy to be derived from conventionalized feminine or masculine actions. Gerald du Maurier plays Lady Fanny who is visited by Captain James, played by Gladys Cooper. Captain James has come to propose marriage to Lady Fanny. Cooper, acting the man, stands with her back to the fire with legs apart and 'flings herself on a couch in a man's careless way', while du Maurier 'trips in an ingenue's impulsive way' and 'glides to the window'. Attention is drawn to the discrepancy between the verbal text and the physical self-presentation of the performers. The actors frequently forget to act the opposite sex; Cooper 'sits in a ladylike way' for instance and 'then remembers he is a man'. The play reveals the constructed nature of gender roles; women and men are parts we learn to play. Both actors constantly correct their body movements as if the visual takes precedence over the verbal. According to the Lord Chamberlain's report, this play was 'good innocent fun'. The actors' distress is comic. As Evreinov's Male Self shows us, the attempt (and failure) to adhere to rigid notions of masculinity and femininity may prove to be fatal. Although *The Fatal Typist* was not played to a Pioneer Players' members-only audience, it is likely that the membership were much in evidence at this highly publicized fund-raising event. For many members of the Pioneer Players, much was to be gained by deconstructing dominant notions of femininity.

The audience for the Pioneer Players' plays was a crucial part of the plays' meanings. The choice of plays would determine, and was determined by, the membership, whose subscriptions constituted the society's income. Like Evreinov, who self-consciously adopted flamboyant dress and was keen to turn his life into a play, some members of the Pioneer Players were alert to the potential power of costume, especially in relation to playing with gender roles, which they did both on and off stage. In 1913 the Pioneer Players held a costume ball, at which prizes were given for the best fancy dress costume. As a photo in the *Tatler* shows, this was an opportunity for cross-dressing and adopting 'futurist' dress (*Tatler*, 25 March, 1914). Edith Craig, formerly a theatre costumier, provided costumes for the Actresses' Franchise League's fancy dress dinner in 1914. In this community or network of women formed around the Pioneer Players, the visual was a medium through which to argue against verbal patriarchal texts as it had been in the street pageantry of suffrage demonstrations. In the women's suffrage culture, 'dressing up' for women was, like the visual art of the suffrage movement, very much part of the challenge of rendering women visible: making a spectacle; producing, simultaneously, a political point and pleasure.

The 'pioneer' in the society's name is a spatial metaphor signifying the important parts of its work. The mode of organization which the society took, placed it outside the commercial theatre, and constituted it as the Other Theatre, while the plays the society produced often explored subject–object relationships. The Pioneer Players was keen to produce plays about pioneering women and plays which showed women transgressing both as characters within particular plays, and as theatre workers operating in the public arena. In one of the society's first plays, *The First Actress*, written by Christopher St. John, there is a reference to Margaret Hughes (first actress on a London stage) as a 'pioneer' transgressing and redrawing the 'archaic map' of separate spheres for women and men. Hughes faced opposition since the notion of a woman playing a female character (the reverse of the dilemma in *The Fatal Typist*) was anathema to contemporary theatrical convention. The metaphor of the 'pioneer' assumed, at this time, a specifically feminist resonance, especially in its notion of space and crossing boundaries: space to be retrieved and occupied; forbidden territory to be reclaimed; the need to understand space as politicized. The pioneer is explicitly the female performer or dancer, a potentially liberating figure.

In many plays performed by the Pioneer Players conventional gender roles were interrogated by juxtaposing conflicting discourses, often showing the inability of men to understand women, as if speaking different languages. Instead of adopting and rewriting Evreinov's technique and controlling what the audience sees, the dramatists show the process of characters' dialogues and exchanges in crisis, where words were exchanged but meanings differed because determined by fundamentally differing world views.

Through the comic form, the manipulation of point of view and juxtaposition, the Pioneer Players' drama often suggested that different points of view produce and reproduce different realities, the results of which have serious, material effects on the lives of women and men. The ideological importance of such a dramatic representation was to attempt to intervene in the reproduction of patriarchal points of view.

The Pioneer Players, when it questioned dominant ideas of femininity and masculinity, was cutting new ground, pioneering the new, not for its own sake, but to engage in an ideological battle of which the enfranchisement of women was but one result. The society's members supported women's rights to independence in employment, as single parents, as workers (including cultural producers) and for some members as lesbians, rejecting heterosexual marriage as the only role for women. The Pioneer Players was unafraid of new ideas and dangerous subjects, appropriately ending its life in 1925 with a production of Susan Glaspell's *The Verge*.[13]

Notes

1. For a discussion of the relationship between theatre and Englishness see Dodd (1986, pp. 1–28).
2. For two differently focused discussions of The Masquers, see Schuchard (1978) and Chapman (1989).
3. Subscription societies such as the Stage Society published their own magazines and established small libraries. The Pioneer Players did not attempt to develop its own cultural practices in this way, but in 1917–18 it subscribed to a publication called *The Plough* which presumably was made available to members.
4. See unpublished memorandum from Gilbert Murray to the Committee of the Masquers, 27 October 1903, 3.598, Edith Craig Correspondence File (ECCF), held at Ellen Terry Memorial Museum, Kent; memorandum from Gilbert Murray, undated, 3.597, ECCF.
5. This subversion of existing forms seems to have been a typical strategy of the women's suffrage artists. It was typical of Cicely Hamilton's aesthetic; Stowell (1992) argues that Hamilton subverted the romantic comedy.
6. A few plays were directed by men, for instance Louis Calvert, and some plays were co-directed by Craig and the (male) dramatist, for instance Laurence Housman.
7. Craig's productions were as follows: Little Theatre, 7 March 1915 subscription performance for the Pioneer Players; Shaftesbury Theatre, 3 December 1915, in aid of Lady Limerick's Free Refreshment Buffet for Soldiers and Sailors at London Bridge Station; Savoy Theatre, 7 April 1916, in aid of wounded soldiers and sailors at home and abroad; Nancy Price's National Theatre, London in the thirties. For a discussion of the controversy surrounding the Pioneer Players' failed production of Evreinov's play at the Alhambra Theatre, see my 1991 article, 'New Light on Edith Craig', *Theatre Notebook*, **45**, 3, pp. 132–42.
8. For instance, Michael Orme's *The Eternal Snows* performed on 28 May 1916 at the Criterion Theatre and Cecil Fisher's *The Great Day* directed by Leonard Craske (who had, on several occasions, played the role of Prejudice in Edith Craig's productions of Cicely Hamilton's *A Pageant of Great Women*) performed on 18

May 1913 at the Little Theatre. In Orme's play the death of the protagonist in a polar expedition, in the manner of Captain Oates in Captain Scott's expedition, is the uneasy solution to a troubled marriage. The explorer's wife and her lover are then free to marry, but the play examines the conventions of chivalry and the consequences of a marriage of convenience. In Fisher's play, unusually for the Pioneer Players with an all-male cast, the nervous breakdown of one of the male insurance clerks is used to dramatize the psychological costs of capitalism.

9   Bakhtin (1981) argues that while a 'unitary language' asserts an authoritative, single ideological perspective, attempting to centralize and limit meaning, it is always subject to interruption, to parodic challenge, from the decentralizing forces of hetero-glossia.

10   Eleanor Elder played the 2nd Concept of the Dancer at the Little, Savoy and Shaftesbury Theatre productions. Ethel Levey played the 1st Concept of the Dancer at the Shaftesbury Theatre production. Margaret Morris played the 1st Concept of the Dancer at the Little Theatre production.

11   On 28 February 1935 Craig gave a lecture in the prestigious series of Shute lectures on *The Art of the Theatre* at Liverpool University. See *Liverpool Post*, 1 March 1935.

12   Miles Malleson's monodrama, *The Little White Thought* was performed in the same bill as the Pioneer Players' production of *The Theatre of the Soul* at Lady Randolph Churchill's charity matinee, 3 December 1915, Shaftesbury Theatre.

13   Edith Craig directed the play, which formed the last Pioneer Players' production, on 29 March 1925 at the Regent Theatre. In November 1919, Susan Glaspell submitted *Bernice* for consideration by the Pioneer Players for a possible production; this was never realized. See copy of play in Edith Craig's archive held at Ellen Terry Memorial Museum, Kent.

References

ASTON, E. and SAVONA, G. (1991) *Theatre as Sign System: A Semiotics of Text and Performance*, London, Routledge.

BAKHTIN, M.M. (1981) 'Discourse in the Novel', in HOLQUIST, M. (Ed.) *The Dialogic Imagination: Four Essays*, translated by EMERSON, C. and HOLQUIST, M., Austin, University of Texas Press.

BARRIE, J.M. *The Fatal Typist*, ADD LCP 1915/31, Lord Chamberlain's Play Collection, British Library.

CARNICKE, S. (1989) *The Theatrical Instinct: Nikolai Evreinov and the Russian Theatre of the Early Twentieth Century*, New York, Peter Lang.

CHAPMAN, W.K. (1989) 'Yeats's "Theatre of Beauty" and the Masque', *Yeats: An Annual of Critical and Textual Studies*, 7, pp. 42–56.

DODD, P. (1986) 'Englishness and the National Culture', in COLLS, R. and DODD, P. (Eds) *Englishness: Politics and Culture 1880–1920*, pp. 1–28, London, Croom Helm.

DORYNNE, J. 'The Surprise of His Life'; typescript 20 pp. held at the Ellen Terry Memorial Museum, Kent.

EVREINOV, N. (1915) *The Theatre of the Soul*, translated by ST. JOHN, C. and POTAPENKO, M., London, Hendersons.

FAULKNER, P. (1977, reprinted 1990) *Modernism*, London, Routledge.

GLOVER, H., 'Pressure', ADD LCP 1915/31, Lord Chamberlain's Play Collection, British Library.

HAMILTON, C., 'A Pageant of Great Women', in GARDNER, V. (Ed.) (1985) *Sketches From the Actresses' Franchise League*, Nottingham, Nottingham Drama Texts.

MORRIS, M. (1928) *The Notation of Movement: Text, Drawings and Annotations*, London, Kegan Paul, Trench, Trubner & Co. Ltd.

MORRIS, M. (1967) *My Galsworthy Story*, London, Peter Owen.

SCHUCHARD, R. (1978) W. B. Yeats and the London Theatre Societies 1901-1904, *The Review of English Studies*, **29**, pp. 415-46.

ST. JOHN, C. (undated) *The First Actress*, London, Utopia Press.

ST. JOHN, C. (1949) 'Close Up' in ADLARD, E. (Ed.) *Edy: Recollections of Edith Craig*, London, Frederick Muller Ltd., pp. 16-34.

Stage Society Annual Reports, held at the British Library.

STOWELL, S. (1992) *A Stage of Their Own*, USA, The University of Michigan Press.

TERRY, E. (1932) *Four Lectures on Shakespeare*, in ST. JOHN, C. (Ed.) London, Martin Hopkinson Ltd.

WILLIAMS, Harcourt, (undated), 'The Duel', in '*Three One Act Plays From Stories by Guy de Maupassant: The Bad Lot, The Minuet and The Duel*', typescript 14 pp., held in the library of the British Theatre Association.

WILLIAMS, R. (1981; 1983 reprint) *Culture*, London, Fontana.

WOOLF, V., "The Higher Court", *New Statesman*, 17 April 1920, in MCNEILLIE, A. (Ed.) (1988) *Essays of Virginia Woolf Vol. III, 1919-24*, London, Hogarth Press, pp. 207-10.

Chapter 11

'Meeting the Outside':
The Theatre of Susan Glaspell

Elaine Aston

Susan Glaspell was a pioneer of the 'new drama' on the American stage. She was born in Davenport, Iowa (probably in 1876), and began her career in journalism and fiction writing. In 1913, after a period of mixing in the artistic circles of Chicago, she married George Cram Cook. The couple took up residence in New York, but spent their summers on the coast in Provincetown, Massachusetts, where in 1915 they co-founded the Provincetown Players: the company which was to become a home for the 'new drama' of the American theatre. Glaspell worked with the Provincetown Players until 1922 when she left for Greece with her husband. Cook died shortly afterwards in 1924, and Glaspell returned to Provincetown. Although she was still involved in theatre in her later years, she was more fully engaged with fiction writing and produced her tenth and final novel a few years before her death in 1948.

Despite Glaspell's pioneering contributions to the American stage during the formative years of the Provincetown Players, her position in the theatrical canon has been a marginal one. This, so this essay will argue, is as a direct result of male-centred critical approaches to Glaspell's work which have failed to understand her theatre: which have judged her drama according to male values, found it wanting, and allowed it to disappear (Ozieblo, 1990, pp. 66–76). Only in recent years has feminist theatre scholarship begun to excavate Glaspell's work and to offer an understanding of her plays based on current ideas and approaches to women's theatre which have raised the question of a 'new poetics'. The concept of a new poetics frames this commentary on Glaspell's theatre in an attempt to expose how it has been betrayed by the values of male criticism, and, most importantly, to show how a woman-centred approach to her work gives her theatre back to the blood-line of women's theatrical history.

The evidence of a male norm against which Glaspell's work is measured began during her lifetime in reviews and commentaries on her theatre. Arthur Hobson Quinn's brief overview of Glaspell's canon in 1927 summarized it as 'more experimental than systematic', which he justified by constrasting her work with that of the playwright Gilbert Emery, described by Quinn as an 'expert crafts*man* who devotes his entire attention to the theatre' (Quinn, 1927, p. 212; my emphasis). Ludwig Lewisohn (1932) offered the following retrospective summary:

> Miss Glaspell had enough metaphysical stamina and disdain of success to produce a small but coherent body of dramatic work. The new stages and the new playwrights plowed up the soil of art and of life and changed the spiritual scene of America. But of all their activity only fragments remain, brilliant but barren fragments, save for the work, with all its shortcomings, of one *man*, of Eugene O'Neill.
>
> (Lewisohn, 1932, p. 401; my emphasis)

Glaspell in fact authored six full-length plays (one of which was co-authored) and seven one-act pieces (two of which were co-authored) for which 'small' hardly seems an adequate description. Furthermore, her work for the theatre also included performing, directing, and reviewing. In sum, she was responsible for an innovatory and significant theatrical output which can hardly be described as fragmentary (Ben-Zvi, 1989, p. 147). (One exception to the contemporary trend of Glaspell criticism was Isaac Goldberg's comparative analysis of Glaspell and O'Neill, which saw their theatre as 'rooted in the difference of sex'. (Goldberg, 1922, p. 472))

The male perspective on and judgement of Glaspell's work persists in modern approaches to her theatre. C. W. E. Bigsby's introduction to the 1987 Cambridge anthology of Glaspell's plays (they had previously been allowed to go out of print), concludes with a statement to the effect that Glaspell 'deserves more than a footnote in the history of drama' (Bigsby, 1987, p. 30). Yet his own introduction is coloured by a male perspective on her work which insists on locating her within a male line. For example, Bigsby quotes from Floyd Dell, editor of the *Friday Literary Review*, and includes the statement that 'the novelists from Fielding to Galsworthy have spoken on behalf of the *man* at odds with society'. Bigsby concurs with this view by commenting that this was 'Susan Glaspell's theme throughout her career' (Bigsby 1987, p. 5; my emphasis). This overlooks Glaspell's central concern which was to speak on behalf of the *woman* at odds with society.

The sourcebook *Women in American Theatre*, even though under a female co-editorship, only makes passing references to Glaspell, and has just two brief entries devoted to *Trifles* (see Chinoy and Jenkins, 1987, pp. 149–51, pp. 253–56). *Trifles* is the one one-act piece which has been widely anthologized since the feminist recovery of Glaspell, mainly as a result of the American 'images of women' style of criticism in the 1970s which saw Glaspell's short story version of *Trifles*, *A Jury of her Peers*, as 'a paradigmatic one for feminist criticism' (Hedges, 1986, p. 90). The sourcebook does not, however, attempt to go beyond this to recover Glaspell's canon of 'lost' theatre.

Other feminist approaches to theatre have been more thorough in their re-charting strategies, and have included a revisioning of the concept of the canon (Schlueter, 1989; 1990). The notion of an 'alternative' canon is not without its own problems given that it runs the risk of sustaining 'the gender assumptions it seeks to question, expose, and disrupt' (Schlueter, 1990, p. 23), but the broad notion of deconstructing male definitions of what is considered a classic or great piece of theatre has been instrumental in foregrounding previously 'lost' women's theatre. In the introduction to *Out from Under*, an anthology of texts by American women performance artists, the editor Leonora Champagne introduces the idea that women's artistic creativities be seen not in canonical terms, but as a 'trail of blood':

> When tracing the course of twentieth-century writing and artwork by women, one often finds a trail of blood. From Susan Glaspell to Marsha Norman, Lillian Hellman to Marguerite Duras, Sophie Treadwell to Irene Fornes, Frida Kahlo to Ana Mendieta, Martha Graham to Pina Bausch, in work after work women's silence implodes into violence, often manifested as murder or suicide. Society's definition of normalcy is represented as distorted or perverted. Home is no haven, but a dangerous place, a suffocating enclosure, a cage to fly from.
>
> (Champagne, 1990, p. x)

Champagne further states of the women artists in her volume that 'beneath the powerful writing is the under-the-skin experience of oppression for being "other" — a Jew, a black, a lesbian, and always, a woman' (*Ibid*. p. x). But she also stresses that these women are fighters, not victims. Seeing Glaspell as part of a blood-line of women's artwork furthers an understanding of her writings as an 'under-the-skin experience of oppression for being "other"', rather than a clever, possibly radical, experimenter who never quite measured up to Eugene O'Neill. Glaspell's theatre is an expression of being a woman, of being 'other', but also of fighting; of struggling to move beyond and outside of male-defined normalcy. To understand Glaspell as a dramatist is to understand her as a woman dramatist, as a woman writing.

The concept of 'other' and the desire to move outside of male structures, is central to contemporary feminist debate about performance practice. In the wake of French feminist theories (especially those of Cixous, Kristeva, and Irigaray), the notion of 'scripting the body' into a performance context has initiated a discussion of the possibilities of a 'female form' or 'feminine morphology' of theatre (Case, 1988, pp. 112–32). If Glaspell's theatre is framed in terms of these new ways of seeing women's theatrical artwork, then her struggle to represent woman at odds with society, desirous of overcoming oppression and speaking out, can be understood.

In terms of her dramatic writing, Glaspell works in a realist (male) mode, but at the same time subverts and rejects the serial construction of well-made actions: the 'phallic experience' of organizing plot into 'complication, crisis and resolution' (Case, 1988, p. 129). Where realist drama is constructed around actions and action initiated through speech, Glaspell's woman-centred drama resists a logical and linear progression towards closure through doing or speaking. Her women desire to 'undo': to 'unspeak'. Because Glaspell's theatre belongs, as Champagne identifies, to the 'setting-out' phase of the twentieth-century female dramatists' blood-line, it is inevitable that her drama will be marked by an expression of the desire for, rather than an attainment of, a new 'female form': by techniques or devices which splinter and fragment male structures in order to point towards the possibility of a female register. By examining aspects of Glaspell's dramatic/theatrical text, specifically her radical use of plot, language, directions, character, and setting, it is possible to substantiate the claims that Glaspell is a pioneering force in women's theatre.

This point is reinforced if one pauses for a moment to examine why it is that Glaspell's *The Inheritors* (1921) attracted considerably more attention and praise from male commentators and reviewers than her other full-length dramas. *The Inheritors* is a highly-charged political piece, speaking out against the activities of the American government in the aftermath of World War One. The drama is woven out of narrative lines which cross three generations of American libertarians, and makes use of a central female protagonist as an instrument of political discontent. There are lines in the play which, as Ben-Zvi comments, were 'liable to bring Glaspell — like her protagonist — a possible fine and jail sentence under the espionage and sedition laws' (Ben-Zvi, 1989, p. 161). Yet, despite its radical political content, and its use of a central female pro/an-tagonist, it is one of Glaspell's least woman-centred plays. The radical content is marred by the conventionality of the play's form which remains tied to the American (male) experience. Hence, for all the failings of the piece, the critics have responded in glowing terms. Lewisohn called it 'in its day and date, a deed of national import' (Lewisohn, 1932, p. 395). J. Ranken Towse, reviewing the play for the New York *Evening Post*, had much to complain of, but ultimately decided that the play was proof of a 'dramatist of ideas' having 'taken her place in the theatre' (Towse, 1921, p. 9). Bigsby, who includes *The Inheritors* in his anthology, acknowledges the play's dramatic weaknesses, stating that the drama, 'perceived as an epic analysis of the decline of American idealism', demonstrates an unresolved 'tension between a radicalism of subject and a conservatism of form'. However, he concludes that 'nevertheless, the sheer scale of the play, its attempts to identify the roots of a national ambiguity of experience and thought, went beyond anything else which she wrote' (Bigsby, 1987, p. 19). Terms such as 'epic', 'sheer scale', going 'beyond' are indicative of a male response. But Glaspell's theatre goes 'beyond' when Glaspell scripts herself, as woman, into her texts: when both form *and* content are encoded with the en-gendered 'otherness' of the writer.

In Glaspell's early experiments in writing for theatre, when she worked in the one-act form, the female quest to move beyond male structures and oppressive systems of closure is taken as subject matter for dramatization. This is the case, for example, in her one-act comedies *Woman's Honor* (which makes fun of male definitions of female purity); *Suppressed Desires* (which laughs at Freudian analysis), and *Tickless Time* (which makes light of the ways in which lives are ordered by the clock). Among these one-act pieces there are two whose encoding of oppression and 'otherness' is registered in terms of both formal properties and ideological content: *Trifles* and *The Outside*.

Trifles raises gender-based issues, specifically the miserable conditions under which rural wives lived, through generically subverting the detective story. The piece has two sets of detectives: the official male investigators (County Attorney Henderson and Sheriff Peters, helped by the neighbouring farmer, Lewis Hale), and the female 'detectives' Mrs

Peters and Mrs Hale. The men are holding an official investigation into the murder of John Wright, which has taken place before the play begins. Mrs Wright has been taken in for questioning. The male investigation fails because the men are unable to decode the domestic trifles which are the clues to solving the puzzle. Downstairs in the farmhouse they see nothing of importance, merely 'kitchen things'. The two wives, however, are able to piece together the domestic trifles and arrive at an understanding of the intolerable conditions under which Mrs Wright had been living: the loneliness, the lack of female company, and the hardness of her husband who had choked the life out of her. These conditions led Mrs Wright to murder her husband. The wives judge the crime of male violence against women to be greater than that of a woman breaking the law, and they remain silent about what they have found out. They are able, as Rachel France comments, to 'band together to protect another woman from what is clearly the injustice of man's law when applied to women' (France, 1981, p. 151).

Generically this play subverts the traditional narrative structure of the detective (subject) who hunts and finds the criminal (object). The structural subversion is encoded and enacted according to Greimas actantial model (Aston and Savona, 1991, p. 37) in the overturning of the narrative male quest by the female quest as follows:

Male Quest
Law (Sender)→Male Investigators (Subject)→to solve crime (Object)→in the dominant (male) interests of society (Receiver). Opposed by Wives. Helped by male forces of law and order and their agents.

Female Quest
Oppression (Sender)→Wives (Subject)→to understand 'crime' (Object)→in the interests of the oppressed, subordinate (female) group (Receiver). Opposed by male forces of law and order. Absence of Helpers.

In this way, Glaspell's first single-authored piece for theatre shows a pioneering grasp of what has become a theoretical exploration in contemporary feminist studies (especially in the field of film): the oppressive positioning and objectification of the female 'subject' in traditional narrative structures and quests of male desire.

Glaspell's rebellion against (male) norms of narrative structuring also extends to her use of dramatic dialogue. She makes use of devices and techniques which de-familiarize language, and expose how its logo-(phallo)centric structures are designed to control and mediate the world on male terms. Glaspell's women, like Claire Archer in *The Verge* for example, frequently express a desire to get 'underneath' words. This is linguistically registered by Glaspell in specific ways which include the use of oppositional terms which cancel each other out and leave a void, the taking of words to mean their opposites, and the breaking up of sentences which punctures and fragments meaning and resists closure. Where language is highlighted as a system of closure which is to be rejected, certain of Glaspell's stage directions point towards the performance potential of using the body of the female performer as a means of inscribing female desire into the theatrical text. This is clearly illustrated in her one-act play *The Outside*.

The setting and context of this drama is as follows. The action takes place in a deserted life-saving station which stands in 'strange forms of sand' where only the 'rude things, vines, bushes' will grow (Glaspell, 1987a, p. 48). Symbolically the set represents the edge of life, and mirrors the struggle for growth which is dramatized. The life-saving station is where Mrs Patrick has chosen to live after having been deserted by her husband. Allie Mayo, who works for her, is a woman whose husband was drowned at sea years ago. Since that time Allie has been silent. The play dramatizes the moment when she begins to speak again in order to encourage Mrs Patrick to share in her own realization that you cannot shut life out. Their coming to life, 'meeting the outside', is juxtaposed with the image of the male life-savers who fail to save the life of a fellow sailor:

ALLIE MAYO: I found — what I find now I know. The edge of life — to hold life behind me —
(*A slight gesture towards Mrs Patrick.*)

MRS PATRICK: (*stepping back*) You call what you are life? (*laughs*) Bleak as those ugly things that grow in the sand!

ALLIE MAYO: (*Under her breath, as one who speaks tenderly of beauty*) Ugly!

MRS PATRICK: (*passionately*) I have *known* life. I have known *life*. You're like this Cape. A line of land way out to sea — land not life.

ALLIE MAYO: A harbor far at sea. (*raises her arm, curves it in as if around something she loves*) Land that encloses and gives shelter from storm.

> MRS PATRICK: (*facing the sea, as if affirming what will hold all else out*) Outside sea. Outer shore. Dunes — land not life.
>
> (Glaspell, 1987a, p. 54)

Various of Glaspell's disruptive language techniques, as previously discussed, are demonstrated in this extract: the oppositional play, for instance, of beauty and ugliness, and the broken sentences indicative of a desire to break out of language. In the stage directions Allie Mayo's desire to 'meet the outside' is registered in the physical instruction *'raises her arm, curves it in as if around something she loves'*. This is a visual, physical realization that the key to life lies in herself, in her own body/self through which she has found 'the edge of life'. Mrs Patrick's initial inability to grasp this is again demonstrated through her body: *'facing the sea, as if affirming what will hold all else out'*. It is important that Mrs Patrick's gradual awareness of self evolves through another woman. They are both women who have lost 'life' through men, but their re-awakening is not effected through a return to the male order — the directions for the final tableau, for instance, indicate that both women shrink away from the male presence which threatens to disrupt the woman-centred stage picture. Their 'life' is found through each other, woman to woman. In the words of Cixous: 'Everything will be changed once woman gives woman to the other woman. There is hidden and always ready in woman the source; the locus for the other' (Cixous, 1976, p. 252).

Glaspell's use of the linguistic sign-system has been centrally misunderstood in critical readings and reactions to her theatre. Reviewers and commentators have insisted on reading her use of dramatic language on male terms: as a medium for constructing an intellectual argument or a set of ideas about the individual subject — assumed to be male, articulate, and capable of communicating his anxiety ridden state. Glaspell's biographer Arthur E. Waterman, for example, states that, 'while Miss Glaspell is of major importance as a dramatist of ideas, she paid a price for this achievement. She had to foresake a lyrical drama for an intellectual one. Consequently, *there are few moving speeches in her plays*' (Waterman, 1966, pp. 89–90; my emphasis). Lewisohn critizes her one-act tragedies for their 'insufficiency of actual speech', and further describes Glaspell as a 'dramatist a little afraid of speech' (Lewisohn, 1932, pp. 393–4). Such commentaries are indicative of a critical value judgement which endorses the verbosity of a text like, for example, O'Neill's *Anne*

Christie (1920), which purports to be a female-centred pleading on behalf of a woman with a past, and which is certainly replete with long speeches — though not necessarily moving ones. It highlights how male readings have failed to grasp that Glaspell is rejecting the linguistic sign-system as a symbolic (in the Kristevan sense) order. The lack of 'moving speeches' is a manifestation of woman's impossibility of taking a place in relation to the system of language.

Glaspell's method of 'unspeaking' is allied to the subversion of the traditional dramatic conventions which govern character. As with language, there are various strategies which Glaspell employs in her construction of character which de-construct the realistic framework of her theatre. In *Woman's Honor*, for example, she moves away from named characters, to a more emblematic naming reminiscent of medieval drama. Her women characters in this play are called The Shielded One, The Motherly One, The Scornful One, The Silly One, The Mercenary One and The Cheated One. (Glaspell also adopts this convention in *The People*. In *Tickless Time* characters have both individual names and labels.)

Glaspell further disrupts the conventions of the 'prisonhouse of realism' by undermining expectations of status. Characters who are traditionally unnamed servant-types and used as peripheral, background figures are upgraded to individuals central to the drama. Such a subversion was not uncommon amongst the European pioneers of the new drama, but in Glaspell's theatre the device is often used to support her project of showing that it is women who are peripheral, who are on the edge of life, but who also because of that are 'capable of shaping it anew' (Dymkowski, 1988, pp. 91–2). This is the case, for instance, in *The Outside* in the mistress-servant relationship between Mrs Patrick and Allie Mayo. *Bernice*, Glaspell's first full-length play, offers an equivalent woman-to-woman awakening sequence between Margaret Pierce and the servant Abbie. In both of these dramas the servant roles were played by Glaspell herself.

Additionally, Glaspell also upsets conventions of character by making off-stage characters who are never seen, and who, traditionally, are of minor importance to the dramatic action of a play, vital to the stage picture. In *Bernice* and *Alison's House* (Glaspell's last full-length play), the central female protagonists are already dead: Bernice has just died; Alison has been dead for eighteen years. Glaspell not only establishes these characters at a linguistic level — as they are talked about — but also encodes their presence in the stage space. *Alison's House*, which was a response to Glaspell's wanting to dramatize something of Emily Dickinson's life, is set for two acts in the library of the old Stanhope homestead — Alison's House:

> ACT 1. SCENE: The library of the old Stanhope homestead...it is the room of people who have lived in comfortable circumstances, and signifies a family of traditions and cultivation.
>
> (Glaspell, 1931, p. 583)

The third act is set in Alison's room, where various members of the Stanhope circle are able to move closer to Alison; to understand 'life'.

Traditional criticism is quick to note the pattern of the absent characters, though not to address the significance of this in relation to female representation. This absence is a further manifestation of the impossibility for women of taking a place in the symbolic order. The unseen presence of Alison, Bernice, or the imprisoned Mrs Wright in *Trifles* also offers a life force which comes from beyond, from the outside and which is shared with other women, in order that they too see beyond.

The question of women seeing beyond is centrally encoded in what is arguably Glaspell's most experimental play and perhaps most significant contribution to the blood-line of women's theatre: *The Verge*. This centres on Claire Archer's desires to create new plant (life) forms. Her desire to get beyond male constructed forms and structures takes her through a series of rejected relationships: rejection of her daughter, husband, lover and a second lover whom she chokes the life out of in order to keep 'living'. Her violent breaking out of the symbolic is an act of *jouissance*, but it is not one which male critics viewed favourably or could come close to understanding.

Quinn saw the play as a study of a 'neurotic woman going insane' (Quinn, 1927, p. 211). Alexander Woolcott's (1921) review in the *New York Times* described the play as a 'study of an abnormal and neurotic woman', and suggested that it could 'be intelligently reviewed only by a neurologist or by some woman who has journeyed near to the verge of which Miss Glaspell writes' (p. 23). Waterman insists that 'we must realize that Claire has gone too far' (Waterman, 1966, p. 81). Even Bigsby states that it is 'tempting to see in Claire the portrait of a man' — specifically her husband (Bigsby, 1987, p. 21). In short, there is nothing among the majority of male critics that suggests that what Glaspell offers in Claire is a portrait of a *woman* who recognizes that she is trapped by the symbolic order, at the same time as expressing the female desire to move beyond it.

As in Glaspell's one-act play *The Outside*, the settings for *The Verge* operate at a symbolic level: in this instance as a visual representation of Claire's struggle for 'otherness'. Acts One and Three are set in her laboratory where she carries out her experiments with the Edge Vine and her new plant 'Breath of Life'. Act Two is set in a distorted tower. The set directions give an indication of the demands which Glaspell made on her set designer, Cleon Throckmorton, demands which would still represent a challenge for any modern designer.

Throckmorton's settings for *The Verge* also provide a clear indication of how Glaspell's pioneering of a new performance poetics was encoded in the theatrical (as opposed to merely dramatic) text. Waterman describes and analyzes the setting for Act Two as follows:

> The most interesting device in the play is the use in the manner of some European playwrights of an Expressionistic setting which is distorted and unrealistic in order to suggest the twisted reachings of Claire and her plants. The set *'is a tower which is thought to be round but does not complete the circle. The back is curved, then jagged lines break from that, and the front is a queer bulging window — in a curve that leans. The whole structure is as if given a twist by some terrific force — like something wrung'*. Better than any other device, the setting suggests the Surrealistic — that is, other-worldliness — of Claire's search and actions.
>
> (Waterman, 1966, p. 82)

Integral to the setting was the lighting design which also functioned as a visual representation of transformational structures. The Provincetown Playhouse, where the play was first performed, had a special dome built, in itself a source of light, which facilitated complicated lighting effects and which, according to company member James Light, changed all the players' 'ideas of setting plays' (Deutsch and Hanau, 1931, p. 62). In this instance, the play of light and shadow was used to contribute to the architecturing of distortion. A watchman's lantern was used to 'throw a marvellous pattern on the curved wall — like some masonry that hasn't been' (Glaspell, 1987b, p.78). Claire herself was seen through the 'queer bulging window': at one level imprisoned in the setting, yet at another, signifying the life force breaking out of it.

Claire's struggle for 'otherness', her fight to move beyond her male prison, is of necessity violent. Violent acts by women are hard to contemplate — for both men and women — and harder still if they are in any way cold-blooded, which is an additional reason why Claire was judged insane. One has only to think of the controversy surrounding the issue of female violence in a feminist film like *A Question of Silence*, or in Wendy Kesselman's play *My Sister in this House* (taken from the *Murderers of Le Mans* case of Christine and Lea Papin), to appreciate the hostility which might accrue to the violent actions of Glaspell's women like Claire, or Mrs Wright in *Trifles*, both of whom are driven to murdering men.

Feminist theatre scholarship has begun to recover Glaspell's theatre in a way which foregrounds its trajectories of female desire, however violent. But recognition for Glaspell is still far from being widely acknowledged (Ozieblo, 1990, p.67; p.75, n.3). The canonical stranglehold of male traditions and values is hard to dismantle. The position is emblematized in the closing tableau of Glaspell's *Alison's House* where Ann Leslie argues that the newly-found love poems of the dead Alison should be given to Elsa, the fallen woman of the family. She meets with patriarchal resistance in the form of Stanhope, who has the power to withold them. But Ann persists in arguing with his male prejudice on the grounds that Elsa should be heir to the letters because they must be left 'to a woman. Because Alison said it — for women' (Glaspell, 1931, p.669). It is high time that Susan Glaspell's plays were left to the blood-line of women's theatre because Glaspell, like the absent Alison, 'said it — for women'.

Notes

A list of Susan Glaspell's plays with first performance dates:

One-Act Plays:

Suppressed Desires, with George Cram Cook, Wharf Theatre, Provincetown, Summer 1915;
Trifles, Wharf Theatre, Provincetown, 1916;
The People, Playwrights' Theatre, 1917;
Close the Book, Playwrights' Theatre, 1917;
The Outside, Playwrights' Theatre, 1917;
Woman's Honor, Playwrights' Theatre, 1918;
Tickless Time, with George Cram Cook, Provincetown Playhouse, 1918.

Full-length Plays:

Bernice, Provincetown Playhouse, 1919;
The Inheritors, Provincetown Playhouse, 1921;
The Verge, Provincetown Playhouse, 1921;
Chains of Dew, Provincetown Playhouse, 1922;
The Comic Artist, with Norman Matson, Strand Theatre, 1928;
Alison's House, Civic Repertory Theatre, 1930.

References

ASTON, E. and SAVONA, G. (1991) *Theatre as Sign-System*, London, Routledge.
BEN-ZVI, L. (1989) 'Susan Glaspell's Contributions to Contemporary Women Playwrights', in BRATER, E. (Ed.) *Feminine Focus*, New York, Oxford, Oxford University Press, pp. 147–66.
BIGSBY, C. W. E. (Ed) (1987) *Plays by Susan Glaspell*, Cambridge, Cambridge University Press.
CASE, S. E. (1988) *Feminism and Theatre*, London, Macmillan.
CHAMPAGNE, L. (Ed) (1990) *Out From Under: Texts by Women Performance Artists*, New York, Theatre Communications Group.
CHINOY, H. K. and JENKINS, L. W. (Eds) (1981, revised 1987) *Women in American Theatre*, New York, Theatre Communications Group.
CIXOUS, H. (1976) 'The Laugh of the Medusa', in MARKS, E. and COURTIVRON, I. (Eds) (1981) *New French Feminisms*, Brighton, Harvester, pp. 245–64.
DEUTSCH, H. and HANAU, S. (1931) *The Provincetown: A Story of the Theatre*, New York, Russell & Russell.
DYMKOWSKI, C. (1988) 'On the Edge: The Plays of Susan Glaspell', *Modern Drama*, **31**, pp. 91–105.
FRANCE, R. (1981), 'Apropos (*sic*) of Women and the Folk Play', in CHINOY and JENKINS, (1981, pp. 145–52).
GLASPELL, S. (1920) *Plays*, Boston, Small, Maynard.
GLASPELL, S. (1931) 'Alison's House', in *Six Plays*, London, Victor Gollancz, pp. 581–672.
GLASPELL, S. (1987a) 'The Outside', in BIGSBY, C. W. E. (Ed.) *Plays by Susan Glaspell*, Cambridge, Cambridge University Press.
GLASPELL, S. (1987b) 'The Verge' in BIGSBY, C. W. E. (Ed) *Plays by Susan Gaspell*, Cambridge, Cambridge University Press.
GOLDBERG, I. (1922) *The Drama of Transition: Native and Exotic Playcraft*, Cincinnati, Ohio Stewart Kidd.
HEDGES, E. (1986) 'Small things reconsidered: Susan Glaspell's "A Jury of her Peers"', *Women's Studies*, **12**, 89–110.
LEWISOHN, L. (1932) *Expression in America*, London, Thornton Butterworth.
OZIEBLO, B. (1990) 'Rebellion and Rejection: The Plays of Susan Glaspell', in SCHLUETER (1990, pp. 66–76).
QUINN, A. H. (1927) *A History of the American Drama: From the Civil War to the Present Day II*, New York, London, Harper.
SCHLUETER, J. (Ed) (1989) *Feminist Readings of Modern American Drama*, London, Toronto, Associated University Presses.
SCHLUETER, J. (Ed) (1990) *Modern American Drama: The Female Canon*, London, Toronto, Associated University Presses.
TOWSE, J. R. (1921) 'The Play', *Evening Post*, New York, March 23, p. 9.
WATERMAN, A. E. (1966) *Susan Glaspell*, New York, Twayne.
WOOLLCOTT, A. (1921) 'The Play: Provincetown Psychiatry', *New York Times*, November 15, p. 23.

Chapter 12

'When This You See Remember Me': Three Plays by Gertrude Stein

Nicola Goode Shaughnessy

Gertrude Stein has been institutionalized as one of the mad women in literature's attic. A writer who is remembered as much for her eccentricity and self-proclaimed stature as a 'genius' as for her literary work, her *œuvre* is usually represented by the 1933 *The Autobiography of Alice B. Toklas* (1966) — which characteristically constitutes an instance of self-mythologization. The commercial and critical success of *Toklas* can be attributed in part to its accessibility and to Stein's teasing literary and artistic anecdotes and cameos. The comparative disregard of her other work — prose fiction, poetry, literary theory and drama — may be due to its capricious, idiosyncratic inaccessibility. In particular, despite the fact that she wrote over a hundred plays, Stein's drama has until recently received remarkably little critical attention, apart from some articles and chapters and a few full-length studies.[1] Similarly, Stein's plays have been as absent from the theatre. However, there are signs that she is beginning to be rehabilitated by the operations of experimental theatre practitioners such as Judith Malina and Robert Wilson. In terms of Wilson's postmodern theatrical project of 'splaying the unitary subject' (Savran, 1993, p. 26),[2] Stein's plays may well be appropriated as explorations of a world of fragmented identity, rampant intertextuality and anarchic disintegration, but in this paper I wish to offer an alternative route into her drama, via the minefield of autobiography. In her early, more ostentatiously and provocatively experimental work (examples of which are found in collections such as *Geography and Plays*, 1922), Stein abandoned narrative, character, the semblance of dramatic dialogue and scenic form in pursuit of an arbitrary, non-representational dramatic technique, throwing out the baby of the self with the bathwater of realist dramaturgy. And yet questions of autobiography and authorship, which are central to the rest of her work, continually resurface throughout Stein's plays. I focus here on several key later works where these concerns become most acute: *Four Saints in Three Acts, Doctor Faustus Lights the Lights* and *The Mother of us All* , written in 1927, 1938 and 1945 respectively.

The opera *Four Saints in Three Acts* is one of Stein's better-known dramatic works. With Virgil Thompson's score, it achieved a considerable degree of commercial success and critical acclaim on its Broadway première in 1934. Much of Stein's writing can be regarded as musical in form, in that it is often more concerned with rhythm and melody than with representational 'sense': *Four Saints* is pivotal in terms of her drama in that from here on she began to conceive of her plays as operas. Virgil Thompson used a musical analogy to describe Stein's method:

> She wrote poetry, in fact, very much as a composer works. She chose a theme and developed it, or rather, she let the words develop themselves through the free expansion of sound essence. Putting to music poetry so musically conceived as Gertrude Stein's has long been a pleasure to me. The spontaneity of its easy flow, and its deep sincerity have always seemed to be just right for music.[3]

Surrendering sense to sound in musical fashion was for Stein a way of evoking the continuous present in the experience of art. It was also connected with her preoccupation with a theatrical and experiential state of *being* rather than *doing*. In *Four Saints* the form was aptly matched to the subject matter, for in the concept of sainthood Stein found a mirror of her own self-defined genius. The saints occupy an ambiguous position on the borderline of culture, serving as a focus for Stein's meditations on identity, philosophy and religion. One of the play's distinctive features is the characteristically Steinian manner in which it foregrounds the presence of the author in the narrative process as the play discloses the mechanisms of its own composition. Stein presents herself as the narrator who finds herself both inside and outside the text, negotiating existing language models in her search for an artistic voice. The opening declares the author's intention to 'prepare for saints', but the narrative falters as she searches for material and inspiration: 'Saint saint/a Saint. Forgotten saint.' (Stein, 1987, p. 11). Acknowledging feelings of barrenness as creator of the drama, the playwright attempts recourse to familiar representational strategies: 'What happened today, a narrative' (p. 11). Anxiety and frustration become a source of dramatic tension as she struggles to form 'a narrative to plan an opera' (p. 14), reflects on the problems of representing Saint Therese and voices her consequent exasperation and despair: 'come panic come'(p. 14). By addressing the audience frequently in this manner, Stein underlines her central, domineering role as the play's creator; a tactic perhaps designed not only to direct attention towards Stein's ever-present public *persona* but also to prevent the spectator from willingly suspending disbelief, encouraging a critical response. Yet in Thompson's stage version, the sustained sections of authorial commentary were divided and assigned to individual characters, thus appropriating artistic control from the singular Stein and redistributing it along more pluralist, multivocal lines.

The autobiographical dimension of *Four Saints* is insistently reiterated in a repeated refrain: 'when this you see remember me.' The recurrent concerns of Stein's prose autobiographies are prevalent in *Four Saints*, in particular her preoccupation with time and mortality. In *Everybody's Autobiography*, Stein notes her 'fear of dying' and refers this ontological insecurity to the circumstances of her own birth:

> Anybody can think if I had died before there was anything but there is no thinking that one was never born until you hear accidentally that there were to be five children and if two little ones had not died there would be no Gertrude Stein, of course not.
>
> (Stein, 1985, p. 97)

If existential disarray is indicated here by the slippage between a first, second and third-person 'Gertrude Stein', and in her early plays by the polyphony of characterless 'voices', in *Four Saints* it is marked by the instability of the *dramatis personae*. From the outset, the gestation of the play is shown to be a troubled one, and as the narrative goes on characters appear and then dissolve: 'Saint Therese come again to be absent' (Stein, 1987, p. 16). Many of the saints are named in the opening scene but never appear on stage; they remain unborn while other characters enter the play who have not been initially introduced. The figures in the play are suspended on the verge of possibility, within an atemporal matrix which is constantly in flux: 'Saint Therese about to be' (p. 16). As Stein saw it, she understood the nature of her genius to be 'existing without any internal recognition of time' (Stein, 1985, p. 210). The tenses of *Four Saints* are constantly shifting along with the play's modes of self-consciousness.

The figure of Saint Therese may be identified as a further version of Stein the creative artist, as she repeatedly questions the progress, shape and rationale of the narrative for which she is both the central focus and the motive force:

Saint Therese. Could Four Acts be three. (Stein, 1987, p. 31)
Saint Cecilia. How many saints are there in it.
Saint Therese. There are as many saints as there are in it. (Stein, 1987, p. 28)
Saint Therese. To be asked how much of it is finished. (Stein, 1987, p. 30)

Saint Therese's identity as a character is radically unstable, for she seems to be continuously in the process of being created: 'Intending to be intending to intending to to to to. To do it for me' (Stein, 1987, p. 41). When the play begins, Saint Therese is presented ambiguously as a half-formed figure:

Saint Therese something like that.
Saint Therese something like that.
Saint Therese would and would and would.
Saint Therese.
Saint Therese half in doors and half out of doors.
Saint Therese not knowing of other saints. (Stein, 1987, pp. 14–15)

Introduced on the threshold of theatrical identity, Saint Therese is realized as a visual icon, a figure in a landscape: 'Saint Therese in a storm at Avila'. In *Lectures in America* Stein explains the origins of her image of Saint Therese:

As it happened there is on the Boulevard Raspail a place where they make photographs that have always held my attention. They take a photograph of a young girl dressed in the costume of her ordinary life and little by little in successive photographs they change it into a nun . . . For years I had stood and looked at these when I was walking and finally I was writing Saint Therese in looking at these photographs I saw how Saint Therese existed from the life of an ordinary young lady to that of a nun. And so everything was actual and I went on writing.

(Stein, 1988, p. 130)

The girl's identity, transformed from 'ordinariness' to that of the nun, is recorded by the photographic medium as an effect of *costume*, an imposed social (or theatrical) role rather than as a sign of sanctified singularity.

The success of *Four Saints* was partly attributable to the influence of Virgil Thompson, who shaped Stein's apparently recalcitrant text into a commercially viable product. As far as Stein was concerned, the experience of seeing *Four Saints* in performance enabled her to begin 'knowing what plays are' (Stein, 1985, p. 167). What this also meant was tailoring her art to the demands of audiences, something which raised for her a conflict between integrity and expediency. The success of *Four Saints* coincided with that of *Toklas*, and with Stein's sudden emergence into the public eye, performing her popular role as literary eccentric on the much-publicized lecture tours of the United States. While she had previously seen herself as free to pursue her sanctified role as artist without taking account of the demands of the public, she was now only too aware of the extent to which her role of genius was dependent upon the belief of her audiences and readers. Developing the religious motif of *Four Saints*, Stein pictured this as a conflict between god and mammon: 'When I say god and mammon concerning the writer writing I mean that any one can use words to say something':

> Mammon may be a success, mammon may be an effort he is to produce, mammon may be a pleasure he has from hearing what he himself has done . . . Now serving god for a writer who is writing is writing directly, it makes no difference what it is but it must be directly.
>
> (Stein, 1988, pp. 23–4)

This conflict is one of the main concerns of *Doctor Faustus Lights the Lights*, written in 1938 but not performed until 1951. Stein uses as her source a popular myth within the male literary tradition, appropriating aspects of Marlowe's and Goethe's versions of the story. Only three principal characters from the traditional legend survive in Stein's play: Faustus, Mephistopheles and Marguerite. All three can be seen as aspects of Stein herself.

When *Doctor Faustus* opens, the protagonist is recorded as having sought public recognition through his invention of the electric light; like Stein, he is a self-made, self-advertising genius who has been dazzled and disorientated by success. Having sold his soul to achieve illumination, he gradually realizes that the power he has is illusory: the lights in the play prove to be volatile and unreliable, the illumination they give out constantly diminishing. Their flickering aptly reflects Faustus's own state of mind. For Faustus, the invention of the electric light is an attempt to manipulate forces which are beyond his control — the electric lights work independently and unpredictably, functioning as characters in a drama who have escaped the control of their author, acting, like his companions the boy and the dog, as rebellious constituents of Faustus's consciousness.

The fluidity of the boundaries of identity was an important issue for Stein, that is, 'it is all a question of the outside being outside and the inside being inside'. She feared that the achievement of public recognition on mammon's terms would disrupt this: 'As long as the outside does not put a value on you it remains outside but when it does put a value on you then it gets inside or rather if the outside puts a value on you then your inside gets to be outside' (Stein, 1985, p. 34). Faustus is haunted by the awareness that his immensely theatrical identity is dependent upon his recognition by others — that in a sense he only exists in others' perceptions of him. The repeated meditation in *Everybody's Autobiography* (Stein, 1985, p. 278) 'perhaps I am not I even if my little dog knows me' also finds its way into *Doctor Faustus* when the protagonist asks 'what is the difference between a man and a dog':

> When I say none do I go away does he go away go away to stay no nobody goes away the dog the boy they can stay I can go away go away . . . am I a boy am I a dog is a dog a boy is a boy a dog and what am I I cannot cry what am I what am I . . .
> (Stein, 1949, p. 213)

The main female presence in *Doctor Faustus* is similarly a projection of Stein, a divided self as her two pairs of names indicate: Margeurite Ida and Helena Annabel. Paradoxically both singular and plural, her (their?) names are themselves subject to dispute: Faustus stresses that 'her name is Margeurite Ida and Helena Annabel' (p. 209), but contradicts himself in dialogue with the dog: 'She will not says Dr Faustus, never, never, never, will her name be Mary Ida and Helena Annabel' (p. 210). Stein foregrounds and interrogates the practice of naming through a form of double double-take, in that the conjunction 'and' which links the names is made central, emphasizing the arbitrary and constructed nature of naming itself as a signifying practice. Her first words are an attempt to locate herself through naming: 'I am I and my name is Margeurite Ida and Helena Annabel, and then oh then I could

yes I could I could begin to cry but why why could I begin to cry'
(p. 210). Her crisis of identity appears to be related to an implied sexual
experience in the 'wild woods' with 'wild animals': she is a fallen woman
who has been stung by a serpent. When Margeurite Ida and Helena
Annabel first meets Faustus, she is perceived as an Eve-like figure, to be
cured of her serpent bite and transformed by Act Two into an angel or
saint: 'a halo is around her not of electric light but of candle light . . . the
chorus sings' (p. 220). In contrast with Faustus's tawdry, flickering
lightbulbs, the candles create a religious aura, as Margeurite Ida and
Helena Annabel is shaped into the *objet d'art* of the eternal feminine.
Mermaid-like, Margeurite Ida and Helena Annabel is able only to sing,
but she is subsequently 'rescued' from her state by the ambiguously
romantic figure of the Man from Overseas, who is keen to merge her
identity with his own: 'She is my love and always mine/ And I am hers
and she is mine' (p. 223). But Margeurite Ida and Helena Annabel
rebuffs his advance, pointing in pantomime fashion to the figure of the
Devil lurking behind him: 'No one is one when there are two, look
behind you look behind you you are not one you are two'; Stein's voice
intervenes triumphantly to declare that 'And indeed behind the man of
the seas is Mephistopheles' (p. 225). Margeurite Ida and Helena
Annabel nonetheless finally surrenders, swooning into the arms of the
Man from Overseas and conflating her voice and identity with his in
androgynous union: 'Pretty pretty pretty dear, I am he and she is he and
we are we' (p. 235). If Faustus can be seen to represent Stein the artist,
the interaction between Margeurite Ida and Helena Annabel and the
Man from Overseas seems to offer a complexly coded allegory of her
sexual identity. The contradictions, divisions and differing gender
positions occupied by these three selves offer an ironic mirror of Stein
and Toklas's lesbian relationship, modelled nonetheless on the
bourgeois heterosexual pattern of marriage (Stimpson, 1986).

In her last full-length play, *The Mother of us All* (1945), Stein
fashions her own idiosyncratic style of geographical dramatic biography
in her portrait of the nineteenth-century campaigner for American
women's suffrage, Susan B. Anthony. The play's title is itself
ambiguous: who is the mother, and who does 'us' include — men as well
as women? Or does the first person plural represent Stein's imperious
use of a kind of royal 'we', rendering the teeming cast of the play as a
proliferation of versions of Stein herself, who is also the mother of
modernist women's writing? Once again the relationship between
identity and naming is signalled from the outset as a fundamental
concern. Stein specifies that all that characters state 'my father's name

was Daniel' (Stein, 1949, p. 160), a running gag which destabilizes the name of Stein's own father and establishes the autobiographical dimension of the play, which is further emphasized by the presence of the character G. S. in the first scene (she also includes her acquaintances Virgil T. and Constance Fletcher).[4] As in *Doctor Faustus*, gender identities are in flux: Daniel Webster refers to Susan B. Anthony using the male pronoun and insists on addressing her in masculine terms, calling her 'the honorable member' and 'gentleman'. Throughout the play, Daniel Webster arrogates to himself the role of the namer of names and definer of identities and genders, as when he introduces Henrietta M.: 'Ladies and gentlemen let me present to you let me present to you Henrietta M' (p. 176). But Stein also makes sure to assert her own authorial presence and power by playing with characters' names: here she identifies 'Daniel' by his forename only, indicating his archetypal function.

In many ways the character of Susan B. Anthony is a mouthpiece for Stein's own convictions about identity and social role; the play is less about Anthony than it is about its author. Stein did not entirely subscribe to Anthony's feminism, since she believed that the struggle for political and economic equality was insufficient in itself: gender identity itself had to be subverted. This is reflected in the play's very form, which adopts the mode of dramatic biography only to question it. The linear and rational model of history is subverted through anachronism, with characters from fact and fiction and from different historical periods placed alongside each other in stage time. This temporal model complements the play's concern with the process of struggle as an activity in the continuous present, rather than a movement towards the achievement of goals. Consequently the play does not develop to a triumphant climax. Indeed, the one historical fact that Stein insists upon is that women's suffrage was not achieved until after Susan B. Anthony's death. When she is assured that the vote for women will be won, she responds that 'by that time it will do them no good because having the vote they will become like men' (p. 193). The silences which end the play poignantly testify to the limitations of Susan B. Anthony's achievement. All the characters gather around a sculpture commemorating Anthony and two other suffrage leaders. The voice of Anthony is heard from behind the statue, reiterating her convictions but continually lapsing into silences more eloquent than words. Stein's protagonist is forced to conclude that 'Going forward may be the same as going backward' (p. 201). Stein's ambivalence about her own achievements as a writer are projected into this ending: perhaps she sensed that she was likely to enter literary history as a marginal or peripheral figure, her difference categorized as eccentricity; her genius revalued as mere self-promotion.

In so far as Stein's drama can be seen as autobiographical, it is in the manner of her better-known prose writing, where the certainties of realist first-person self-narration are playfully subverted but also transformed into myth. *The Autobiography of Alice B. Toklas* may be the quintessential modernist autobiography in this respect, in that it shows Stein at her happiest in colonizing the space of her significant Other in a bravura feat of impersonation: her plays develop this strategy, dramatizing the constituents of Stein's psyche and what she sees as her own archetypal genius. By refusing to disappear conveniently into the wings of her own dramas, Stein takes the idea of authorial omniscience to its logical limit, firmly positioning herself centre stage. Given that much of Stein's own life was something of a virtuoso performance anyway, her autobiographical drama seems a fitting memorial.

Notes

1 Stein's plays are discussed briefly in Bridgman (1970), DeKoven (1983), Hoffman (1976), Stewart (1967) and Sutherland (1951). Full-length studies are provided by Alayne Ryan (1984) and Palatini Bowers (1991).
2 David Savran refers here to the compatibility of Stein's 'construction and deconstruction of being' with Wilson's postmodernist interrogation of the subject.
3 This comment is taken from Virgil Thompson's sleeve notes to the 1964 RCA LP record of *Four Saints in Three Acts* (RCA Victor Red Seal LM 2756).
4 Constance Fletcher, the author of *Kismet*, was a close friend of Stein from 1912 onwards.

References

ALAYNE RYAN, B. (1984) *Gertrude Stein's Theatre of the Absolute*, Ann Arbor. UMI Research Press.
BRIDGMAN, R. (1970) *Gertrude Stein in Pieces*, Oxford, Oxford University Press.
DEKOVEN, M. (1983) *A Different Language: Gertrude Stein's Experimental Writing*, Madison, University of Wisconsin Press.
HOFFMAN, M. (1976) *Gertrude Stein*, Boston, Twayne.
PALATINI BOWERS, J. (1991) *They Watch Me as They Watch This: Gertrude Stein's Metadrama*, Philadelphia, University of Pennsylvania Press.
SAVRAN, D. (1993) 'Whistling in the Dark', *Performing Arts Journal*, **15**, 1, pp. 25-7.
STEIN, G. (1922) *Geography and Plays*, Boston, Four Seas.
STEIN, G. (1949) *Last Operas and Plays*, VAN VECHTEN, C. (Ed), New York, Rinehart.
STEIN, G. (1966) *The Autobiography of Alice B. Toklas*, Harmondsworth, Penguin.

STEIN, G. (1985) *Everybody's Autobiography*, London, Virago.

STEIN, G. (1987) *Operas and Plays*, New York, Station Hill Press.

STEIN, G. (1988) *Lectures in America*, London, Virago.

STEWART, A. (1967) *Gertrude Stein and the Present*, Cambridge, Mass. Harvard University Press.

STIMPSON, C. (1986) 'Gertrude Stein and the Transposition of Gender', in MILLER, N. (Ed) *The Poetics of Gender*, New York, Columbia University Press. pp. 1–18.

SUTHERLAND, D. (1951) *Gertrude Stein: A Biography of her Work*, New Haven, Yale University Press.

Notes on Contributors

Elaine Aston is a lecturer in Theatre Studies at Loughborough University. She is the author of *Sarah Bernhardt* (Berg, 1989), and the co-author of *Theatre as Sign-System* (Routledge, 1991). With Gabriele Griffin she co-edited two volumes of plays by women, *Herstory* vols. 1 and 2 (Sheffield Academic Press, 1991).

Katharine Cockin is working on a cultural history of the Pioneer Players for her doctoral thesis at Leicester University, where she also teaches part-time. An article on Edith Craig, director of the Pioneer Players, has recently been published in *Theatre Notebook* (Vol. XLV, No. 3, 1991) and since 1989 she has been working on a descriptive catalogue of Edith Craig's documents, held at the Ellen Terry Memorial Museum.

Mary Condé is a Lecturer in English and American Studies at Queen Mary and Westfield College, University of London. She has published articles on African-American, Caribbean, Canadian and Malaysia-Singapore women writers. She is currently working on a book on Caribbean women writers.

Nicola Goode Shaughnessy is a Senior Lecturer in English and Drama at Worcester College of Higher Education. She is currently working on a study of modernist women's dramatic writing.

Gabriele Griffin is a Reader in Women's Studies at Nene College, Northampton. She has contributed to *What Lesbians Do In Books* (eds. Elaine Hobby and Chris White, Women's Press, 1991), *Insights into Blackwomen's Writing* (ed. Gina Wisker, Macmillan, 1993) and to *Teaching Women* (eds. Ann Thompson and Helen Wilcox, Manchester University Press, 1989). She is the author of *Heavenly Love? Lesbian*

Images in Twentieth Century Women's Writing (Manchester U₁
Press, 1993), and edited *Outwrite: Lesbians and Popular Culture*
Press, 1993). Together with Elaine Aston, she also edited two vo₁
of plays by women, *Herstory* vols 1 and 2 (Sheffield Academic P₁
1991).

Penelope Kenrick is a Senior Lecturer in the Department of Arts an·
Letters at Anglia University, teaching Art History and Women's
Studies. She has produced educational videos on Susan Hiller. Her
research interests focus on contemporary feminist artists such as Mary
Kelly and Barbara Krüger.

Jan Montefiore has lectured at the University of Kent in Canterbury in
English Literature since 1978 and in Women's Studies since 1980. She is
the author of *Feminism and Poetry* (Pandora, 1987) and of essays on
women's writing and critical theory. She is now at work on a major
study of gender in the history of British writing in and of the 1930s.

Andrew Thacker is a lecturer in English at Wolverhampton University.
His doctoral research at the University of Southampton was on the
Imagist poets and he has published in the areas of modernism and
postmodernism. He is now writing a book entitled *Reifications of
Language: Gender and Modernism in Imagist Poetry* and researching
modernist little magazines.

Deborah Tyler-Bennett is currently teaching part-time at Loughborough
University and is in the process of finishing her PhD on the works of
Djuna Barnes. She is feminist fiction editor for the magazine *Topical
Books* and has had work published in *Writing Women* and in the
anthology *Scarlet Women*.

Joss West-Burnham is Subject Leader in Cultural Studies at Crewe and
Alsager Faculty, Manchester Metropolitan University. Current research
strands include Victorian religion and the woman writer, popular
narratives 1880–1920, and the writings of Pat Barker. She is also coordinator of the 'Gender and the Body' network. Publications include
articles on George Eliot's poetry, *The Lady* newspaper, and feminist
intervention in Cultural Studies.

Gregory Woods teaches in the Department of English and Media Studies
at Nottingham Trent University. He is the author of *Articulate Flesh:*

Male Homo-eroticism and Modern Poetry (Yale University Press, 1987) and of a collection of poems, *We Have The Melon* (Carcanet, 1992). His essays and reviews on gay culture and on the AIDS epidemic have been published in books and journals in Britain, Italy and the US. He has been a regular contributor to the gay press in Britain for over a decade, and has also written for the *New Statesman and Society, The Times Higher Educational Supplement* and *The Times Literary Supplement.*

Sue Wragg is a Senior Lecturer in the History of Art and Design at Nene College, Northampton, where she also contributes to American Studies. Her current research interests focus on feminist art theory, Orientalism, and European depictions of the native peoples of America 1500–1700.

Index

Note: **Bold** numbers denote pages on which references are given particular attention.

Index

GLASGOW
Departmental
Libraries
UNIVERSITY